history *in focus*

ESSENTIAL modern world history

history in focus

ESSENTIAL modern world history

Ben Walsh

Are YOU in this?

JOHN MURRAY

Note: Some written sources have been adapted or abbreviated to make them accessible to all students, while faithfully preserving the sense of the original.

Words printed in SMALL CAPITALS are defined in the Glossary on page 219.

First published in 2002
by John Murray (Publishers) Ltd
50 Albemarle Street
London W1S 4BD

Layouts by Fiona Webb
Illustrations by Oxford Designers and Illustrators
Cover design by John Townson/Creation
Picture research by Liz Moore
Typeset in Garamond by Wearset Ltd, Boldon, Tyne and Wear
Colour separations by Colourscript Digital Ltd, Mildenhall, Suffolk
Printed and bound in Spain by Bookprint, S. L., Barcelona

A CIP catalogue record for this book is available from the British Library.

ISBN 0 7195 7715 2
Teacher's Resource Book ISBN 0 7195 7716 0

Contents

Chapter 5 Weimar and Nazi Germany 1918–45

LEAGUE OF NATIONS
ARBITRATION
"PLEASSE, MISS, I HAF LEARNT DER LESSON. MAY I GET DOWN?"

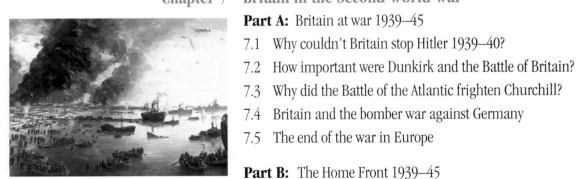

Chapter 6 The road to war 1929–39

Chapter 7 Britain in the Second World War

H
H

1 Britain and the Great War

1.1 Why did Europe go to war in 1914?

Here is the bottom line for this topic. Give four examples of TENSION between countries that helped to lead to the Great War.

Key words **alliance; arms race; colony; empire; tension**

SOURCE 1

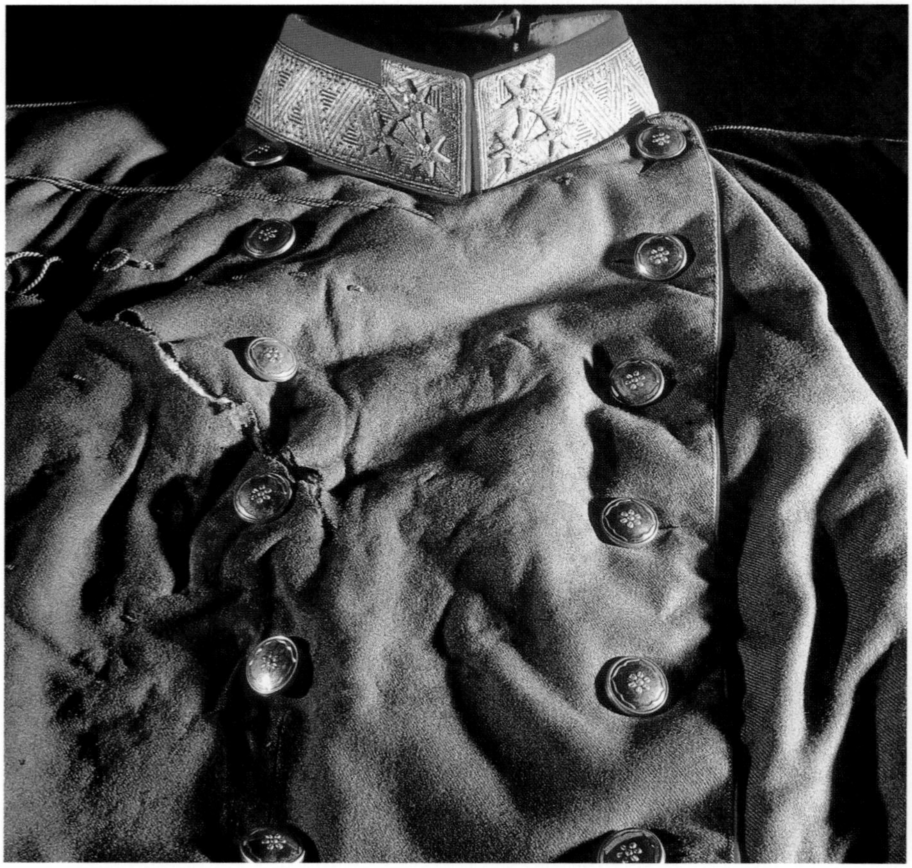

The uniform that Franz Ferdinand, Archduke of the Austrian empire, was wearing when he was assassinated in Sarajevo in 1914.

Look at Source 1. It is dramatic, maybe even a bit shocking, to be looking at the clothes that a man died in. The murder of Franz Ferdinand in June 1914 led to the deadliest war the world had ever seen. We call it the First World War. It is also often called the Great War.

But it was not just the murder of the Archduke that caused the war. To find out the real causes, you have to look back many years.

The fuse is laid

Tension between countries in Europe had been building for years.

- **There was tension over COLONIES.** For the previous fifty years, European countries had been competing with each other to build bigger EMPIRES, especially in Africa.
- **There was an ARMS RACE going on.** Most countries were building up their armies. Britain and Germany were building up their navies, too.
- **Europe was divided into rival ALLIANCES** (see Source 2). In an alliance, each member promises to help the others if there is a war. France, Britain and Russia made an alliance, called the 'Triple Entente', because they were scared of Germany. Germany felt that the Triple Entente was an attempt to encircle it so it made an alliance, called the 'Dual Alliance', with Austria–Hungary!

SOURCE 2

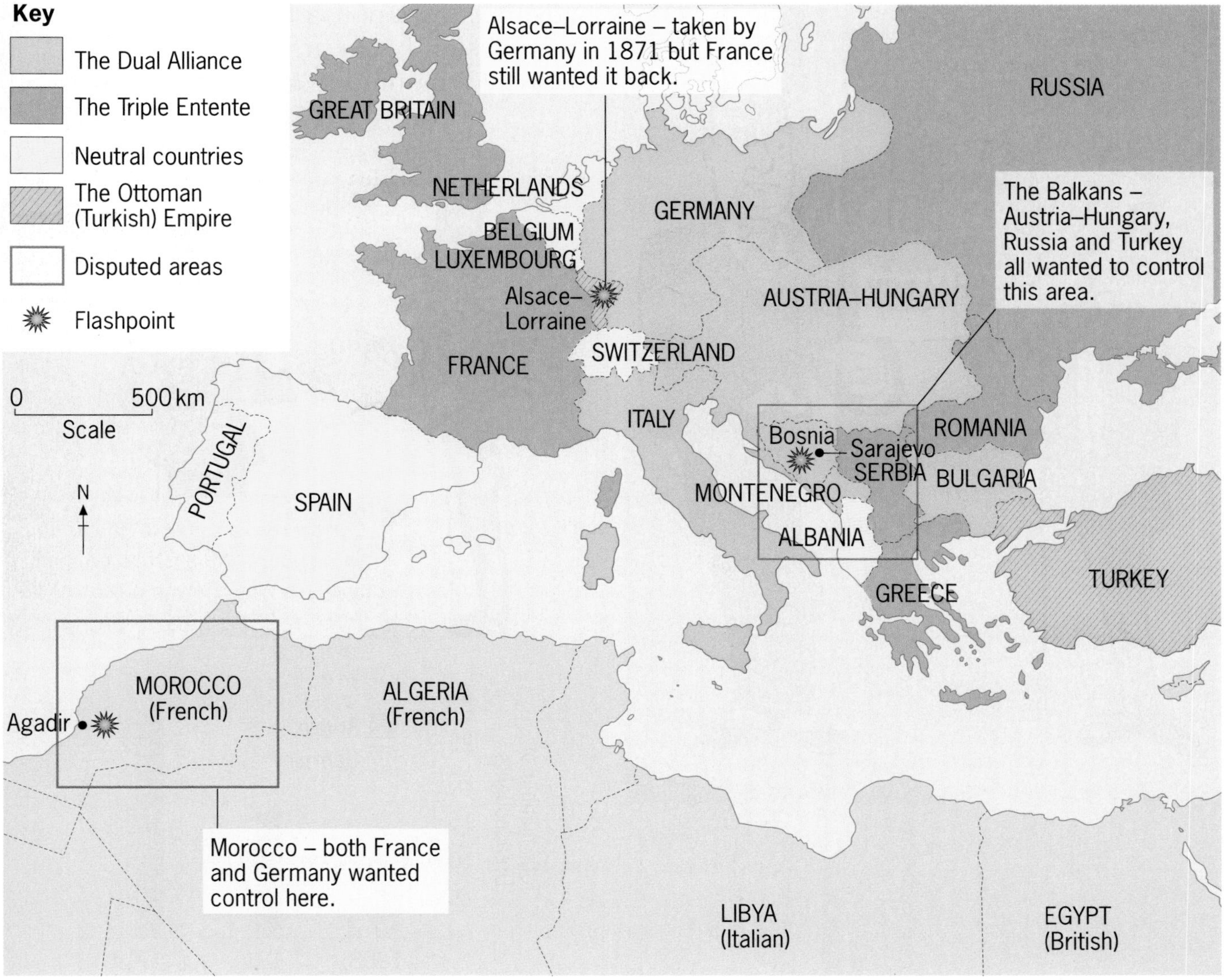
Key
The Dual Alliance
The Triple Entente
Neutral countries
The Ottoman (Turkish) Empire
Disputed areas
Flashpoint
0 500 km
Scale
N
Alsace–Lorraine – taken by Germany in 1871 but France still wanted it back.
GREAT BRITAIN
RUSSIA
NETHERLANDS
GERMANY
BELGIUM
LUXEMBOURG
Alsace–Lorraine
AUSTRIA–HUNGARY
The Balkans – Austria–Hungary, Russia and Turkey all wanted to control this area.
FRANCE
SWITZERLAND
ITALY
PORTUGAL
SPAIN
Bosnia
Sarajevo
SERBIA
ROMANIA
BULGARIA
MONTENEGRO
ALBANIA
GREECE
TURKEY
MOROCCO (French)
Agadir
ALGERIA (French)
Morocco – both France and Germany wanted control here.
LIBYA (Italian)
EGYPT (British)

A map of Europe in 1914 showing the two alliances.

Key words **ally; ethnic**

The tension builds

From time to time, these tensions brought countries close to war.

***Germany versus France:* Morocco**

In 1905, then again in 1911, France tried to take over Morocco. Germany wanted to control Morocco as well, as it was trying to build up its own African empire at this time. So it sent a warship to Agadir (in Morocco) to stop France. It looked like there might be a war but a conference was held and a compromise was reached. France got Morocco, but Germany got some land in Central Africa instead.

They're getting far too arrogant. It's none of their business what we do here in Morocco.
FRANCE
GERMANY
We've got as much right to be in Morocco as they have.

***Germany versus Britain:* Dreadnoughts**

Britain had the strongest navy in the world. It needed a strong navy to control its massive overseas empire. When Germany started to build up its navy, Britain was very suspicious that Germany might try to take over some of its colonies.

From 1906, the arms race entered a new phase. Germany and Britain competed to build new super battleships called Dreadnoughts. They were the most advanced weapons of their time. They were faster, better armed and more heavily armoured than any other ships.

What do you need that navy for? You don't have an overseas empire to protect.
BRITAIN
GERMANY
Our overseas trade is nearly as big as yours. We need to protect our ships. Why are you objecting to our navy?

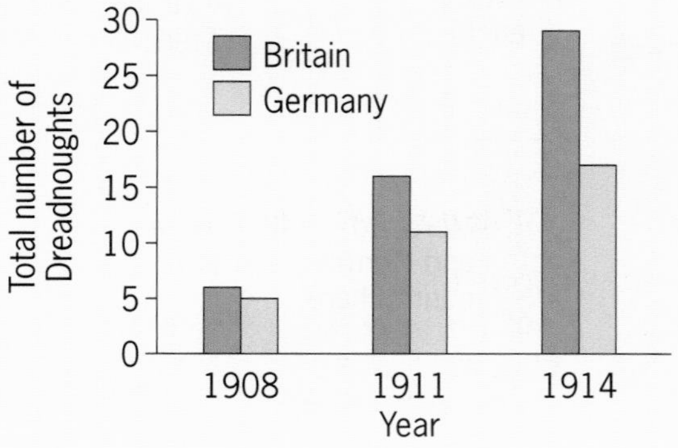
Britain
Germany
Total number of Dreadnoughts
0
5
10
15
20
25
30
1908
1911
1914
Year

Austria–Hungary versus Russia: the Balkans

The Balkans was a very unstable area. Different ETHNIC groups were mixed together, and they distrusted each other.

Russia and Austria–Hungary both wanted to control this area so that they could have access to the Mediterranean Sea. In 1908, Austria–Hungary unexpectedly took over Bosnia. Russia (and its close ALLY, Serbia) protested, but then backed down when Germany made it clear it would support Austria–Hungary if they attacked. Russia did not want to fight Germany as well as Austria–Hungary.

From then on, Russia distrusted Austria-Hungary and began to build up its army so that it could fight in the future.

With Germany on our side we can do what we want.
AUSTRIA-HUNGARY
RUSSIA
They'll not get away with it next time.

Germany, France and Russia: massive armies

With all this tension around, all the great powers built up their armies and navies.

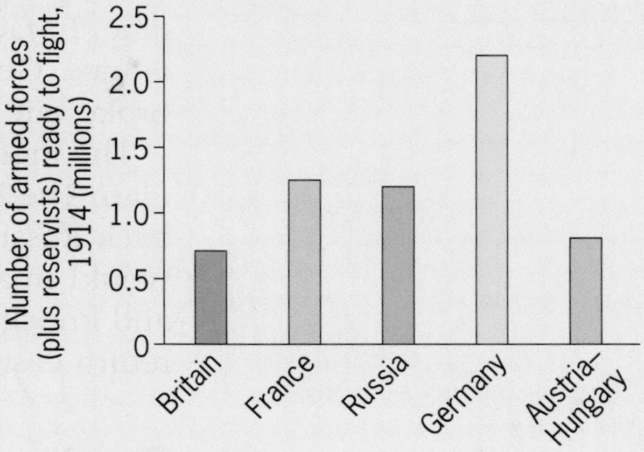
Number of armed forces (plus reservists) ready to fight, 1914 (millions)
2.5
2.0
1.5
1.0
0.5
0
Britain
France
Russia
Germany
Austria–Hungary

The really big armies were in Germany, France and Russia. Germany felt very threatened surrounded by two enormous armies that belonged to a rival alliance.

What do you need that huge army for?
FRANCE
GERMANY
RUSSIA
To defend my country from your huge armies.

Focus task

Why did Europe go to war in 1914?

1 Make your own copy of this table.
2 Fill out the blue shaded areas with examples of tension between those countries. You can get ideas from pages 2–5.

	Germany	Austria-Hungary
France		
Russia		
Britain		

Explain in less than twenty words why the shooting in Sarajevo set off the First World War.

Key word trigger

Plans for war

Many people expected there to be a war in Europe at some time. In fact, some people even wanted one. Britain, France, Germany and Russia all made plans in case war broke out.

The most controversial plan was Germany's Schlieffen Plan. The idea was to keep a small army in the east to hold back Russia. Meanwhile, the rest of Germany's armies would smash through Belgium, defeat France and Britain and knock them out of the war. Then Germany could return east to defeat the Russians.

1 Historians often describe the murder in Sarajevo as a TRIGGER rather than an actual cause of the war. Explain this.

The fuse is lit: Sarajevo and the July Crisis

The atmosphere in Europe at this time has been compared to a bonfire waiting to be lit or a bomb ready to be set off. All it needed was a single spark to set it alight.

On 28 June 1914, the Archduke Franz Ferdinand of Austria–Hungary visited Sarajevo in Bosnia. Some young Bosnian Serbs were waiting for him. They hated Austria and wanted to be part of Serbia.

This is what happened next:

28 June Princip, a Serbian, shoots dead the Archduke and his wife.
28 July Austria–Hungary blames Serbia for the murder and declares war on it.
29 July Russia gets ready to help the Serbs – this worries the Germans. The Schlieffen Plan will not work if Russia has time to organise its armies.
1 August Germany declares war on Russia.
3 August Germany declares war on France and attacks France through Belgium. The Schlieffen Plan goes into action.
4 August Britain declares war on Germany.
6 August Austria–Hungary declares war on Russia.

Activity

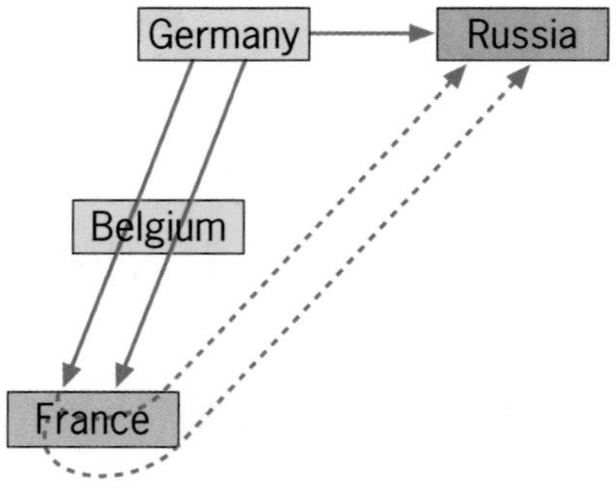

Germany
Russia
Belgium
France

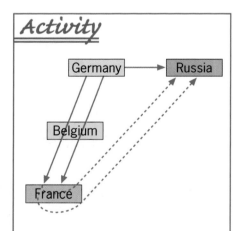

1 Copy and complete this diagram to explain the Schlieffen Plan. Label the arrows to show:
- how the plan dealt with Russia
- how the plan dealt with France
- how Belgium was involved
- what would happen to France when it was defeated.

2 Add to your chart anything that you think could go wrong with this plan.

Focus task

Why did Europe go to war in 1914?

On page 5 you completed a table to show some tensions that built up in Europe in the years before 1914. Unfortunately, you cannot draw a set of boxes in an exam! So, you are going to turn the information in the table into a piece of writing. Use your own copy of this writing frame.

Start with a clear introduction that sums up what you are going to say.	I am going to explain why there were tensions between countries in Europe and why they led to war in 1914.
Now write a paragraph describing one cause of tension. Try this approach . . . • State the cause of tension. • Add an example – and explain <u>why</u> that example caused tension (who felt angry or worried about what).	For years before 1914, tension had been building in Europe. One cause of tension was overseas colonies. For example, Germany and France clashed over . . .
Once you've done one paragraph, it gets easier! Just repeat the above for a different cause of tension. I'll leave you to choose which causes to use in the next two paragraphs. You could use the arms race or the alliances.	Another cause of tension was . . . For example . . . Yet another cause of tension was . . . For example . . .
Tensions make war possible, but they don't actually cause a war. It needs a trigger. Now it's time to explain that trigger . . .	This tense situation made war likely, but it still needed an event to trigger it off. This happened in . . . This sparked off war because . . .

1.2 Why did all the military plans fail in 1914?

Key words **artillery; barbed wire; barracks; bombardment; front; infantry; land mine; machine gun; outflank; recruitment; shellfire; stalemate; trenches; volunteers**

Your teacher will (rightly) tell you that you should learn all this stuff. If it won't stay in your head, concentrate on three reasons why the Schlieffen Plan failed.

Diary of Billy Wilson

Billy Wilson is a captain in the Staffordshire Regiment. He comes from a soldiering family: his brother is a major in another regiment; his father is a senior officer. Billy is a top-class officer and well respected by the men he commands. His family connections also mean that he knows a bit more about the events of 1914 than the average captain.

Billy Wilson's war, August 1914

4 August 1914: War fever
Well, it looks like we're going to war: we were called back to our BARRACKS two days ago. On my way I passed hundreds of VOLUNTEERS trying to join up at the RECRUITMENT offices. I have heard it is like this in Russia, France, Germany and Austria.

5 August 1914: The BEF
We have moved to a training camp in Norfolk. We've been told that we are to be part of the British Expeditionary Force (BEF) led by General Sir John French.

I must say I'm looking forward to getting at the Germans. I've just read in the papers that they have invaded Belgium. It's part of their Schlieffen Plan to knock us and France out of the war quickly.

15 August 1914: Belgium holds out
We're all bored and fed up. We are still in Norfolk while other units are going over to France. Our colonel told us that the Belgians have put up a tremendous fight. They've put the Schlieffen Plan back twelve days.

19 August 1914: Russians attack early
We're still stuck here, but there's some interesting news from the FRONT. The Russians invaded eastern Germany yesterday. The Germans did not expect them to be ready so quickly. The Schlieffen Plan is looking a bit shaky.

24 August 1914: The battle at Mons
We finally made it to France and were very soon in action.

We gave the Germans a nasty shock at Mons yesterday. Our rapid rifle fire really cut them down. Even so, we could not stop them like we planned to. We had to pull back. There were so many of them! I must admit I'm a bit worried.

25 August 1914: Plan 17 fails
We met up with some French troops today. It has not gone well for them. Their Plan 17 involved a big INFANTRY charge against the German border a few days ago. They were cut to bits by MACHINE GUNS and SHELLFIRE before they even got to the German line – there were 200,000 casualties apparently.

Billy Wilson's war, September–December 1914

10 September 1914: The Battle of the Marne

I am exhausted. We have been fighting the Germans at the River Marne for five solid days now.

The Germans' original plan was to encircle Paris and cut off the city. Instead they turned straight towards it. They thought that we and the French were beaten. It was their first really big mistake. They got a nasty shock when we attacked them on 5 September.

The French were amazing. They pulled together their exhausted troops and saved Paris! The government even took control of all the taxis in Paris to take troops out to meet the German advance. We have wrecked the Schlieffen Plan. But what will happen now?

13 October 1914: The race to the sea

Fritz [the Germans] keeps trying to OUTFLANK us. We try to do the same to him. Gradually we are moving towards the coast and the English Channel. I think Fritz is trying to capture the ports which bring our supplies and reinforcements. So it's a race to the sea.

At the moment we are near Ypres, alongside an Indian regiment. The fighting is very heavy.

30 October 1914: The Battle of Ypres

Lots of things have changed: the weather's turning cold and wet; the lovely town of Ypres is now a wreck; the fighting is very different – we do more digging and sheltering from ARTILLERY than face-to-face fighting. Losses are getting really heavy, mainly because of BOMBARDMENTS. I have a feeling that we will have to get used to life in these TRENCHES.

12 November 1914: Stalemate

Both sides have given up trying to take Ypres. We can't shift the Germans, but they can't shift us either. We attack their trenches, they drive us back. It's the same for them. We just keep digging deeper and stronger trenches. We have also put BARBED WIRE barriers up along the entire trench line, and LAND MINES. I can't see how it will end.

25 December 1914: Christmas

They said it would all be over by now, but I reckon we'll be here next Christmas, too. It's still STALEMATE in our part of the line. We get new troops and supplies but so do the Germans.

The French tried to drive the Germans out of Artois last week but they lost thousands.
I am told that the trenches now run from here all the way to Italy.

Focus task

Why did the Schlieffen Plan fail?

1 Read through Billy's diary entries. Try to find reasons why the Schlieffen Plan failed. List as many as you can. Once you have made a list, decide whether each reason was an example of:
- factors that the Germans did not expect
- mistakes by the Germans
- the effectiveness of the Germans' opponents.

2 Add two more sentences to your work, explaining why the war was at stalemate by the end of 1914.

A common exam question is 'How RELIABLE is Source X?' 'Reliable' means you can trust the source to tell you the truth. Examiners usually want a 'balanced' answer (looking at both the strengths and weaknesses of the source). These two pages help you think this through.

Billy Wilson's diaries: using historical sources on the Great War

Key words **evidence; reliable; source**

I hope you found Billy Wilson's diaries interesting and useful. The aim was to help you to get an idea of the main events of 1914. However, it's confession time: I made up Billy Wilson. I thought the diary extracts would be an interesting way to learn about the war. But I used a wide range of original SOURCES, textbooks and other materials to make Billy's diaries realistic and also useful. Now it's time to think about how I used the sources.

Activity

1 Look at Sources 1–5 on page 11. These are some of the sources the author used to create Billy Wilson's diaries (but they are not in the right order). Decide how the author made use of each source. You could use a table like this to help you.

Source	**Which diary extract it was used for**	**Explain how you know the author used this source**
1		
2		
3		
4		
5		

2 All historians use sources. However, they don't usually create fictional characters. In pairs or small groups, work out your view on this question:

The diary of Billy Wilson is fictional so it is unreliable. Do you agree?

You could present your view in a class discussion or write a short paragraph to explain your view. Try to think in terms of 'balance'.

Before you reject the diary entirely, think about these questions:
- The diary is fiction – does that mean the information is wrong?
- The diary is based on original sources – would it have been more helpful if the author had just given you the sources?
- The author has added Billy's thoughts and views – do you think he has got EVIDENCE for them or did he just make them up?
- Does the diary sound and feel right? How did you reach that decision?

SOURCE 1

A volley of bullets whistled past our noses and cracked into the trees behind . . . More firing, closer now and tearing into our ranks . . . the 160 men that left the wood with me had shrunk to less than 100.

We had to go back . . . A bad defeat, there could be no arguing. In our first battle we had been badly beaten, and by the English – by the English whom we had laughed at a few hours before.

From the diaries of Walter Bloem, a young soldier in the German army in 1914. Here he describes his first taste of action at Mons.

SOURCE 2

14 August 1914

This has been a truly painful week waiting for orders to move, getting troops trained, etc., etc. Rumour has it we are to be left in England as Home Defence, which would be just awful.

From the diary of Billy Congreve, a young junior officer in the British army.

SOURCE 3

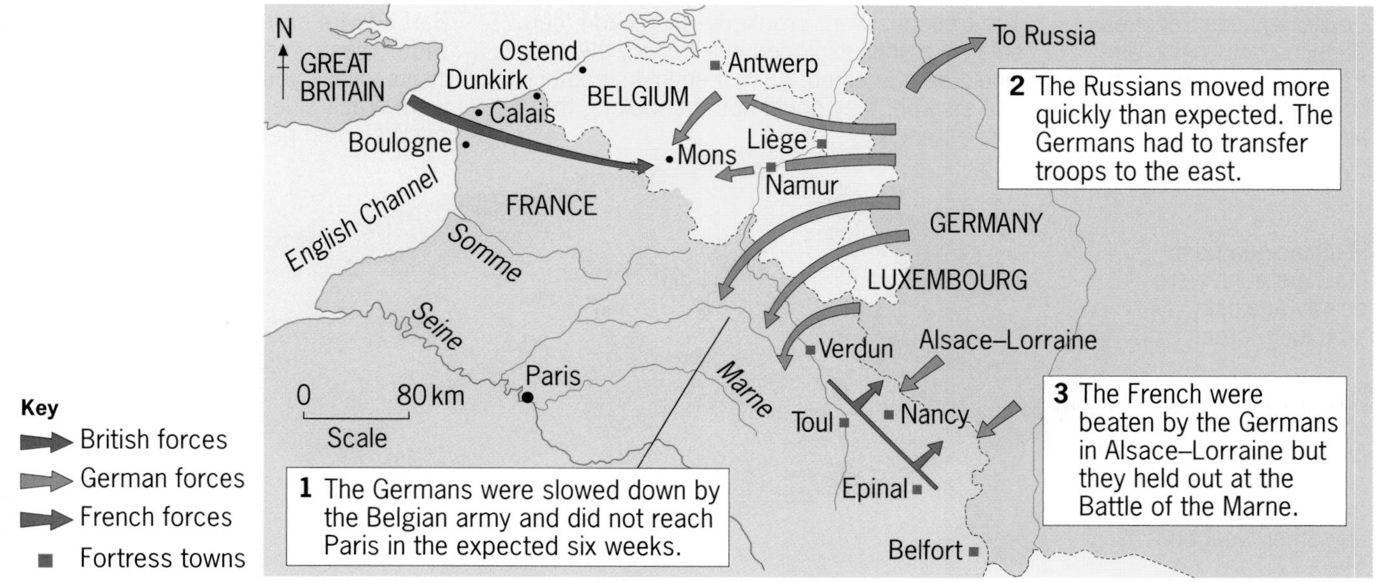
N
GREAT BRITAIN
Ostend
Dunkirk
Calais
Boulogne
Antwerp
BELGIUM
Mons
Liège
Namur
FRANCE
English Channel
Somme
Seine
Marne
Paris
0 80 km
Scale
To Russia
2 The Russians moved more quickly than expected. The Germans had to transfer troops to the east.
GERMANY
LUXEMBOURG
Verdun
Alsace–Lorraine
Toul
Nancy
Epinal
Belfort
3 The French were beaten by the Germans in Alsace–Lorraine but they held out at the Battle of the Marne.
1 The Germans were slowed down by the Belgian army and did not reach Paris in the expected six weeks.
Key
British forces
German forces
French forces
Fortress towns

A map showing the movement of the British, French and German armies in 1914.

SOURCE 4

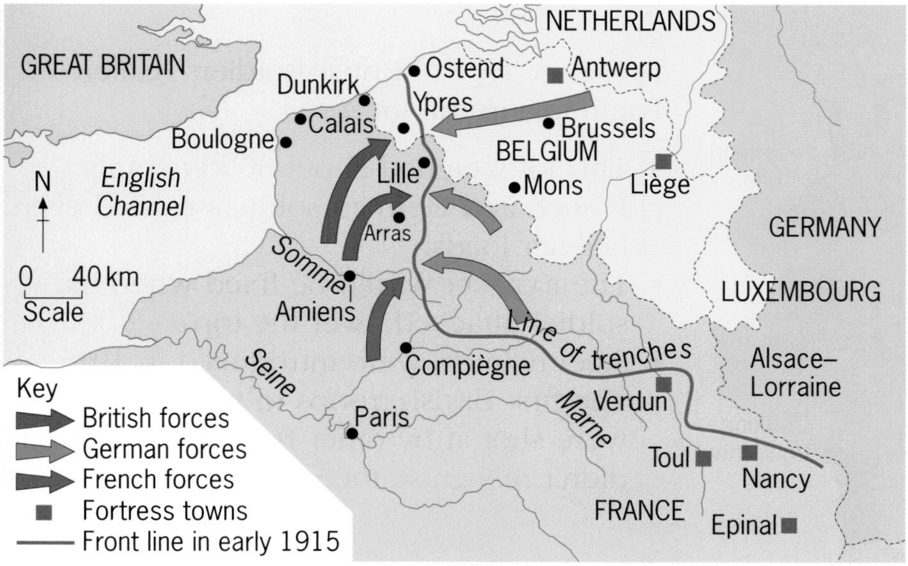
NETHERLANDS
GREAT BRITAIN
Dunkirk
Ostend
Antwerp
Ypres
Calais
Boulogne
Brussels
BELGIUM
Lille
Mons
Liège
N
English Channel
Arras
Somme
0 40 km
Scale
Amiens
GERMANY
LUXEMBOURG
Line of trenches
Compiègne
Alsace–Lorraine
Seine
Verdun
Marne
Paris
Toul
Nancy
FRANCE
Epinal
Key
British forces
German forces
French forces
Fortress towns
Front line in early 1915

A map showing the race to the sea in 1914.

SOURCE 5

That French soldiers who have retreated for ten days, sleeping on the ground and half dead with fatigue, should be able to take up their rifles when the bugle sounds is a thing which we never expected.

German army commander General von Kluck commenting on the actions of French soldiers at the Battle of the Marne.

1.3 A tour through the trenches

One important skill of an historian is to describe past situations accurately. Before you turn over to the next spread, try to memorise five important things about the trenches.

Key words **Allies; ammunition; bayonet; blast; censor; communications; duck boards; dugout; No Man's Land; 'over the top'; parapet; psychological; sewage; shell shock; shrapnel; sniper**

From 1914 to 1917, the Great War was bogged down in a stalemate. Neither side could defeat the other. Both the Germans and the ALLIES dug large, well-defended trenches.

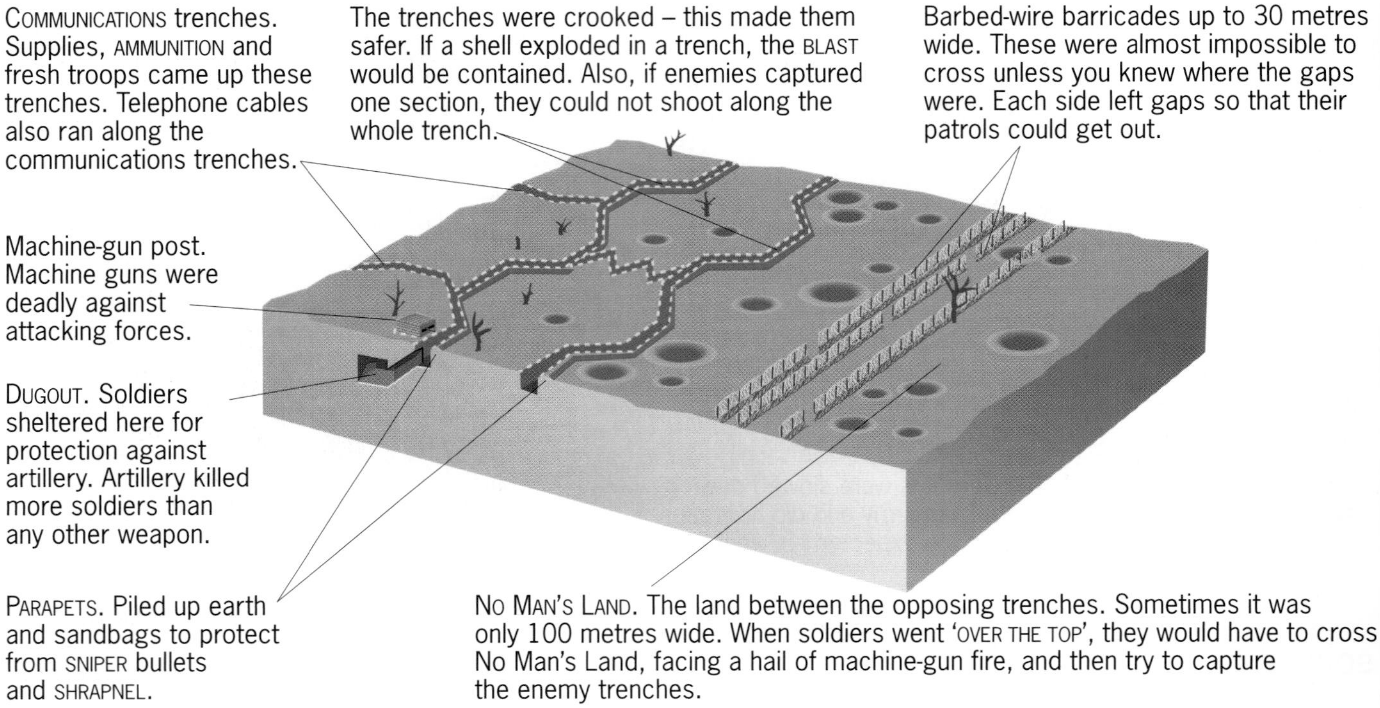

COMMUNICATIONS trenches. Supplies, AMMUNITION and fresh troops came up these trenches. Telephone cables also ran along the communications trenches.
The trenches were crooked – this made them safer. If a shell exploded in a trench, the BLAST would be contained. Also, if enemies captured one section, they could not shoot along the whole trench.
Barbed-wire barricades up to 30 metres wide. These were almost impossible to cross unless you knew where the gaps were. Each side left gaps so that their patrols could get out.
Machine-gun post. Machine guns were deadly against attacking forces.
DUGOUT. Soldiers sheltered here for protection against artillery. Artillery killed more soldiers than any other weapon.
PARAPETS. Piled up earth and sandbags to protect from SNIPER bullets and SHRAPNEL.
NO MAN'S LAND. The land between the opposing trenches. Sometimes it was only 100 metres wide. When soldiers went 'OVER THE TOP', they would have to cross No Man's Land, facing a hail of machine-gun fire, and then try to capture the enemy trenches.

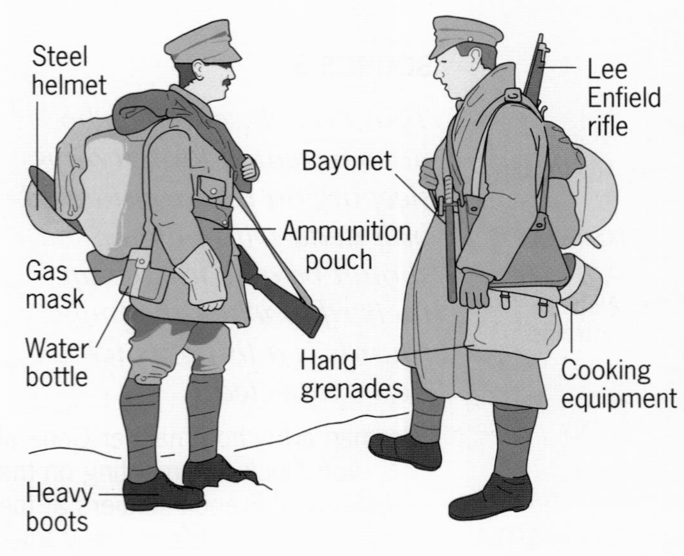

Steel helmet
Gas mask
Water bottle
Heavy boots
Bayonet
Ammunition pouch
Hand grenades
Lee Enfield rifle
Cooking equipment

These are typical British soldiers (called Tommies) in full kit.

- This kit weighed about 30 kilograms. French and German soldiers carried even heavier loads.
- The BAYONET would be fixed when the soldier attacked 'over the top'.
- Steel helmets were introduced in 1915. The first British troops to wear them were shot at by other British troops who didn't recognise them!

The soldiers' clothing was usually infested with lice, or 'chats' as the soldiers called them.

This officer is speaking to headquarters on a field telephone.

Letters from home were crucial to soldiers' spirits.

One thing this picture can't show you is the smell, which was awful, particularly in summer. There were thousands of horses and thousands of unwashed soldiers. At times, there were unburied human corpses. There were no toilets – at best, soldiers had to use a bucket which was emptied whenever possible.

This is a repair party. Tommies spent a lot of time digging or repairing trenches.

The constant bombardment of artillery could cause PSYCHOLOGICAL problems. This was usually called SHELL SHOCK. Soldiers suffering from shell shock often became totally confused or lost their memories.

This patrol is waiting for complete darkness. Then they will go out into No Man's Land to look at and listen to enemy trenches.

In winter, trenches flooded. Trench water could be contaminated with sewage. Crates, pieces of wood or DUCK BOARDS were laid down in the trenches to create a surface above the mud.

The bodies, SEWAGE and rubbish meant that the trenches were infested with millions of rats.

Boredom was a big problem. Soldiers played card games and bingo. Some took up courses to pass the time. Many took up sketching. Others, like Wilfred Owen, wrote poetry about the horrors of war.

An imaginative reconstruction of a British trench at the time of the Battle of the Somme.

Activity

1 You are a young soldier in 1916. You volunteered for the army and have been in the trenches for a few months. Write a letter home explaining what trench life is like. Write at least two sentences about each of these topics:

- the physical features of a trench (for example, the dugouts, the parapets)
- living conditions in the trenches
- the work you have to do
- the dangers you face
- how you pass the time.

NB If you use a word-processor to do this task, question 2 will be easier.

2 All letters that soldiers sent home from the trenches were censored. The CENSOR crossed out any information that might help the enemy, or any bad news that might discourage people back home.

You are now the censor. You will be given one letter from someone else in the class. Delete any details from it that you think you should. (If you are working on a word-processor, make sure that you save a copy of the original letter first!)

In this section, aim to:
- list at least three reasons why British soldiers were able to stand the trench conditions
- use at least two sources to support your reasons.

Why did the Tommies put up with it?

Key words battalion; comradeship; court-martial; mutiny; patriotic; rations

Life in the British trenches was pretty tough. The Germans, French, Russians, Italians (and, later, Americans) all suffered similar conditions. But there was no big MUTINY at all in the British army during the war. Why did the soldiers put up with the conditions?

One explanation is army discipline. Any soldier who disobeyed orders, or tried to run away, would be COURT-MARTIALLED, and could be executed. In fact, 3080 British soldiers were condemned to death for cowardice and similar offences during the Great War and 346 actually had the sentence carried out.

But discipline is not the only reason. Historians have looked at thousands of letters and diaries of ordinary soldiers and have found that other, more positive factors were just as important in keeping the Tommies motivated. This is what they have found out.

Factors that kept the Tommies motivated

1 Adventure

- **Travel:** most soldiers were ordinary working-class men. They had not travelled much before the war. The fighting took them to France and Belgium, the Middle East and Africa – places they would not otherwise have visited.
- **Excitement:** some men actually enjoyed the risk and the thrill of war.
- **Challenge:** most people like a challenge. War was the ultimate challenge. In war-time, many soldiers achieved things they would never have dreamt possible. It may have been an act of bravery or simply putting up with pain or hardship.

2 Comradeship

- **Old friends:** many BATTALIONS were made up of close friends who all joined the army together. Soldiers relied on each other totally. They did not want to let each other down. After the war, many soldiers said they greatly missed the sense of COMRADESHIP they had experienced during the war.
- **New friends:** Allied soldiers came from all over the world. British soldiers met Canadian, Australian, South African, New Zealand, Indian, West African and Caribbean soldiers. They also met many other British people.

3 Patriotism

The soldiers on all sides were generally PATRIOTIC. Whatever the horrors of war, most believed they were there to do a job for their country and that the job was worth doing well.

SOURCE 1

Four of us were talking and laughing on the road when a dozen bullets came within a whistle. We all dived for the nearest door, which happened to be a lav, and fell over each other, yelling with laughter . . . I adore war. It is like a picnic without the pointlessness of a picnic. I have never been so well or so happy. Nobody grumbles at being dirty.

Julian Grenfell, a British soldier serving in 1915, commenting on his experience of war.

1 Which of the factors 1–5 do Sources 1 and 2 support? Write two sentences to explain your answer.

SOURCE 2

My dear father and mother
Should this letter reach you, you will know that I have made the greatest sacrifice that it is possible for a lad to make for his country in her time of need, and in the struggle to free the world of its greatest curse – German militarism [military aggression].

I do not begrudge [resent] for a moment the price which has been demanded of me, as to serve in the greatest cause is indeed worthwhile. I hope you will not grudge the offering which this means you will make.

Part of a letter written by Private George Marriott in July 1915. The author volunteered for service. He was killed in action soon after he wrote this letter.

4 Comforts

- **RATIONS:** for British troops, food rations were generally good. Soldiers complained about always having tinned beef and jam, but they knew they were better off than French soldiers, and even French civilians, and they were *much* better fed than the Germans.
- **Letters:** soldiers received regular letters and parcels from home.
- **Luxuries:** they also received lots of little luxuries such as chocolate, cigarettes and alcohol.

5 Humour

Finally, we should not underestimate the importance of humour in keeping up morale! For example, 'Old Bill' was a cartoon soldier created by Captain Bruce Bairnsfather (see page 16). Old Bill grumbled and complained, but then got on with the job. He was very popular with soldiers. He helped them to laugh at their situation and therefore to rise above it.

Focus task

The Trench Top Ten

Once you have read page 16, look back over all of your work on pages 12–16. You could also do some extra research of your own for this task.

1. Make a list of the top ten facts you think are most important about life in the trenches.
2. Put a star next to any of your top ten facts that only the soldiers would know about (because of the censors).
3. Underline facts that you think are negative about life in the trenches.
4. Highlight facts that show positive aspects of trench life.
5. Finally, as a class, decide what are the five things every GCSE student should know about the trenches.

Activity

The trench experience

SOURCE 3

Bruce Bairnsfather

In and Out (I)

That last half-hour before "going in" to the same trenches for the 200th time

Bruce Bairnsfather

In and Out (II)

That first half-hour after "coming out" of those same trenches

Cartoons by Bruce Bairnsfather.

Source 4 (below) gives the view of one serving soldier on Bairnsfather's cartoons in Source 3.

1. Explain why the lieutenant in Source 4 felt that the cartoons were so accurate. (Mention at least three details in the cartoons that fit with your knowledge of trench life.)
2. The cartoons do not show every aspect of life in the trenches. What is not shown in the cartoons? (Mention at least two things you have come across that are not shown in the cartoons.)

SOURCE 4

You may have seen Captain Bruce Bairnsfather's two pictures showing the hour before going into the trenches and the hour after coming out. Well, they are absolutely it. Lord, how we laughed over them in the front line . . . Take it from me, he is one of the people who by supplying roars of laughter and joy to the troops are helping to win the war.

A letter to *The Outlook* magazine from a lieutenant in the British army.

1.4 How did they break the stalemate on the Western Front?

Your main aim on this page is to remember the major reason why there was a stalemate.

Key words camouflage; commander; Hindenburg Line; offensive; poison gas; tank

Why was there a stalemate?

From late 1914 until March 1918, there was stalemate on the Western Front. Why?

The biggest problem was that trenches were easy to defend. That is why they were dug in the first place! For both sides, the main method of attack was an artillery bombardment followed by an infantry attack (soldiers on foot). But immediately a bombardment finished, defenders would race to set up their machine guns. One machine gun could mow down hundreds of advancing soldiers.

Sometimes an attack did succeed and infantry would capture enemy frontline trenches. However, they found it almost impossible to hold on to them.

SOURCE 1

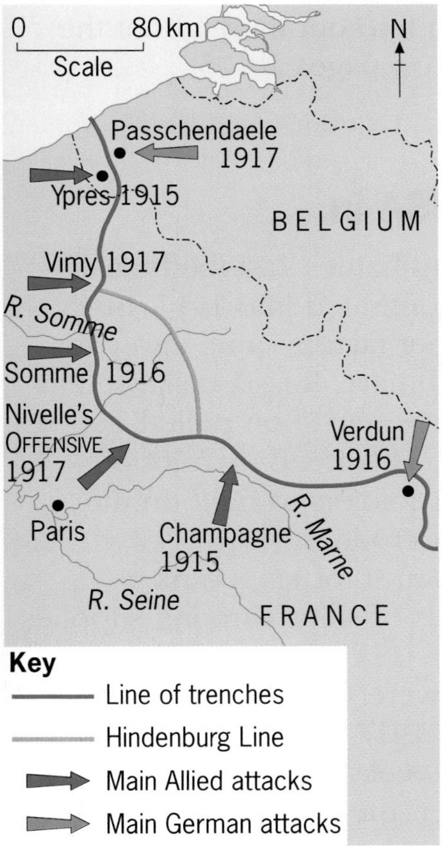
0
80 km
Scale
N
Passchendaele 1917
Ypres 1915
BELGIUM
Vimy 1917
R. Somme
Somme 1916
Nivelle's Offensive 1917
Verdun 1916
Paris
Champagne 1915
R. Marne
R. Seine
FRANCE
Key
Line of trenches
Hindenburg Line
Main Allied attacks
Main German attacks

The main battles on the Western Front 1915–17. The HINDENBURG LINE was a heavily defended line of forts, dugouts and trenches.

New techniques and ideas

Many people, both now and at the time, criticise the military COMMANDERS. They say that their tactics were useless and they did not care about soldiers' lives.

However, that is not quite fair. Throughout the war, new ideas were tried.

- Both sides used new weapons. The Germans first used POISON GAS in April 1915. The British used TANKS in 1916.
- Both sides used CAMOUFLAGE to disguise soldiers and guns.
- Both sides used aeroplanes.
- Artillery became more and more accurate.

Unfortunately, none of these ideas could break the stalemate.

Gas could only be used in the right weather conditions. Soldiers on both sides were soon issued with effective gas masks.

Tanks could make advances but they could not hold a captured trench. Anyway, they often broke down and became easy targets for German gunners.

- *Aim to give one reason why each of the following was important: Verdun; the Somme; the HUNDRED DAYS.*
- *If you're on good form, try to remember two examples of important technology.*

Key words **armoured car; attrition; blockade; breakthrough; general; Hundred Days; parachute; revolution; storm troopers; submarine**

1916: The war of Attrition

No one could break through so the war became a war of ATTRITION. Attrition means trying to win by killing enemy soldiers. At the Battle of Verdun (February–July 1916), the Germans caused 542,000 French casualties. They suffered 434,000 of their own. The slaughter continued at the Battle of the Somme, July–November 1916. French and British losses were over 600,000. German losses were 500,000. Germany lost many of its best soldiers at Verdun and the Somme. You can find out more about the Somme on pages 20–25.

1 Write your own definition of the term 'war of attrition'.

1917: Russia out, the USA in

The giant battles and the huge losses continued into 1917. But then other factors came into play.

In February, Russia collapsed in REVOLUTION and soon pulled out of the war. This freed up a lot of German soldiers to fight on the Western Front.

German SUBMARINES sank hundreds of ships carrying supplies from the USA to Britain. These attacks were very effective. At one stage in 1917, Britain was down to just six weeks' supply of food. However, the attacks had an unwelcome effect on Germany itself. The German submarines destroyed so many American ships that the USA entered the war against Germany in April 1917.

2 Explain why some historians call 1917 the year of crisis.

March 1918: the German breakthrough and the end of the stalemate

The Germans decided to try to win the war before American soldiers could arrive in large numbers. They moved troops from the Eastern Front to the Western Front and they trained special STORM TROOPERS to break through enemy defences. The Germans attacked in March 1918 very successfully. They broke through British lines in many places and the most successful attackers almost reached Paris. However, they stretched themselves too far. They were short of supplies because of the British naval BLOCKADE. Even if they had supplies, their soldiers had advanced so far it was difficult to get supplies to them.

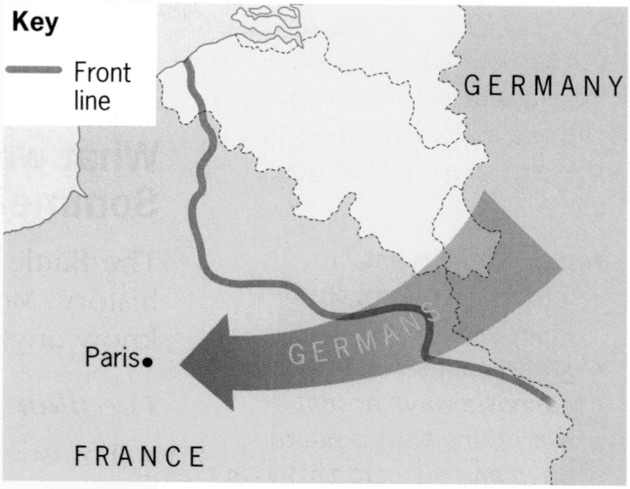

Key
Front line
GERMANY
GERMANS
Paris
FRANCE

3 Why did the German offensive fail?

August 1918: the Hundred Days

The Allies held their line and began to drive the Germans back. The British army took on the main role. The period August to November 1918 is known as the Hundred Days. In that time, Sir Douglas Haig led the British army brilliantly. It used accurate artillery barrages to destroy the heavily fortified Hindenburg Line. It captured nearly 190,000 enemy troops and 2800 guns. The British army used aircraft, ARMOURED CARS, tanks and radio communications. It dropped supplies to troops by PARACHUTE. It even used the lifejackets from cross-channel ferries to help soldiers cross the Saint Quentin canal! The Hundred Days was a period of outstanding victories.

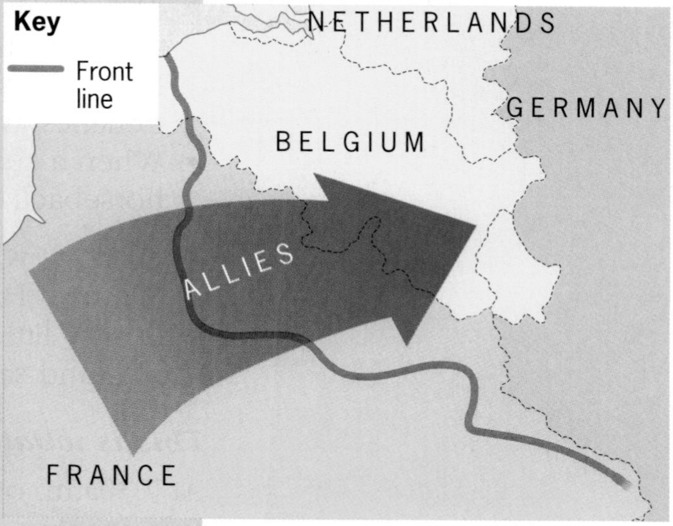

Key
Front line
NETHERLANDS
GERMANY
BELGIUM
ALLIES
FRANCE

4 Why were the Allies successful in the Hundred Days?

Focus task

The stalemate 1914–18

Prepare a short ICT presentation for a museum exhibit about the Great War.

Your presentation should have three 'pages'.

1 Why a stalemate developed (key words: defence, machine gun, artillery).

2 How the GENERALS tried to break the stalemate but failed (key words: gas, tanks, attrition).

3 How the stalemate was finally broken (key words: BREAKTHROUGH, Hundred Days).

For each 'page', you should write at least two bullet points and choose one picture from pages 17–19 or your own research. In your bullet points, make sure you use each of the key words.

1.5 The Battle of the Somme

During your course, you will have to use original sources. The two main aims in doing this are to show that you can:

- pick out relevant information from the sources
- give reasons why historians cannot always accept everything that a source says and support this with examples from the source.

These pages give you an opportunity to practise these skills.

Key words **barrage; cavalry; division; landmark; objective**

What went wrong on the first day of the Somme?

The Battle of the Somme was a LANDMARK event in Britain's history. Most people have heard of it, even if they don't know anything about it. The battle began on 1 July 1916.

The plan

- For one week, British guns would bombard German-held trenches with heavy artillery.
- The British bombardment would destroy the German trenches and blast the German barbed wire to pieces.
- German troops would be shell-shocked and would surrender.
- At 7.30a.m. the BARRAGE would stop and British soldiers would walk into No Man's Land. Some would carry heavy packs full of equipment to rebuild the German trenches as they captured them.
- When a suitable gap opened up, CAVALRY (soldiers on horseback) would be used to gain ground.

The troops who put this plan into action were commanded by General Haig. Most of the soldiers were young recruits with very little experience so the general kept his orders simple and said that they were to be obeyed strictly.

This is what happened

At 7.30a.m. on 1 July the attack began exactly as ordered. But, within minutes, it was clear that the German positions were not deserted. The slaughter was horrendous – the worst casualties of any single attack by a British army ever. By the end of the day, 20,000 soldiers were dead and 40,000 were wounded. Very few of the first day OBJECTIVES had been achieved. It was a military disaster. What went wrong?

The inquest

The army soon began an investigation. Page 21 gives you some of the evidence that would have been available to the army on or soon after 1 July 1916. See if you can work out what went wrong. The task on pages 22–23 will help you to analyse these sources.

SOURCE 1

I . . . joined this battalion on 13 June 1916. Previous to this attack [1 July] I had only been in the trenches for two days – I am 18 years of age.

From evidence given to the army inquiry by an officer, 2nd Lieutenant G.H. Ball, most of whose platoon were killed on the first day of the Somme.

SOURCE 2

The first wave of troops went over the parapet walking as they had been ordered. The ones who went over later were more canny. They did not stand up and get shot, they rolled over on their sides. Machine-gun fire caught a lot of men as they climbed over the parapet and some of them fell shot at our feet.

From the memoirs of a soldier from the Fermanagh and Donegal Volunteers, the 36th Ulster Division.

SOURCE 3

General Rees says that our barrage was accurate and severe. Despite our heavy fire, he saw the Germans, standing up above the parapet, fire very rapidly at our advancing infantry. He was amazed at the bravery of those Germans . . .
The result of this was that hardly any of our men were able to reach the German front line trenches. He saw lines which advanced according to their orders melting away under the fire. Yet not a man wavered, broke the ranks, or attempted to come back.

An account of a report from Brigadier General Rees, 1 July 1916, on events at Serre.

SOURCE 4

I LIE IN BED AND THINK ?
HOW A BATTALION OF THE SKIN'S LAY IN
ALL NIGHT LONG ..... THEN ATTACKED AT ZERO HOUR.
STORMING THE GERMAN TRENCHES IN A WILD FRENZY.
NO TIME FOR THE WOUNDED WE MUST KEEP ON.... ON .....
ALONE! ALONE! THE LAST OF ..... THIRTEEN ....
ALL SENSE OF RIGHT AND WR
FORGOTTEN ... KILL ... KILL ...
A LITTLE FAT SERGEANT THEN PUT THEM IN ORDER ... IN HIS OWN WAY.
POOR "KID LEWISS" ESCORTED THEM BACK. IT WAS HIS LAST TRIP.
THE SUN BEATS DOWN. WE DIG IN. WATER! WATER!
HOW THAT GLORIOUS 107th BRIGADE SWEPT THROUGH ... AND ONWARD.
GRANDCOURT LAY BENEATH US IN THE SUNLIGHT. A MARVELLOUS FEAT.
WONDERFUL DUGOUTS GERMAN THOROUGHNESS
A BIG BLACK BEARDED GERMAN BOMBER CAUSES HAVOC IN OUR RANKS
CAPT RENWICK GROWS DESPERATE HE STANDS UP AND SHOOTS ....
SURRENDER TO THOSE B— DAMN THE FEAR BOYS!
GOD ABOVE ME! THIS IS WAR.
HOW AN UNKNOWN FRIEND DRAGS ME TO THE SUNKEN ROAD ......
AT THE TOP OF ELGIN AVENUE ..... A WELL KNOWN VOICE ... OUR ADJUTANT CAPT MULHOLLAND ... IMPLORES ......
· ALL SKETCHES BY JIM MAULTSAID.

A sketch of the German dugouts by Private Jim Maultsaid of the 36th Ulster Division. The 36th was one of two units to make major advances on the first day of the Somme. This was partly because their commander did not follow orders. He sent his men into No Man's Land early. This allowed them to reach the German trenches before the Germans could emerge from their deep dugouts.

SOURCE 5

- *Reports up to 8a.m. seemed most satisfactory. Our troops had everywhere crossed the enemy's front trenches.*
- *By 9a.m. I heard that our troops in many places had reached the 1.20 line [the place they were supposed to reach after one hour, twenty minutes]. The 29th Division was held up just south of Hawthorne Ridge, but the 31st Division was moving into Serre village. This was afterwards proved to be incorrect.*
- *Hard fighting continued all day on front of Fourth Army. On a sixteen-mile front of attack varying fortunes must be expected! It is difficult to summarise all that was reported.*

Extracts from the diary of General Sir Douglas Haig for 1 July 1916. He wrote up his diaries after the battle and added extra details as they became clear.

Focus task

What went wrong on 1 July 1916?

Key word **inference**

When you use sources in an enquiry, work in four steps.

Use a table like this to record your findings.

Source	Comprehension	Connection (and inference)	Evaluation
	What does the source tell me?	This might have made things go wrong on 1 July 1916 because . . .	Reasons to accept or be careful with this source

Step 1 Comprehension: look at or read each source to understand what it is saying.

Step 2 Connection: connect the source to your enquiry question. In this case your enquiry question is 'What went wrong on 1 July 1916?' Sometimes this connection might be obvious. Sometimes you will need to 'read between the lines' (INFERENCE). For example, you might read Sources 1–5 and think to yourself:

Looks like communications were very poor – that would lead to problems.

The volunteer soldiers were very inexperienced. Maybe they were not up to the job.

The orders were very strict. The people who survived best were those who did not follow orders.

The leaders underestimated the German defences.

The bombardment does not seem to have worked very well.

Which of Sources 1–5 might support each of these inferences (things suggested by the source)?

Step 3 Evaluation: sources are your friends! Usually you can accept what they say. However, you should still check each source. It's always worth asking some questions about the source **in this order**:

- *Does the source sound or look trustworthy?* (Common sense)
- *Does the source fit with what I already know?* (Knowledge)
- *Does it fit with or clash with any of the other sources?* (Cross reference)
- *Does the language or look of the source seem suspicious (for example, does it try to justify or criticise something or someone)?* (Tone)
- *Who has produced the source and why?* (Provenance)
- *Was the person in a good position to know what was happening?* (Provenance)

Here is how you might fill out your table for Source 1.

Source	Comprehension	Connection (and inference)	Evaluation
1	This officer had only been in the trenches for two days. He was only eighteen years old.	Young, inexperienced officers might make bad decisions that lead to high casualties.	Accept source: From my background knowledge, I know that soldiers were mainly young volunteers without much experience. Careful with source: Only one officer in one unit – his evidence might not be typical of all officers.

Step 4 Cross referencing: when you have finished your table, think about cross referencing. Use a coloured pen to draw lines between points that back each other up. Use a different coloured pen to draw lines between points that contradict each other.

Step 5 Writing up your conclusions: now it is time to use your completed chart to help you to write a balanced answer to the enquiry question.

To test you a little we are not going to ask you simply to describe what went wrong on 1 July 1916. Instead we want you to consider this question, which is more like what you may face in the exam. (In an exam you are usually given a one-sided statement to agree or disagree with.) 'The first day at the Somme was a disaster for the British army because the generals were ineffective. How far do the sources agree with this view?'

To produce a balanced answer, you should use your table to help you:

- choose two sources that support the view
  - explain how they support the view
  - explain whether they are reliable sources
- choose two sources that do not support the view
  - explain what view these sources support
  - explain whether they are reliable sources.

Was the Battle of the Somme a disaster?

Your aim here is to:

- remember at least two interpretations of the Somme
- explain why each one has at least some evidence to support it.

Key word **hindsight**

Was the Battle of the Somme a disaster? This might sound like a pretty strange question after what you have found out about 1 July 1916. After five months of battle, the Allies had won a strip of land just 25 km long and 6 km wide. It had cost 420,000 British casualties (and 200,000 French casualties).

However, there are plenty of historians who argue that if you look at the bigger picture, the Somme was not a military disaster.

There are two claims to balance against each other.

The main aim was achieved ...

- The aim at the Somme was to save the French at Verdun. This was achieved.
- Haig always warned that casualties would be heavy but politicians didn't listen.

... but Haig did make expensive mistakes

- Haig had too much faith that the artillery would destroy German dugouts.
- Too many shells were duds.
- Early reports from the battle were over-optimistic so people had unrealistic hopes.

The Somme changed British attitudes to the war. Until this battle, the British public still hoped that some glorious victory would achieve a breakthrough and win the war. The Somme brought home to many people what kind of war this was – a long, grim war of attrition.

The battle also shook confidence in the army. Haig was criticised after the battle by his own soldiers, by politicians and in the newspapers. He gained the unwanted title of 'The Butcher of the Somme'. The relationship between Haig and the British Prime Minister David Lloyd George was particularly poor.

Focus task

Look at the planning mistakes mentioned on pages 20–25 then discuss these questions.

1. Which of these errors can only be seen with the benefit of HINDSIGHT? Which could be seen at the time?
2. Which of these mistakes were things under Haig's control and which were not?
3. Read Source 6 on page 25. Who is Lloyd George blaming for the casualties at the Somme – himself or Haig?
4. Study Sources 6–10 on page 25. On which side of the scales should each one go?

SOURCE 6

Should I have resigned rather than agree to this slaughter of brave men [at the Somme]? I have always felt there are solid grounds for criticism of me in that respect. My sole justification is that Haig promised not to press the attack if it became clear that he could not attain his objectives.

From the war memoirs of David Lloyd George, the British Prime Minister during the war.

SOURCE 7

An aerial view of German trenches under British bombardment in the days before the attack.

SOURCE 8

By 1918, the best of the old German army lay dead on the battlefields of Verdun and the Somme . . . As time passed, [casualties] were replaced by young fellows of the very best will, but without sufficient knowledge.

A German opinion on the German army of 1918.

SOURCE 9

Reg. No.	Rank.	Name.	Date of Death.
12/288	Pte.	Bagshaw, William	1/7/16
12/289	"	Bailey, Joseph	1/7/16
12/291	"	Barlow, Wilfred	16/5/16
12/294	"	Batley, Edward	1/7/16
12/296	"	Baylis, Lawrence	1/7/16
12/307	Cpl.	Braham, George	1/7/16
12/310	Pte.	Bramham, George	13/10/18
12/314	C.S.M.	Bright, Arthur Willey	12/4/18
12/318	Pte.	Brookfield, Fredk. Harold	1/7/16
12/591	"	Bedford, Norman	1/7/16
12/593	"	Beniston, Aubrey	1/7/16
12/597	L/Cpl.	Blenkarn, William	10/9/16
12/600	Pte.	Bowes, Frank	1/7/16
12/604	"	Bratley, Clifford William	11/4/18
12/606	"	Brindley, Charles W.	14/3/17
12/607	"	Brown, Arthur	1/7/16
12/608	"	Brown, Samuel	6/12/17
12/611	"	Busfield, Harry Craven	18/5/17
12/862	L/Cpl.	Barnsley, Frank	1/7/16
12/865	Pte.	Barrott, John Henry	1/7/16
12/867	"	Barton, John Arthur	1/7/16
12/870	"	Bennett, Joseph Arnold	1/7/16
12/871	L/Cpl.	Binder, Walter Bertram	1/7/16
12/874	"	Bland, Ernest	1/7/16
12/879	Pte.	Brammer, Archie	1/7/16
12/882	"	Brown, Stanley	1/7/16
12/887	"	Buttery, John Arnold	1/7/16

A page from the list of dead and wounded suffered by the Sheffield Pals Battalion on the first day of the Somme. The Sheffield Pals suffered 548 casualties on the first day of the battle.

SOURCE 10

We all admired him [Haig] tremendously, you know. In my opinion, whatever Lloyd George and all those other people said about him, if it hadn't been for Dougie we shouldn't have won the war.

A comment about Sir Douglas Haig from Reginald Haine, a soldier in the battle and winner of the Victoria Cross, the highest award for bravery.

1.6 Should the Great War really be called a world war?

At the end of this section, you should be able to:

- list three areas where fighting took place apart from the Western Front
- explain two reasons why the Great War can be called a world war.

Key words **airship; loan; U-boat**

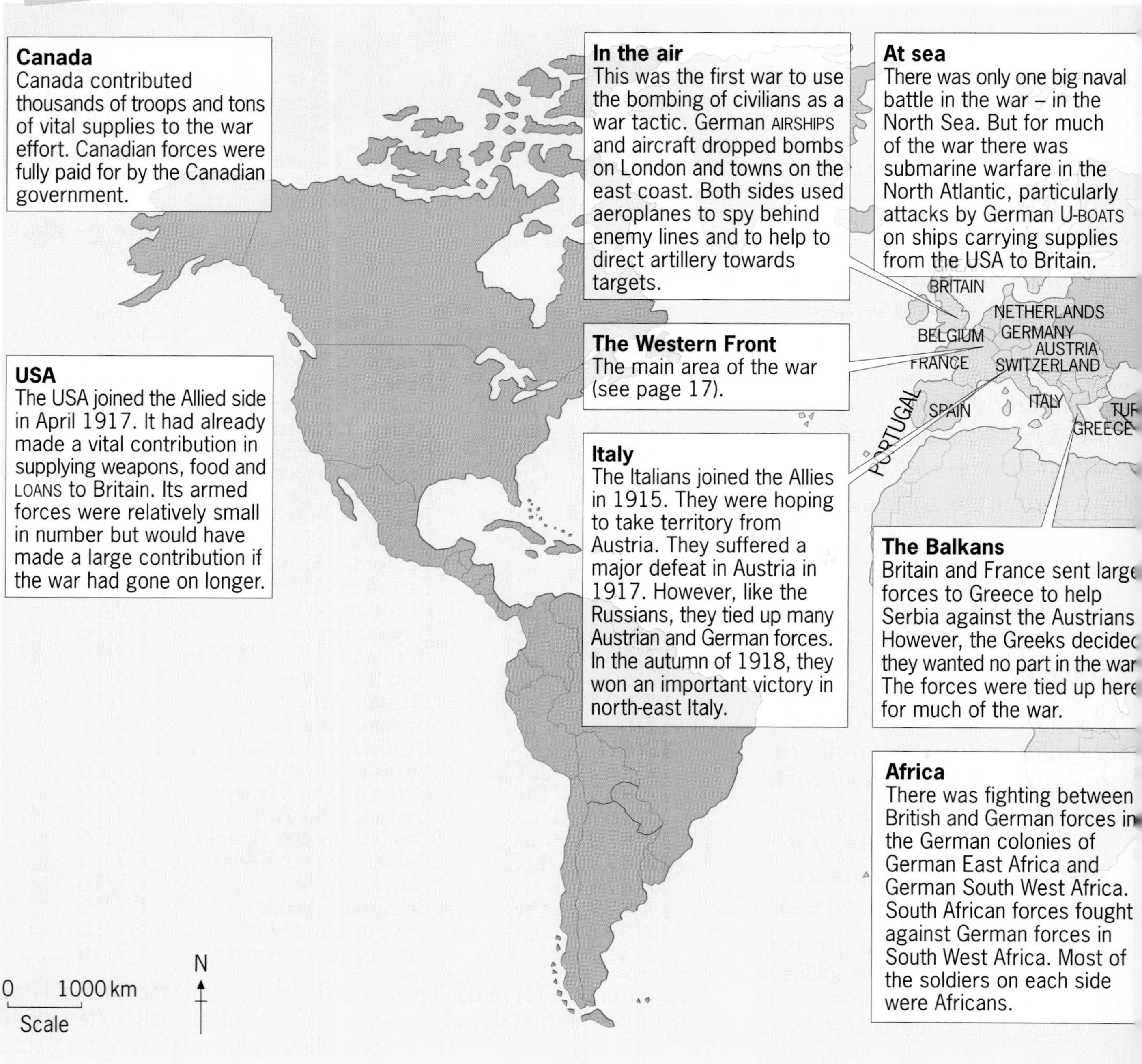
BRITAIN
NETHERLANDS
BELGIUM
GERMANY
AUSTRIA
FRANCE
SWITZERLAND
PORTUGAL
SPAIN
ITALY
TUR
GREECE
0 1000 km
Scale
N

Canada
Canada contributed thousands of troops and tons of vital supplies to the war effort. Canadian forces were fully paid for by the Canadian government.

USA
The USA joined the Allied side in April 1917. It had already made a vital contribution in supplying weapons, food and LOANS to Britain. Its armed forces were relatively small in number but would have made a large contribution if the war had gone on longer.

In the air
This was the first war to use the bombing of civilians as a war tactic. German AIRSHIPS and aircraft dropped bombs on London and towns on the east coast. Both sides used aeroplanes to spy behind enemy lines and to help to direct artillery towards targets.

The Western Front
The main area of the war (see page 17).

Italy
The Italians joined the Allies in 1915. They were hoping to take territory from Austria. They suffered a major defeat in Austria in 1917. However, like the Russians, they tied up many Austrian and German forces. In the autumn of 1918, they won an important victory in north-east Italy.

At sea
There was only one big naval battle in the war – in the North Sea. But for much of the war there was submarine warfare in the North Atlantic, particularly attacks by German U-BOATS on ships carrying supplies from the USA to Britain.

The Balkans
Britain and France sent large forces to Greece to help Serbia against the Austrians. However, the Greeks decided they wanted no part in the war. The forces were tied up here for much of the war.

Africa
There was fighting between British and German forces in the German colonies of German East Africa and German South West Africa. South African forces fought against German forces in South West Africa. Most of the soldiers on each side were Africans.

Focus task

Should the Great War really be called a world war?

The Great War is now more often called the First **World** War. Do you think this is an accurate name for it?

Write each of the fourteen titles from the map on a separate piece of card. Work with a partner to put each of these fourteen cards into one of the following categories:

- places where there was fighting
- places that supplied troops
- places that were affected in some other way.

Then write a paragraph to explain whether the Great War was really a world war.

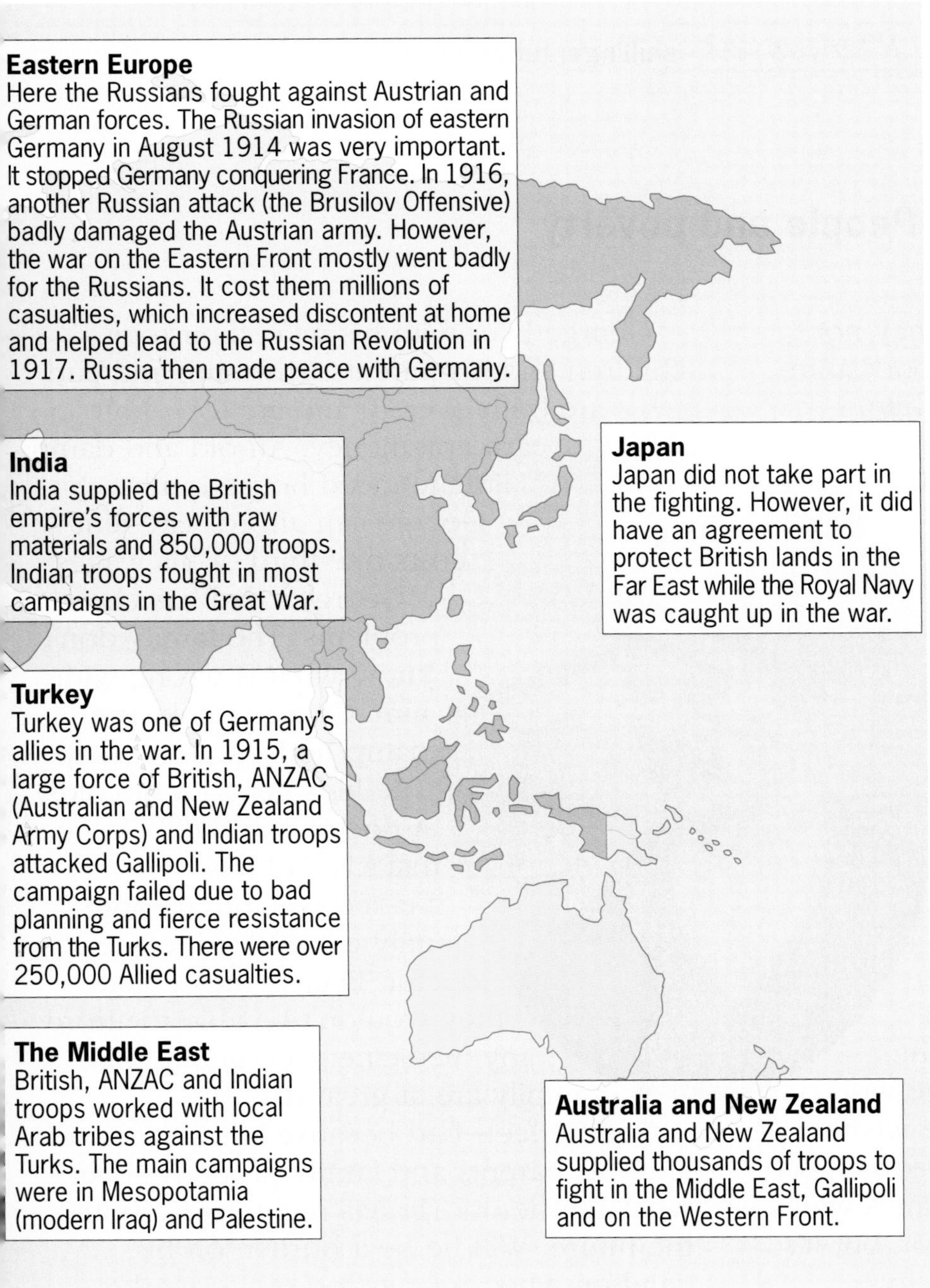

Eastern Europe
Here the Russians fought against Austrian and German forces. The Russian invasion of eastern Germany in August 1914 was very important. It stopped Germany conquering France. In 1916, another Russian attack (the Brusilov Offensive) badly damaged the Austrian army. However, the war on the Eastern Front mostly went badly for the Russians. It cost them millions of casualties, which increased discontent at home and helped lead to the Russian Revolution in 1917. Russia then made peace with Germany.

India
India supplied the British empire's forces with raw materials and 850,000 troops. Indian troops fought in most campaigns in the Great War.

Japan
Japan did not take part in the fighting. However, it did have an agreement to protect British lands in the Far East while the Royal Navy was caught up in the war.

Turkey
Turkey was one of Germany's allies in the war. In 1915, a large force of British, ANZAC (Australian and New Zealand Army Corps) and Indian troops attacked Gallipoli. The campaign failed due to bad planning and fierce resistance from the Turks. There were over 250,000 Allied casualties.

The Middle East
British, ANZAC and Indian troops worked with local Arab tribes against the Turks. The main campaigns were in Mesopotamia (modern Iraq) and Palestine.

Australia and New Zealand
Australia and New Zealand supplied thousands of troops to fight in the Middle East, Gallipoli and on the Western Front.

Review task

You have been commissioned to produce a new TV series on the Great War. It will consist of two programmes of 50 minutes each. That makes a total of 100 minutes. You have to decide how much time should be spent on each of the following topics.

- The origins of the war
- Why the war became a stalemate
- Conditions in the trenches
- The Battle of the Somme
- How the stalemate was broken.

You could summarise your ideas as a pie chart using ICT. Enter the number of minutes per section on a spreadsheet and the spreadsheet will draw the chart for you.

Revision task

Throughout this book, there are little yellow notes at the beginning of each section. The notes contain advice and ideas about important issues in each section. At the end of each chapter in the book, work in small groups to prepare a class quiz based on these notes. Your teacher can give you a sheet to help you.

2 British depth study: Britain 1906–18

Part A The Liberal Party's welfare reforms 1907–11

2.1 Why did the Liberals introduce welfare reforms?

By the end of the next page, aim to be able to list three main problems faced by the poor around 1906.

Key words **shillings; tuberculosis**

People and poverty

This is George Meredith. You may not realise it, but he was pretty important in 1906. George, and people like him, inspired Britain's government to bring in a range of new ideas and policies. Of course, George didn't know much about this either. He was too busy getting on with his life. And his life was pretty tough.

George is a builder's labourer in York. He generally carries bricks and mixes mortar for bricklayers. The bricklayers get about 38 SHILLINGS a week. George receives less than half that sum.

George faces other problems, too. If he is ill or has an accident, he doesn't get any money. If the work dries up, he gets nothing. If the weather is too bad to work, guess what George gets? That's right, nothing! He sometimes walks for ages to try to find other work, but it's pure luck whether he is successful.

George lives with his wife, their four children and his parents. His mum and dad are both over 70 and are too old to earn any money. An old and damp little terraced house is all George can afford. The rent costs one-third of his wages.

George's dad has chest problems. The family don't know what is wrong with him. George thinks the damp house doesn't help. The kids get a lot of colds. A doctor could tell George that his dad has TUBERCULOSIS, but George's family can't afford to see a doctor. Even if they could, they wouldn't be able to afford any medicine. George and his family are at great risk.

George feels bad because he cannot look after his parents and family properly – but what can he do? He has nightmares about the future. Will he be a burden on his children when he gets too old to work?

Activity

1 The diagram below shows some of George's problems. Make your own copy of the diagram.

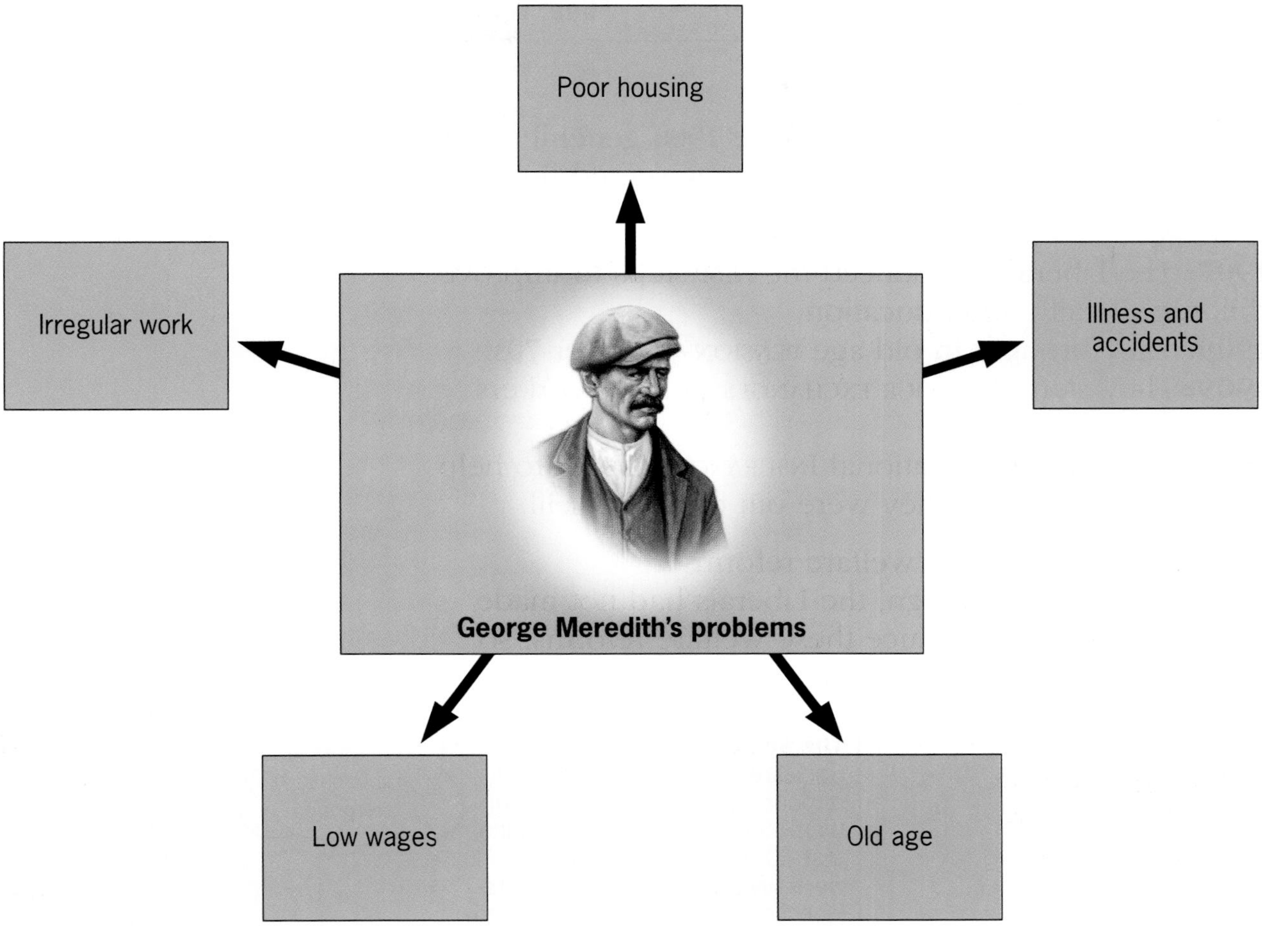

Poor housing
Irregular work
Illness and accidents
George Meredith's problems
Low wages
Old age

2 Add notes to explain why each issue is a problem for George.

3 With a partner discuss how one problem can make other problems worse – for example, housing and illness.

4 Add your conclusions to your chart.

5 Discuss the following questions with your partner.
- Do the problems facing George still exist today?
- If they don't, why don't they?
- If they do, are they as bad today?

6 How would you advise the government in 1906 to help George with his problems? List all the ideas you can think of. Then choose the three that you think are the most important. Later, you will see if you came up with the same ideas as the government.

Extension

7 Do you think your ideas would work? Write a few sentences about each of your important measures:
My first/second/third measure would be . . .
I think this might work because . . .
On the other hand, it might not work because . . .

Why?

Now make it your goal to explain two reasons why the LIBERAL government introduced WELFARE REFORMS.

Key words **Boer War; economic; insurance; Labour; labour exchanges; Liberal; pension; poverty line; reform; welfare**

The Liberals won a huge victory in the 1906 general election. Soon after they took power, they started helping poor people.

- **1907:** The Liberals introduced the first steps to improve children's health and education.
- **1909:** They brought in old age PENSIONS for over-70s.
- **1909:** They started LABOUR EXCHANGES to help workers find work.
- **1911:** They started a National INSURANCE scheme to help workers get by when they were out of work or ill.

These are known as their 'welfare reforms'.

In their election campaign, the Liberals had not made any big promises to introduce these welfare reforms, so why did they do it? Here are some of the reasons.

It's not their fault they are poor.
Rich people should help poor people.

The social reformers

Social reformers studied the lives of poor people in Britain. One of them, Seebohm Rowntree, found that 30 per cent of people in York were living below the POVERTY LINE (see Source 1). He also produced evidence that people like George Meredith were not poor because they drank too much or gambled – they were poor because of things they could not control, like the economy's ups and downs.

POVERTY

SOURCE 1

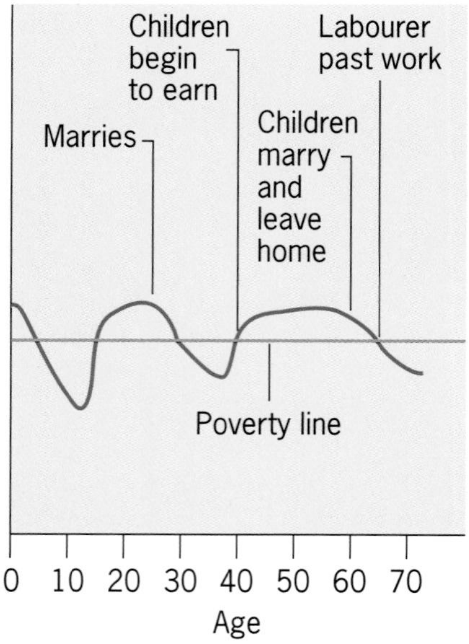
Children begin to earn
Labourer past work
Marries
Children marry and leave home
Poverty line
0
10
20
30
40
50
60
70
Age

Seebohm Rowntree's poverty line. Rowntree was a member of the famous chocolate-making family.

Idealism

Like many Liberals David Lloyd George thought the rich had a duty to help the poor. He felt it was right to tax the rich to raise money to look after the poor. He was able to persuade other people of his point of view.

Focus task

Why did the Liberals bring in welfare reforms?

The diagram below gives five reasons why the Liberals brought in welfare reforms.

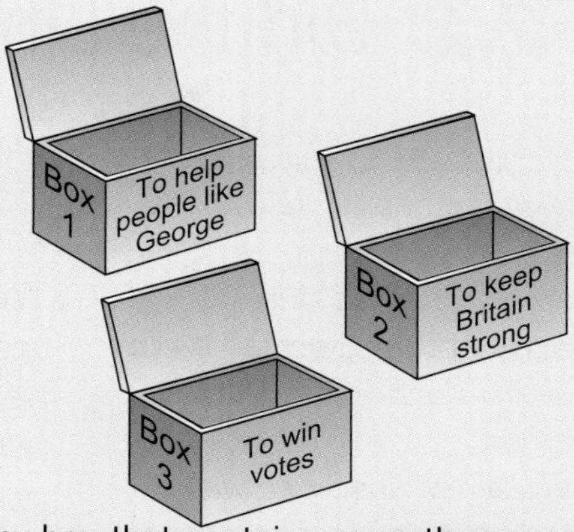
Box 1
To help people like George
Box 2
To keep Britain strong
Box 3
To win votes

1 Write each reason on a separate piece of card.
2 Add to the card your own one-sentence explanation of **why** this led them to bring in welfare reforms. Add at least one example or piece of evidence that supports your explanation.
3 These five reasons are connected. Which of the cards would you put in each of the boxes here? Some cards could go in more than one box.
4 Choose any box that contains more than one card and write a paragraph to explain how these cards are connected.

If there is another war, Britain will need these people to be soldiers.

The army
Between 1899 and 1902, Britain had fought the BOER WAR. In one big city (Manchester), only ten per cent of the army's recruits were found to be fit enough to be in the army. Men like George Meredith would never be fit enough to fight in Britain's army or navy.

Britain needs healthy workers.

Industry
Britain had lost its place as the world's top ECONOMIC power. The USA was already ahead and Germany was catching up fast. Germany had good welfare schemes for workers and German workers were healthier and better educated than British workers. Britain would lag behind unless it did something about it now.

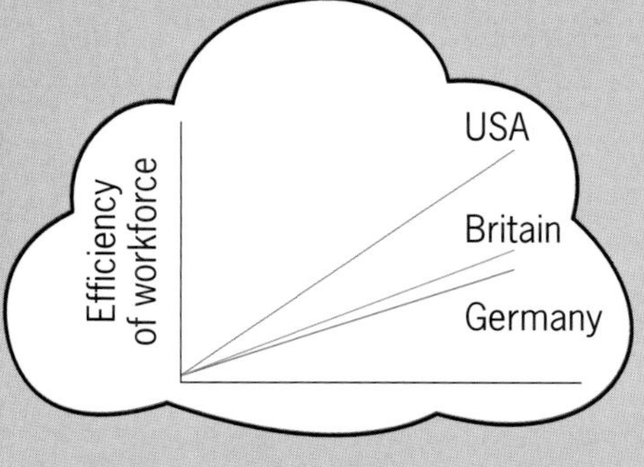
Efficiency of workforce
USA
Britain
Germany

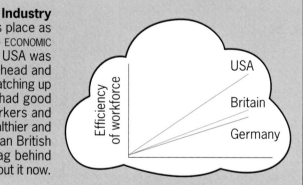

These people can vote now.

The Labour Party
Millions of men like George Meredith were not just workers – they were also voters. The Liberals were worried about the small (but growing) LABOUR Party. If Labour promised better welfare reforms, then men like George would support Labour rather than the Liberals.

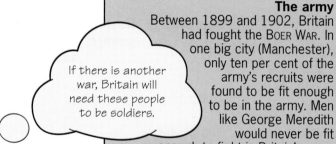

2.2 Did the Liberal welfare reforms work?

Set yourself some new goals. Aim to:

- explain at least one success the Liberals had in helping children and the elderly
- explain at least two ways in which the measures were weak or unsuccessful.

Key words **council; reality; workhouse**

The Liberal Party's welfare reforms have caused lots of arguments. Some people talk about the reforms as if they helped change the world. Others say that the reforms were useful, but were really just a drop in the ocean in solving poor people's problems.

As you find out what the Liberals did, see what you think.

Focus task

On pages 32–35, you are going to find out about the main measures the Liberals passed. After each measure there is a source or two reacting to it. These sources make some kind of claim about the measure. You have to decide where the claim fits on this REALITY scale:

-5	0	5
Over the top – negative	Reasonable	Over the top – positive

Use a table like this to record your answers:

Sources	Basic point(s)	My comments on source being made	Place on the reality scale (-5 to +5)
Children			
Old people			
Unemployed and workers			

To help you decide where to put the source on the scale, see how it stands up to the source tests that you first used in step 3 on page 23.

Children

Most people at the time felt that families were responsible for children. Churches and local COUNCILS provided schools and looked after orphans, but that was about it.

- In 1906, the Liberals passed an Education Act. This *allowed* local councils to provide free school meals *(but it did not force them)*. The idea was that if schools provided meals then poor children would do better at school.
- In 1907, councils *were forced* to provide school medical services. They had to provide check-ups but not treatment. After 1912, they were supposed to provide treatment too, but they *were not forced* to do so.
- In 1908, the Liberals passed the Children and Young Persons Act which made children 'protected persons'. Parents could be prosecuted (taken to court) for ill-treating children. There were also other measures such as regulations on children working.

SOURCE 1

The Children's Act makes parents responsible for finding food and clothing and other necessaries for children. We find that the Act has not to any large extent been enforced by the London county council, or by most local authorities outside London.

An extract from a petition sent to the government in 1911 by the Charity Organisation Society.

1 Fill in the first row of your table to judge Source 1. Source 2 should help you decide how realistic it is.

SOURCE 2

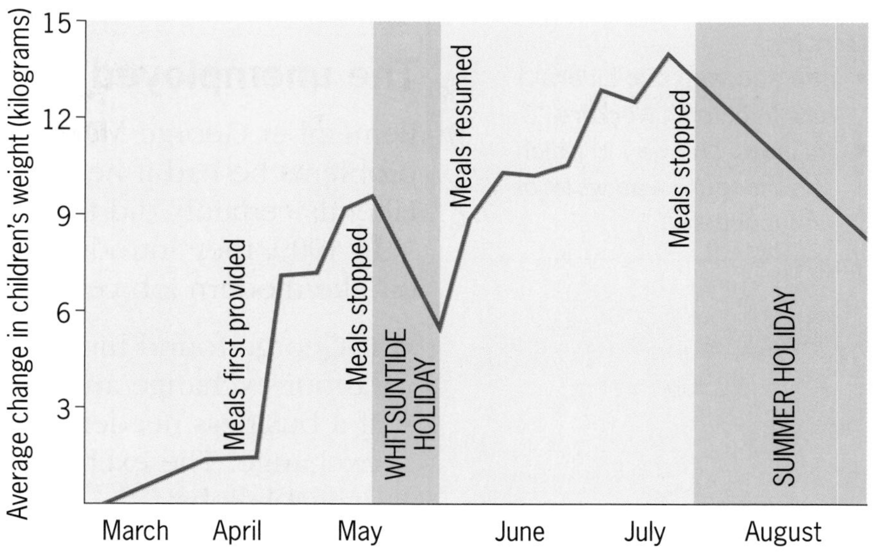

Average change in children's weight (kilograms)
15
12
9
6
3
Meals first provided
Meals stopped
WHITSUNTIDE HOLIDAY
Meals resumed
Meals stopped
SUMMER HOLIDAY
March
April
May
June
July
August

A graph drawn from government figures showing children's weight at different times of the year.

SOURCE 3

Old age pensioners greeting David Lloyd George at Morriston near Swansea in Wales.

2 Fill in the second row of your table to judge Source 4. Source 3 should help you decide how realistic it is.

Old people

Most poor people dreaded old age. They did not earn enough to save for a pension. When they were old, most of them depended on their families. Many others had to live in a WORKHOUSE.

- In 1909, the Liberals brought in the Old Age Pensions Act.
- Anyone over 70 who had no other income was given five shillings per week.
- A married couple received 7s 6d per week.

It was *not exactly a fortune* and *you had to live to 70* to get it. On the other hand, think what kind of difference this pension might have made to a family like George Meredith's.

SOURCE 4

When the old age pensions began, life was transformed . . . They [the old people] were relieved of anxiety. They were suddenly rich! Independent for life! As they first went to the Post Office to draw their pension tears of gratitude would run down the faces of some . . . There were flowers and apples from their gardens for the girl who simply handed them their money.

From *Lark Rise to Candleford* by Flora Thompson. In 1909, she ran a post office where she had to give out pensions.

From these two pages, identify:
- one success the Liberals had in helping workers
- at least one way in which the measure was weak or unsuccessful.

Key words benefit; short term; unemployment

The unemployed

Remember George Meredith? Do you remember the problems he had if he was ill, or his work dried up? The Liberals certainly did not forget people like George.

In 1909, they introduced labour exchanges. These were a bit like modern job centres.

- If George found himself short of work, he could go to a labour exchange and sign on.
- If a business needed workers, it told the labour exchange. The exchange then told George about any available jobs.
- By 1913, the exchanges were finding jobs for 3000 workers every day. However, many of the jobs were SHORT TERM and low paid.

Workers

In 1911, the Liberals passed the National Insurance Act.
- Part I aimed to protect workers against illness.
- Part II tried to help workers cope with UNEMPLOYMENT.

NATIONAL INSURANCE

Part I

- **Workers had to pay 4d out of their weekly wages to the government (*not popular at all with people like George – he felt his wages were small enough without the government taking money out of them*). Employers had to pay 3d and the government added 2d. This built up a fund.**
- **If workers were off work because of illness, the fund gave them money to live on and provided medical care for thirteen weeks.**

Part II

- **Workers, employers and the government all put in 2½d per week (*more money out of George's pay packet!*)**
- **If workers were out of work, they got unemployment BENEFIT. This was 7s 6d for fifteen weeks.**
- **The benefit was paid for fifteen weeks only, because the government did not want the unemployed to become too comfortable!**

Despite all this action, the Liberals did not do much about George's other problems, such as his low wages or his damp and expensive house. Even the leading Liberal MP, Lloyd George, admitted in 1911 that they had a long way to go (see Source 6).

SOURCE 5

THE DAWN OF HOPE.

NATIONAL INSURANCE AGAINST SICKNESS AND DISABLEMENT

Mr. LLOYD GEORGE'S National Health Insurance Bill provides for the insurance of the Worker in case of Sickness.

Support the Liberal Government in their policy of SOCIAL REFORM.

A poster produced by the Liberal Party for the 1911 general election.

SOURCE 6

I never said that the National Insurance Bill was the final solution. I am not putting it forward as a complete remedy. It is one of a series. We are advancing on the road, and it is an essential part of the journey.

From a speech by senior Liberal MP David Lloyd George. He was Chancellor of the Exchequer and one of the most important figures in getting the Liberal Party to pass welfare measures.

1 Fill in the third row of your table to judge Sources 5 and 6.

Most source-based exam papers end with a question like the one in the Focus Task. The trick is to use sources **and** your own knowledge to produce a **balanced** answer. Look back at pages 22–23 for advice.

Activity

You work in the press department of the Liberal Party. You have to feed good news about the welfare reforms to the newspapers. Remember that the papers will be read by people like George Meredith who want to know exactly how the measures will help them.

Work in groups of five. One of you write a press release for each of the following years: 1906, 1907, 1908, 1909 and 1911.

You will need to:

a) work out from pages 32–35 what the Liberals did in that year

b) summarise in three or four bullet points how this will help George Meredith's family.

Focus task

'In the early 1900s, the Liberals failed to improve life for the poor.'

Use Sources 1–6 and your own knowledge to write a balanced view of this statement. You will need to divide your answer into sections.

1 A section that disagrees with the statement
- Explain at least two ways in which the Liberals improved life for workers, the elderly or children.
- Make sure you use at least one source and one piece of factual knowledge.

2 A section that agrees with the statement
- Explain two ways in which Liberal reforms did not really solve the main problems of workers, the elderly or children.
- Make sure you use at least one source and one piece of factual knowledge.

Part B Votes for women

2.3 Votes for women: for and against

As you read this information, aim to be able to:

- list two arguments **for** women's SUFFRAGE which were put forward at the time
- list two arguments **against** women's suffrage which were put forward at the time.

Key words **campaigner; election; suffrage**

Background

In 1906, most (but not all) men could vote in general ELECTIONS to elect Members of Parliament (MPs). However, no women could vote in general elections. Between 1906 and 1918, women's suffrage (the right to vote) became one of the most important issues in British politics. It was not a simple issue:

- Some *women* were opposed to women getting the vote.
- Many women CAMPAIGNERS for the vote wanted only *some* (wealthy and respectable) women to get the vote.
- Lots of *ordinary* working women did not care whether they got the vote or not.
- Most men were opposed to women getting the vote.
- Some *men* tried to get women the vote.
- Some men thought it was the right idea *but* they thought that giving women the vote needed to be done slowly.

The arguments for and against women's suffrage

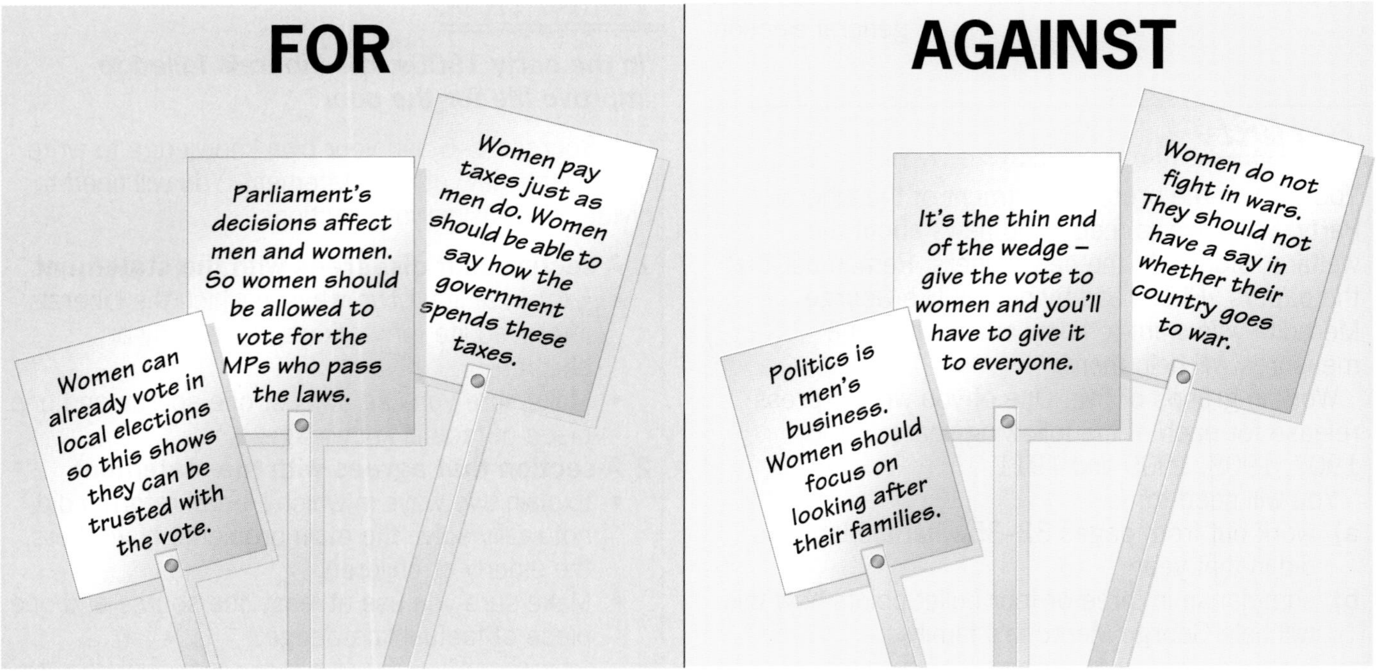
FOR
Women can already vote in local elections so this shows they can be trusted with the vote.
Parliament's decisions affect men and women. So women should be allowed to vote for the MPs who pass the laws.
Women pay taxes just as men do. Women should be able to say how the government spends these taxes.
AGAINST
Politics is men's business. Women should focus on looking after their families.
It's the thin end of the wedge – give the vote to women and you'll have to give it to everyone.
Women do not fight in wars. They should not have a say in whether their country goes to war.

Source activity

How did each side try to win support?

SOURCE 1

What a Woman may be, and yet not have the Vote
MAYOR
NURSE
MOTHER
DOCTOR or TEACHER
FACTORY HAND
What a Man may have been, & yet not lose the Vote
CONVICT
LUNATIC
Proprietor of white Slaves
Unfit for Service
DRUNKARD

A postcard published by the National Union of Women's Suffrage Societies (NUWSS) in the early 1900s. The NUWSS was the largest organisation that campaigned for women's suffrage.

1 Look closely at Source 1.

a) What impression is the artist trying to give of women? Explain your answer by mentioning details such as facial expression, clothes, actions and objects in the cartoon.

b) What impression is the artist trying to give of men? Explain your answer by mentioning details such as the men chosen, expressions, actions, etc.

c) Write a sentence to sum up the main argument of Source 1. Does this argument appear in the list of arguments for women's suffrage on page 36?

2 Now look closely at Source 2.

a) What impression is the artist trying to give of women? Explain your answer by mentioning details such as facial expression, clothes, actions and objects in the cartoon.

b) What impression of women do we get from the caption?

c) What impression is the artist trying to give of men?

d) Write a sentence to sum up the main argument of Source 2. Does this argument appear in the list of arguments against women's suffrage on page 36?

SOURCE 2

POST
EARLY
VOTE

'WHAT'S THE DISTURBANCE IN THE MARKET PLACE?'
'IT'S A MASS MEETING OF THE WOMEN WHO'VE CHANGED THEIR MINDS SINCE THE MORNING AND WANT TO ALTER THEIR VOTING-PAPERS.'

A cartoon from *Punch* magazine published in 1918. Some women gained the vote in 1918. This cartoon suggested what would happen when women were finally allowed to vote in elections.

2.4 The fight for the vote: Suffragists and Suffragettes

On these pages, you will practise the skill of getting information from sources.

Key words Suffragettes; Suffragists

There were two groups campaigning for the vote between 1900 and 1914 – the SUFFRAGISTS and the SUFFRAGETTES. What can you work out about them from these two sources?

The Suffragists

Questions

Is this all they did?

Inferences

Used peaceful methods.

Information

Supported by both men and women.

SOURCE 1

NATIONAL UNION OF
WOMEN'S SUFFRAGE SOCIETIES
LAND'S END TO LONDON.

Suffragists begin their Pilgrimage to London, 18 June 1913. For six weeks, Suffragists from all over the country marched to London. The Pilgrimage ended in Hyde Park with a meeting of around 50,000 men and women supporters of women's suffrage.

The Suffragettes

SOURCE 2

VOTE
VOTES
VOTES

Membership card of the Women's Social and Political Union (WSPU) from 1909.

Activity

Imagine that Sources 1 and 2 are the only pieces of evidence that exist about the Suffragists and Suffragettes. Get your own copies of these sources from your teacher and paste them in the centre of a sheet like Source 1. For each source follow these steps.

- Make a list of all the things you can *definitely* tell from the source. Write those in the inner rectangle.
- Make a list of all the things you can *probably* tell from the source – your inferences. Write these in the middle rectangle.
- Make a list of all the questions you would like to ask about this source. Write these in the outer rectangle.

Some labels have been added to Source 1 to get you started.

Key words militant; moderate

As you read these pages, try to remember one thing the Suffragists and Suffragettes agreed about and one thing they disagreed about.

The Suffragists – moderates

In the 1800s, various groups supported women's suffrage. In 1897, they joined to form the National Union of Women's Suffrage Societies (NUWSS). They were usually called the Suffragists. Their leader was a determined campaigner called Millicent Fawcett.

The NUWSS was an impressive organisation. It had over 500 local branches around the country. It organised rallies and marches, which were often reported in the newspapers. The rallies were orderly and well organised. Even people who disagreed with the Suffragists admired their organisation and discipline. In 1913, the NUWSS ran a campaign of over 400 meetings around the country.

Millicent Fawcett and other Suffragists wrote thousands of letters to MPs. They went to meetings of all the political parties and asked questions about women's suffrage. Everybody in Parliament knew who Fawcett was and what her movement wanted. MPs were constantly under pressure from Fawcett and her supporters. When the Liberals came to power in 1906, about 400 MPs (a big majority) supported the idea of giving the vote to some women.

SOURCE 3

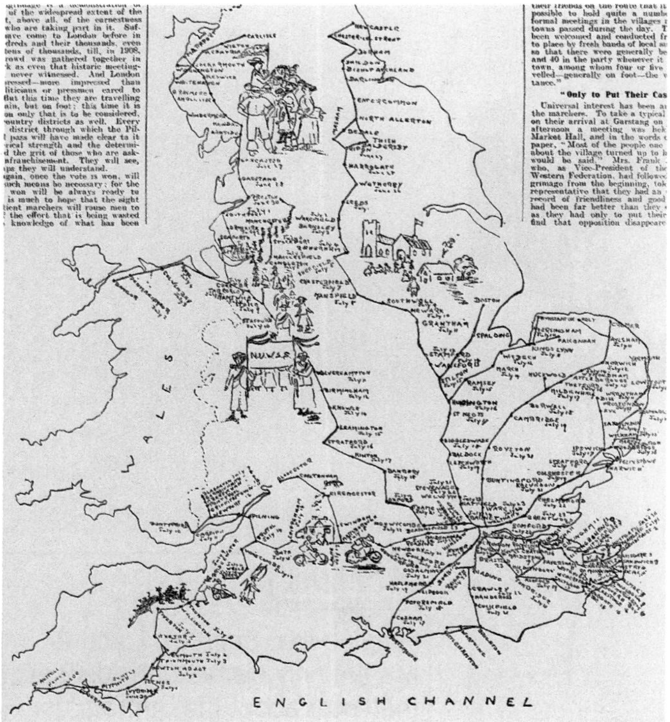
ENGLISH CHANNEL

A map from the magazine *Votes for Women* showing the groups involved in the Suffragist march to London, July–August 1913.

SOURCE 4

I was deeply interested in the work of the National Union of Women's Suffrage Societies and so I decided to take a job with the organisation. I became editor of the NUWSS's newspaper, The Women's Franchise, *and I learned by experience how to select, produce and edit material . . . I also organised petitions, deputations [a group of people acting on behalf of others] and processions.*

The memories of Suffragist, Margery Corbett Ashby. She joined the NUWSS while she was a student at Cambridge University.

1 Look at Source 4. What does it tell you about the
- aims
- motives
- methods

of the Suffragists?

Explain your answer by referring to the source.

Fawcett believed that her MODERATE methods worked. The movement, she felt, was like a glacier – it was huge and unstoppable. One day women would succeed – they would get the vote. But, like a glacier, the movement was also very slow. Far too slow for some . . .

The Suffragettes – militants

Progress was certainly too slow for Emmeline Pankhurst. In 1903, she formed a new organisation called the Women's Social and Political Union (WSPU). The *Daily Mail* called its members 'the Suffragettes' and the name stuck. Pankhurst and her daughters believed that the campaign for votes for women should be MILITANT.

- They disrupted political meetings, especially when government ministers were speaking. In 1908, Emmeline Pankhurst and her daughter Christabel even tried to barge into the House of Commons.
- Many Suffragettes were arrested. This was a deliberate tactic. Getting arrested got maximum publicity and also embarrassed the government.
- Once in prison, the Suffragettes went on hunger strike and were force fed.

Between 1906 and 1913, new laws to give women the vote were put forward six times. Each time they failed. With each defeat, the Suffragettes became more violent. The worst year of violence was 1913 (see Source 5 for an example). Suffragettes attacked government property and property belonging to opponents of women's suffrage. Suffragettes themselves were often attacked by crowds who opposed them. They got little protection from the police. Indeed, some were violently mistreated by police.

Perhaps the most extreme event of all came in June 1913 at the Derby horse race. The Suffragette Emily Davison tried to pin a banner on the King's horse as it thundered by. The horse was brought down and Emily was killed. There was enormous publicity for this sensational event.
To start with, all the publicity was hostile but, later, the fact that Davison was (apparently) prepared to die for her beliefs made a real impact. So, too, did the orderly and impressive procession at Emily Davison's funeral.

SOURCE 5

SUFFRAGETTES
BURN
ANOTHER
CHURCH
Evening
News
6.30

A newspaper poster from the West Midlands. The church was burned down by Suffragettes, on 18 June 1913, as a protest against Parliament refusing to give votes to women.

2 'We should not blame the Suffragettes for the violence in 1913. We should blame the politicians for not giving women the vote.' Do you agree?
3 Look back at the Activity on page 39. How many of your questions can you answer now?
4 On the last four pages we have given the same amount of space to the Suffragettes as to the Suffragists. Do you think this is right?

Back to the sources! On page 40 you used just one source to answer a question. Your main aim now is to use more than one source to answer a question.

Were the Suffragettes effective campaigners?

The Pankhursts believed militancy worked. They got huge publicity – much more than the Suffragists. Parliament seemed to take the issue more seriously once the violent actions started. However, violence also made the government very stubborn. They did not want to give in to violence from women. They feared that, if they did, other groups would use violence to get their way. Some people said that once the campaign turned violent, there was no chance of women being given the vote.

SOURCE 6

The procession was an impressive pageant [parade]. It was watched by dense crowds . . . Nearly five thousand members from all over the country marched in undisturbed quiet and orderliness behind the coffin.

Description of Emily Davison's funeral in the *Manchester Guardian*, 16 June 1913. The Suffragettes planned this event carefully. They organised two funerals – one in Morpeth and one in London.

SOURCE 7

FEMALE SUFFRAGE
GREAT LIBERAL MEETING
TO-DAY AT 3.
Bernard Partridge

THE SHRIEKING SISTER.

THE SENSIBLE WOMAN. "YOU HELP OUR CAUSE? WHY, YOU'RE ITS WORST ENEMY!"

A cartoon from *Punch* magazine, 1906, by the artist Bernard Partridge, who opposed women's suffrage. The title, 'The Shrieking Sister', refers to the woman on the right, who is a Suffragette.

SOURCE 8

A deed of this kind, we need hardly say, is not likely to increase the popularity of any cause with the ordinary public. Reckless fanaticism [thoughtless enthusiasm] is not regarded by them as a qualification for the franchise [vote] . . . Persons who destroy property and endanger innocent lives must be either desperately wicked or entirely unbalanced.

From *The Times*, 6 June 1913, following the death of Emily Davison at the Derby horse race.

SOURCE 9

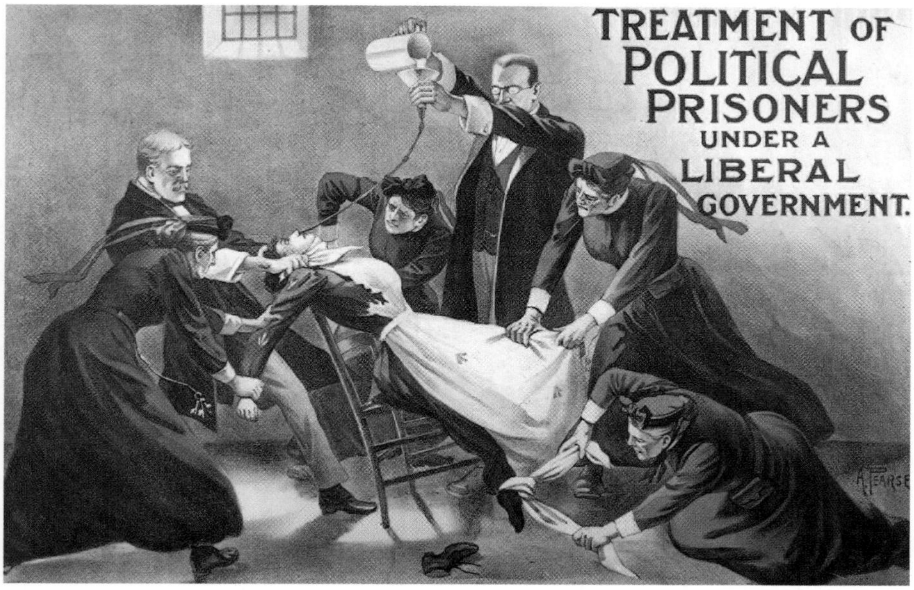
TREATMENT OF
POLITICAL
PRISONERS
UNDER A
LIBERAL
GOVERNMENT.

A Suffragette poster criticising the force feeding of Suffragettes in prison. Force feeding created sympathy for the Suffragettes. As a result, the government allowed Suffragettes on hunger strike to go home and then come back to prison when they had recovered. Suffragettes called this the Cat and Mouse Act.

SOURCE 10

Haven't the Suffragettes the sense to see that the very worst kind of campaigning for the vote is to try to blackmail or intimidate a man into giving them what he would otherwise gladly give?

Liberal politician David Lloyd George speaking in 1913.

SOURCE 11

The formation of the NUWSS [Suffragists] gave the women's movement more focus but the militant tactics of the WSPU [Suffragettes] gained much greater publicity. In the ten years before the First World War the 'woman issue' was rarely out of the headlines. Historians, like people at the time, have debated ever since whether militancy did more to advance the cause or hold it back.

University historian Professor Eric Evans, writing in an A level textbook in 1997.

SOURCE 12

On Saturday the pilgrimage of the law-abiding advocates [supporters] of votes for women ended in a great gathering in Hyde Park attended by some 50,000 persons. Proceedings were quite orderly . . . and were as much a demonstration against militancy as one in favour of women's suffrage. Many bitter things were said of militant women.

From a report in *The Times*, 26 July 1913, commenting on the Suffragist Pilgrimage to London (see Source 1 on page 38).

Source activity

Explain all your answers fully with reference to the sources.

1 Sources 6 and 8 have different attitudes towards the Suffragettes. Is this just because they come from different newspapers?
2 Is the artist of Source 7 keener on the Suffragettes or the Suffragists?
3 Explain how the artist in Source 9 tries to:
   a) gain sympathy for the woman
   b) show the government as cruel and inhumane.
4 Does the evidence of Sources 7 and 9 suggest that the Suffragettes were effective campaigners?
5 Do Sources 10, 11 and 12 agree or disagree about militancy?
6 Using all the sources and your knowledge from earlier pages, explain how far you agree or disagree with this statement: 'The Suffragettes were more effective campaigners than the Suffragists.'

Extension

Look carefully at Source 7.
Is this a fair picture of the Suffragettes and Suffragists in the early 1900s? Produce some extended writing to tackle this question. Your teacher can give you a writing frame to help you.

2.5 Why did some women get the vote in 1918?

You need to be able to:

- explain at least one way in which the war changed attitudes to women
- explain at least two reasons why women got the vote in 1918.

Key words **householder; munitions; representation**

In 1918, Mrs Fawcett's glacier finally reached its destination. The REPRESENTATION of the People Act gave the vote to around nine million women:

- all women over the age of 30
- women over 21 who were HOUSEHOLDERS or married to householders.

Why, after all the disappointments of the previous twenty years, did women get the vote in 1918? You might think it was because of the war. And you would not be wrong, but it is not quite that simple.

Stage 1: 1914–15 – women support the war effort

When war broke out in 1914, the campaign for women's suffrage was interrupted. Differences between Suffragists and Suffragettes were forgotten. Both Suffragettes and Suffragists supported the war effort. Their members set up organisations to help find homes for refugees who lost their homes in the fighting. They also raised money for women who were left behind when their men went off to fight. The Pankhursts encouraged young men to volunteer for the army.

As hundreds of thousands of young men went off to fight, hundreds of thousands of working women found themselves with new opportunities. The Pankhursts campaigned for women to work in the factories. From 1914 to 1918, an increasing number of women started work in offices, MUNITIONS factories, the armed forces and in medical services. Many took over jobs that were traditionally done by men. You can read more about this on pages 54–56. The really important thing is that women in these jobs showed that they were responsible, competent and vital to the war effort. Many of the sexist arguments against women's suffrage melted away in the face of such evidence.

The campaign by the Suffragists and Suffragettes did not end altogether, but there was no more Suffragette violence after August 1914. They kept up the pressure for the vote – but in a subtle way.

1 The caption at the bottom of Source 1 says – The Anti-Suffragists used to allege, as one reason for refusing women the protection of the vote, that women were already protected by men's chivalry – as in a shipwreck, when the women are always saved first. When the hospital ship *Anglia* went down, last week, the women nurses refused life belts, saying, 'Wounded men first'. Is the claim for women's votes based just on the sinking of the *Anglia*?

SOURCE 1

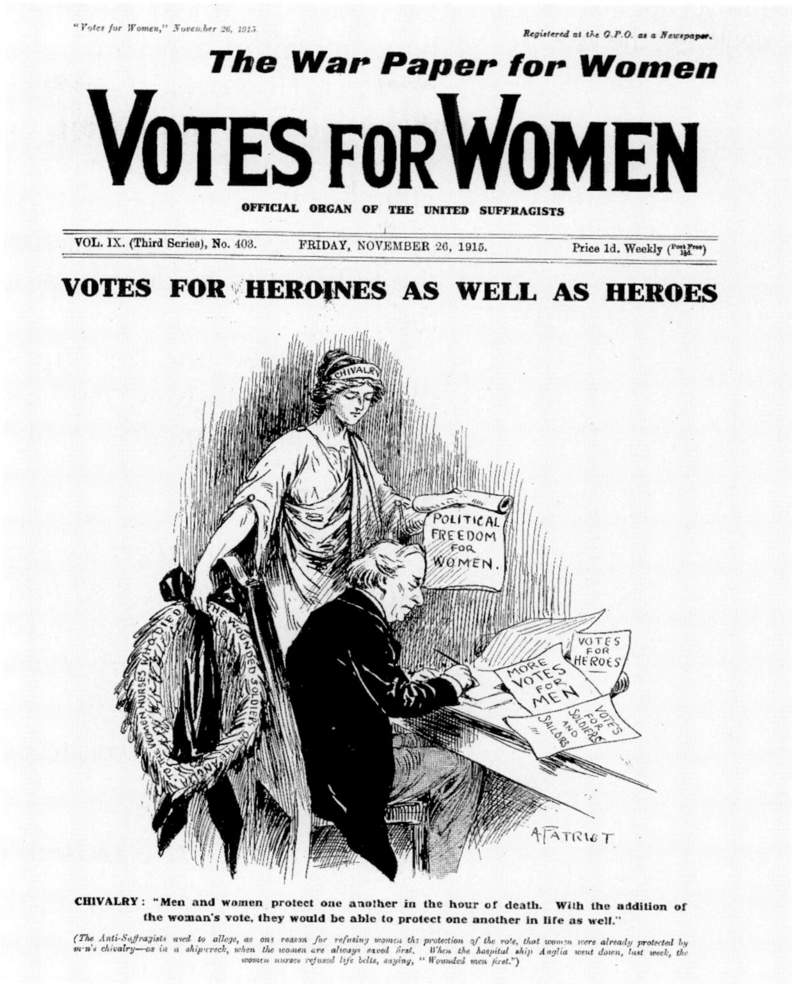

"Votes for Women," November 26, 1915. *Registered at the G.P.O. as a Newspaper.*

The War Paper for Women

VOTES FOR WOMEN

OFFICIAL ORGAN OF THE UNITED SUFFRAGISTS

VOL. IX. (Third Series), No. 403. FRIDAY, NOVEMBER 26, 1915. Price 1d. Weekly (Post Free 1½d.)

VOTES FOR HEROINES AS WELL AS HEROES

CHIVALRY
POLITICAL FREEDOM FOR WOMEN.
VOTES FOR HEROES
MORE VOTES FOR MEN
VOTES FOR SOLDIERS AND SAILORS
A PATRIOT

CHIVALRY: "Men and women protect one another in the hour of death. With the addition of the woman's vote, they would be able to protect one another in life as well."

(The Anti-Suffragists used to allege, as one reason for refusing women the protection of the vote, that women were already protected by men's chivalry—as in a shipwreck, when the women are always saved first. When the hospital ship Anglia went down, last week, the women nurses refused life belts, saying, "Wounded men first.")

The front cover of the magazine *Votes for Women*, November 1915.

SOURCE 2

Former opponents are now declaring themselves on our side, or at any rate withdrawing their opposition. The change of tone in the press is most marked. The view has been widely expressed in [the media] that the continued exclusion of women from representation will be an impossibility after the war.

From an article by the Suffragist leader Millicent Fawcett in the magazine, *Common Cause*, 1916.

2 What two events in 1916 helped the women's cause?

Stage 2: 1916 – an opportunity arises

In 1916, the government decided that a new voting law was needed. Millions of ordinary men were serving their country in the trenches. Under the current law, they did not have the right to vote. That seemed very unjust. The government drafted a new Representation of the People Act that allowed *all men* to vote. The women campaigners saw their chance. They argued that the act should also be changed to give *women* the vote.

In December 1916, David Lloyd George became the new Prime Minister. He was less hostile to women's suffrage than the former Prime Minister, Asquith, but he had been very put off by Suffragette violence before the war (see Source 10 on page 43). Women had to campaign hard to convince him. The leader of the Northern Federation for Women's Suffrage wrote to Lloyd George in 1916. She said that if the government failed to give women the vote in a new law then they were worse than the Germans!

1 Explain why Mrs Fawcett was prepared to accept that not all women would get the vote.

Stage 3: 1917 – the House of Commons agrees

By June 1917, most members of the government seem to have accepted that some women would get the vote in the new act. However, there was a lot of argument over the detail. Some women were upset by the plan that not all women would get the vote. However, Suffragist leader Millicent Fawcett decided to accept the restrictions because it would be an important first step. She also thought that if the Suffragists made a fuss, it would turn opinion against them.

Mrs Fawcett and her supporters sat tensely in the House of Commons in June 1917 as MPs debated the new law. In the end, it was passed easily by 385 votes to 55.

SOURCE 3

Some years ago I used the expression 'Let the women work out their salvation'. Well they have worked it out during the war. When the war is over the question will arise about women's role in society. I would find it impossible to oppose them getting the vote.

Former Prime Minister Asquith speaking in 1917. Before the war, he was opposed to votes for women.

Stage 4: 1918 – the House of Lords agrees (just!)

There was one last obstacle. In January 1918, the act had to be passed by the House of Lords. Before the war, the House of Lords had been even more fiercely opposed to female suffrage than the House of Commons. Even in 1918, there was much opposition. Lord Curzon, President of the Anti-suffrage League, said that the 'act will be the ruin of the country; women are politically worthless and the whole women's movement is disastrous and wrong'. Despite the opposition, the bill was finally passed by 134 votes to 71.

The Representation of the People Act finally became law in February 1918. Women voted in their first elections in December 1918. Ten years later, the vote was extended to all women over 21. Of course, not everyone was convinced, even then . . .

SOURCE 4

I am against the vote for all women. I shall always be against it. It was in 1918 that the disaster took place. Had it not been for the war we could have resisted votes for women successfully for ever.

Conservative politician, Lord Birkenhead, speaking in 1928.

2 Choose three words to describe the general tone of Source 5 from the following: relief, triumph, celebration, joy, worthiness, sorrow, humour.
3 Explain which parts of the cartoon show the words you chose.

SOURCE 5

PUNCH, OR THE LONDON CHARIVARI.—January 23, 1918.
Woman's Franchise
AT LAST!

Cartoon from *Punch* magazine, 1918, celebrating women being given the vote.

Focus task

Why did some women get the vote in 1918?

Here are two views on this question:

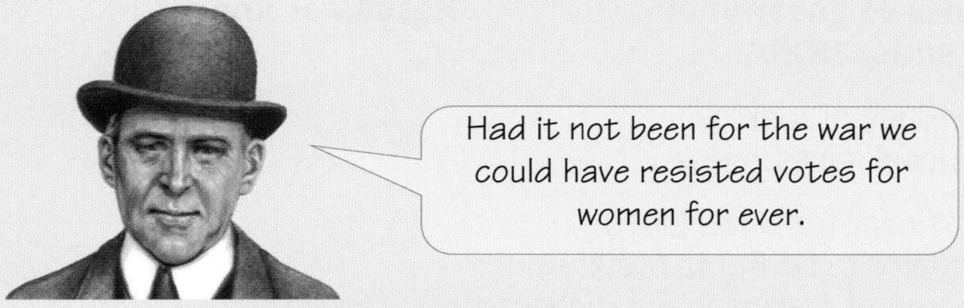
Had it not been for the war we could have resisted votes for women for ever.

Lord Birkenhead

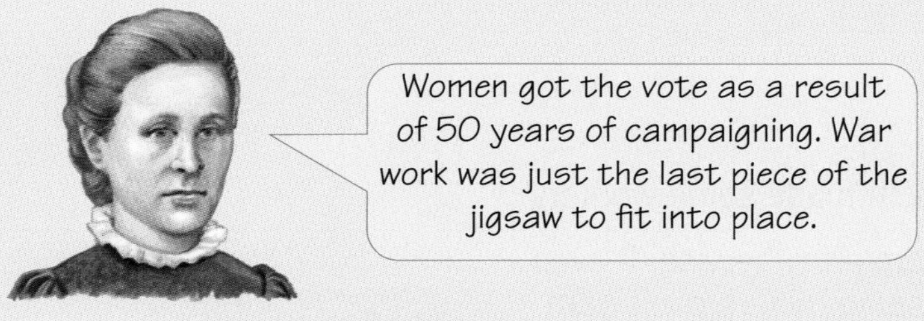
Women got the vote as a result of 50 years of campaigning. War work was just the last piece of the jigsaw to fit into place.

Millicent Fawcett

Which view do you support? Work in stages:

1 Write each of the following factors on a separate piece of paper or card:
- Suffragist campaigning
- Suffragette campaigning
- War work.

2 On each card, write your own notes explaining how the factor helped to achieve the vote for women.
3 Take one card away. Explain whether women could have got the vote with just the remaining two factors.

Part C Britain at war

2.6 How did DORA get Britain organised for the Great War?

Test your understanding by trying to:

- sum up the aims of DORA in one sentence
- name two ways in which DORA was used to control industry.

Key words censorship; exempt; propaganda; trade union

If you have a picture in your head of a little old lady called Dora fighting on the Western Front, then forget it! DORA stands for Defence of the Realm Act. Its aim was to organise Britain for war. In this section, we will look at the terms of the act and how it, and the war, affected Britain.

DORA

The Defence of the Realm Act was passed on 8 August 1914. It was extended several times during the war to give the government more powers. It meant that:

- the government could take control of land, buildings and even whole industries
- the government controlled food production and food consumption
- the government controlled information through PROPAGANDA and CENSORSHIP.

Controlling industry

The war created huge demands on industry. The government had to make sure that the demands were met, especially for munitions. That was where DORA came in.

In some industries the government controlled prices. In others, the government distributed materials. The government even ended up negotiating with TRADE UNIONS over pay and conditions, and bringing over one million women into the workforce (see pages 54–56).

CONTROLLING INDUSTRY		
Challenges to be met	**Examples of government action under DORA**	**Results or impact**
Industry needed huge amounts of coal and steel.	The government took over Britain's coal mines.	
?	Munitions minister David Lloyd George (later to be Prime Minister) took charge of munitions production. He even set up government-run munitions factories.	
Industry needed workers to replace the men joining the army.	?	
Industry needed skilled workers.	Government made some workers	
	EXEMPT from army service. It even brought some miners back from the front.	

1 Look carefully at Source 1. Explain what it says about:
- the cartoonist's attitude towards strikers during the 1914–18 war
- the public's attitude towards strikers in the 1914–18 war
- industrial relations during the war.

2 Look again at your answers to question 1 and discuss:
- whether you based your answers on the details of the cartoon
- whether you based your answers on the information provided in the source caption
- if one was more useful than the other.

Focus task A

How well did DORA work? Part 1

1 Make your own copy of the 'Controlling industry' chart on page 48. Use the information on pages 48–49 to help you:
   a) fill in the two boxes marked with a question mark
   b) add details to the third column to show the achievements of DORA
   c) add other rows to the chart.

Of course, not everything ran smoothly. Munitions factories were often unsafe. For example, there was a huge explosion at Silvertown munitions factory in the East End of London in January 1917. There were also rather more strikes than the government liked to admit (see Source 1). The government sometimes clashed with employers as well. However, industry did deliver the goods. Most historians agree that Britain's war economy performed better than Germany's.

SOURCE 1

FOR SERVICES RENDERED.
A GERMAN DECORATION FOR BRITISH STRIKERS.

A cartoon from *Punch* magazine, 1917, called 'For Services Rendered'. The cross is the German medal, the Iron Cross. The man with the pipe is an industrial worker who has gone on strike. Workers resented this kind of image. They felt that they had the right to make good wages out of the war because so many businessmen made vast profits from war contracts.

SOURCE 2

1915
machine guns 1,700
Bullets 369 million
Shells 2 million
1917
Machine guns 19,000
Bullets 619 million
Shells 23 million

Munitions production, 1915–17. Achievements like these meant that the government had co-ordinated the raw materials (like coal and steel), the workers, the employers and the transport industries to deliver the equipment the army needed.

Aim to remember two ways in which DORA controlled Britain's food supply.

Focus task B

How well did DORA work? Part 2

1 Look back at your chart from Focus task A on page 49.
2 Read through the next two sections on controlling food and controlling information. Make two more charts, one for food and one for information, to summarise what the government did in these areas. Use the same three column headings.

CONTROLLING . . .		
Challenges to be met	**Examples of government action under DORA**	**Results or impact**

Key words allotment; rationing; Trades Union Congress

Controlling food

Obviously, it was essential to feed people during the war. From 1914 to the end of 1916, the food supply was not a major concern. However, by April 1917, U-boat attacks on Britain's supplies led to a crisis. At one point, Britain had only six weeks' food left. Workers went on strike because food prices rose rapidly.

In May 1917, the government took charge. It increased wages for workers. It also introduced *voluntary* RATIONING. The royal family tried to set an example by following the rations. The government put an extra 2.5 million acres of land into agricultural production. Ordinary people used their own gardens or started up ALLOTMENTS or even ploughed up playing fields to grow food. Many women joined the new Women's Land Army to take the place of farm workers who were in the army.

Despite these measures, food still ran short, and the poor suffered most. In January 1918, the government introduced *compulsory* rationing of all the main foods. This meant a weekly ration of meat, butter, margarine, cheese and sugar. Rationing generally solved the problems of shortages. Even so, the government still had to clamp down on people who abused the system (see Source 3).

SOURCE 3

DEFENCE OF THE REALM. E.P. 6.

MINISTRY OF FOOD.

BREACHES OF THE RATIONING ORDER

The undermentioned convictions have been recently obtained:–

Court	Date	Nature of Offence	Result
HENDON - -	29th Aug., 1918	Unlawfully obtaining and using ration books -	3 Months' Imprisonment
WEST HAM -	29th Aug., 1918	Being a retailer & failing to detach proper number of coupons	Fined £20
SMETHWICK -	22nd July, 1918	Obtaining meat in excess quantities - - -	Fined £50 & £5 5s. costs
OLD STREET -	4th Sept., 1918	Being a retailer selling to unregistered customer	Fined £72 & £5 5s. costs
OLD STREET -	4th Sept., 1918	Not detaching sufficient coupons for meat sold -	Fined £25 & £2 2s. costs
CHESTER-LE-STREET	4th Sept., 1918	Being a retailer returning number of registered customers in excess of counterfoils deposited - - - -	Fined £50 & £3 3s. costs
HIGH WYCOMBE	7th Sept., 1918	Making false statement on application for and using Ration Books unlawfully - - - - - - -	Fined £40 & £6 4s. costs

Enforcement Branch, Local Authorities Division,
MINISTRY OF FOOD.
September, 1918.

A government notice published under DORA in 1918.

SOURCE 4

RSP
Are YOU in this?

A government poster.

Controlling information: propaganda and censorship

The government, newspapers and even private individuals produced propaganda publications and films. In the early stages of the war, these tried to get men to join the army. Propaganda posters tried to make war seem exciting (see Source 4). They also tried to get the nation to pull together. As the war went on, propaganda became more serious. The government film *The Battle of the Somme* was grim and fairly realistic (although some scenes were staged). By late 1916, people knew that the war would be a long, hard struggle. Government propaganda reflected this.

It is impossible to say for sure whether government propaganda was effective. In 1915 and 1916 the TRADES UNION CONGRESS (TUC) responded to appeals for workers not to take their holidays (see Source 6). We know that support for the war stayed firm despite the casualties. Sales of newspapers went up during the war, and millions flocked to see films like *The Battle of the Somme*.

Government censors checked books, newspaper articles and even advertisements in case they contained information that might help the enemy. In 1917, the censors told one Manchester engineering firm to scrap an advertisement for this reason. All they were advertising was spark plugs!

1. Look at Sources 4, 5 and 6. One is from early 1915, the other two are from the second half of 1916. Which one is which?
2. Explain how you knew the answer to question 1. Explain how these things helped you:
   - the content and style of the source
   - background knowledge.

SOURCE 5

A still from a government propaganda film about the Battle of the Somme.

SOURCE 6

NO HOLIDAYS
"Fritz! Fritz! are those British munition workers never going to take a holiday!"

A government poster urging women in munitions factories not to take their holidays.

Aim to recall one argument in favour of CONSCRIPTION and one argument against. As an added bonus, you could look at the sources on conscription and think about why they might be useful to historians.

How did they get enough soldiers?

Key words conscientious objector; conscription; minister; Socialist

A volunteer army

The British army needed millions of soldiers. Before the war, Britain was the only major European power that relied solely on volunteers to join the army. In 1914 and 1915, it still did. Lord Kitchener, the government MINISTER for war, organised the campaign to get men to volunteer (see Source 7). To start with, it was very successful.

SOURCE 7

BRITONS
"WANTS
YOU"
JOIN YOUR COUNTRY'S ARMY!
GOD SAVE THE KING
Reproduced by permission of LONDON OPINION

A recruitment poster from 1914 showing the face of Lord Kitchener.

SOURCE 8

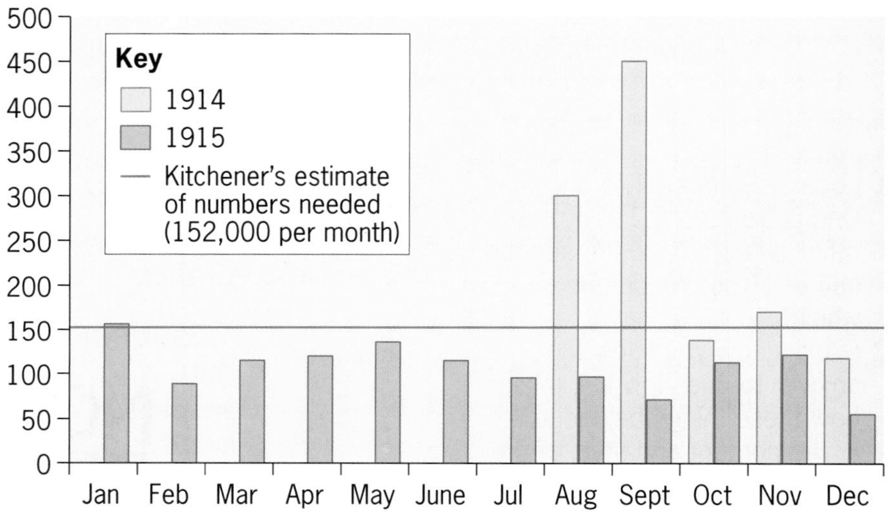
500
450
400
350
300
250
200
150
100
50
0
Key
1914
1915
Kitchener's estimate of numbers needed (152,000 per month)
Jan
Feb
Mar
Apr
May
June
Jul
Aug
Sept
Oct
Nov
Dec

Numbers volunteering for the armed forces in 1914 and 1915.

Was voluntary recruitment working?

By the end of 1915, the number of volunteers was worrying the government (see Source 8). Falling numbers of recruits was not the only problem. There was a strong feeling that not all men were doing their share. Essex farm workers, for example, complained that they were working all hours to grow food for everyone yet they were also being deluged with recruiting posters making them feel guilty for not volunteering for the war.

Many people wrote to the government saying that conscription would be much fairer. It would cover all men, whether they were rich or poor, in or out of work, according to what the country needed.

1 Look at Source 7. Explain whether you think it is useful to historians in terms of:
   a) methods used by the government to recruit soldiers
   b) how successful the government was in recruiting soldiers.
2 Look at Source 8. Explain why this source is useful for historians investigating why conscription was introduced.

SOURCE 9

COMPULSION BILL
WORKER
(BRAIN OR HAND)
(MARRIED OR SINGLE)
"GOT HIM"
Reproduced from the "Workers' Dreadnought"

A cartoon from the Socialist newspaper, *The Workers' Dreadnought*, 1916.

Conscription

So, in January 1916, the government introduced conscription. All men aged 18–40 had to register for war work and could be called up to fight or do any other job the government wanted them to do.

Of course, some people opposed conscription. In Canada, it was not introduced until 1917, after a very close referendum (people's vote). In Australia, there were two votes. It was rejected narrowly both times. In Britain, some political groups, such as the SOCIALISTS, opposed it. They felt that the war only helped the rich. They said it was unfair that working men should fight this 'rich man's war' (see Source 9).

The most notable opponents of conscription were the CONSCIENTIOUS OBJECTORS (conchies). These men refused to fight because of strong moral or religious views. Many served in the trenches as stretcher-bearers or did war work in Britain. Some were sentenced to hard labour. Conchies were generally seen as cowards (see Source 10) and treated very harshly. Some conchies were probably looking for a way out, but many were prepared to suffer for their beliefs and bravely faced the punishments they were given.

3 Study Source 9 carefully. It is a biased view of conscription.
  a) Explain why and how it is biased (mention at least two details from the source).
  b) Does its bias mean it is of no use in studying how people felt about conscription? Explain your answer.

SOURCE 10

Sir
What right have 'conscientious objectors' to live in this country whose safety is only protected by the fighting men of our Army and Navy?
G. Moor, 3 Silverfields, Harrogate

A letter written to the *Daily Mail*, 10 January 1916.

Focus task

How well did DORA work? Part 3

1 Look back at your chart from Focus task A on page 49.
2 Make a final chart to sum up the information about recruitment and conscription on pages 52–53.
3 Below are four men who lived through the First World War (you will look at women on the next page). What might each one say about how DORA has changed his life?
Choose one character and write two speech bubbles for him – one for 1915 and one for 1917.

Essex farm worker	Lancashire miner	London journalist	Midlands publican

2.7 How did women contribute to the war effort?

When you've finished this section, check that you can:

- list two ways women contributed to the war effort
- give examples of each type of contribution
- explain the importance of at least one type of contribution.

Key words domestic service

Before the Great War, the majority of women worked as housewives (often taking in additional work like washing), or in DOMESTIC SERVICE (as maids, cooks, etc.).

For many women the war changed all that.

Women on the front line

Although women did not fight in the trenches, women worked close to the front line.

- Thousands of women served in the Women's Auxiliary Army Corps (WAAC). It was formed in 1918. Its members were mainly drivers, secretaries or officials.
- Many women served in women's hospital units. By the end of the war there were many of these in France, Serbia and Russia.
- Thousands of women worked in voluntary organisations near the front line. The Salvation Army organised kitchens, many of which were run by women.
- When the Germans invaded Belgium and northern France in 1914, civilians there faced chaos. The suffrage movements turned themselves into organisations to feed, house and reunite people with their families.

SOURCE 1

I suddenly saw my job in domestic service as a useless one – doing things for lazy people that they could quite well do for themselves . . . There was talk of 'jobs of national importance' for women as well as men.

Winnifred Griffiths talking in an interview about her feelings during the Great War.

SOURCE 2

RA1039

Nurses working on their ambulance in 1917. These women had to maintain the ambulance as well as do their jobs as nurses.

Women on the home front

Women played a key role in recruiting soldiers for the army. The Active Service League encouraged young men to enlist. The Mothers' Union published posters criticising mothers who stopped their sons joining up. The government also made use of women in their propaganda posters (see Source 3).

In many towns there were Womens' Patrol Movements. These volunteers patrolled the streets, dealing with minor issues such as lost children or litter. This freed up the police for more important work.

SOURCE 3

TO THE
YOUNG WOMEN OF LONDON
Is your "Best Boy" wearing Khaki? If not don't YOU THINK he should be?
If he does not think that you and your country are worth fighting for—do you think he is WORTHY of you?
Don't pity the girl who is alone—her young man is probably a soldier—fighting for her and her country—and for YOU.
If your young man neglects his duty to his King and Country, the time may come when he will NEGLECT YOU.
Think it over—then ask him to
JOIN THE ARMY TO-DAY

A poster issued in 1915 by the government's Parliamentary Recruiting Committee.

SOURCE 4

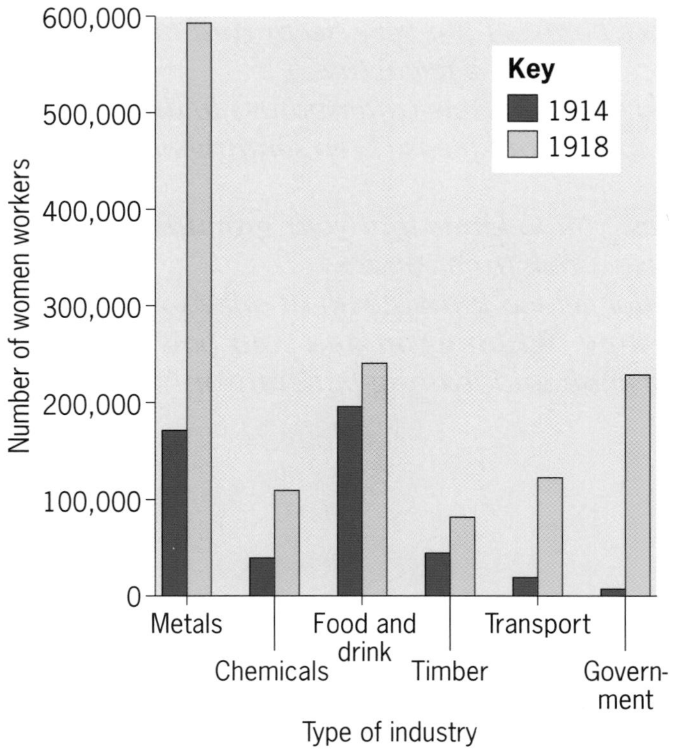
600,000
500,000
400,000
300,000
200,000
100,000
0
Number of women workers
Key
1914
1918
Metals
Chemicals
Food and drink
Timber
Transport
Govern-ment
Type of industry

Women workers in the Great War.

Women in industry

As the war went on, the government needed more men to fight. This meant that women took over many important jobs. Government departments employed 200,000 women during the war.

There was a bit more resistance to women workers in industry. However, by the end of the war, hundreds of thousands of women were working in traditionally 'male' jobs. For example, 800,000 women worked in engineering by 1918. Around 260,000 women worked on Britain's farms in the Women's Land Army. Women even kept some of the works' football teams going during the war!

Aim to explain one advantage and one disadvantage for women working in munitions factories.

Key word munitionettes

Women making weapons

Thousands of women worked in private and government-owned munitions factories. Many women enjoyed the status and the wages the work gave. Official war paintings provided a romantic view of these 'MUNITIONETTES'. On the other hand, it was dangerous work. There were several bad accidents and many women suffered ill health because of chemicals in the explosives.

SOURCE 5

Somewhere in France
June 1917
My dear Miss Chapman,

Pardon me for taking the liberty of writing again, but it may interest you to know that some of the 'Mills Grenades', which I presume you helped make, were used with good effect in the last push in April.

Probably you may remember putting your name on the inside of a base plug of one of these bombs which I had the pleasure of using.

It may give you a hint to keep making these bombs as they are very useful pals at all times and Fritz [Germany] wishes to inform you that he don't like them at all. (Excuse mistakes here as I am very sleepy and must try and find a place soon for a few winks.)

Probably you will find time (after hours) to drop me a line in answer to this and please keep sending out those bombs.

It may interest you to know that your grenades were used driving Fritz back from Arras.

Now I must not get too intimate all at once so I will have to stop writing. Wishing you and your pals every success in your work and waiting patiently on your reply.

I remain
Yours sincerely
Walter P. Miles

P.S. A hundred kisses to be distributed among the munition girls.

A letter from a soldier in the BEF to a munitions worker in 1917.

SOURCE 6

TO THE MEN OF LIVERPOOL WHO FELL IN THE GREAT WAR
AND ALL WHO HAVE FALLEN IN CONFLICT SINCE
AND THE VICTORY THAT DAY WAS TURNED INTO MOURNING UNTO ALL THE PEOPLE

A memorial outside St George's Hall in the centre of Liverpool.

Focus task

Look closely at Source 6. It is part of a memorial to the men of Liverpool who fought and fell in the Great War. Many villages, towns and cities have similar memorials.

Your task is to design a memorial to commemorate the contribution of women to the Great War.

It could be:

- a monument like Source 6
- an object such as a medal or coin
- a poem or song
- a combination of these, or another idea.

Your memorial should cover the main ways in which women contributed to the war. You could research the work done by women in your local area and add that to your memorial.

Design the memorial by sketching it by hand or on computer, or write a plan of the monument. You may be able to use ICT to make a presentation explaining what your memorial will be like and how it shows the contribution of women.

Revision task

It is now time to prepare your class quiz, based on the yellow notes at the beginning of each section. Your teacher can give you a sheet to help you.

3 Making peace 1919–23

3.1 Prospects for peace

The key thing to grasp is that the end of the war did not end the hatred. Try to remember at least two major problems that concerned people at the end of the war.

Key words **armistice; ceasefire; democratic; humiliated; Kaiser; League of Nations; President**

Factfile

The cost of the Great War

- ★ Troops killed: 8 million.
- ★ Troops wounded: 21 million.
- ★ Casualties for selected countries: Germany – 2 million; Russia – 1.75 million; British empire – 3.2 million.
- ★ France lost 250,000 buildings and 8000 square miles of agricultural land. Around 60 per cent of France's young men were either killed or wounded.
- ★ Britain spent around £9 billion on the war.
- ★ Germany, Russia and the Austrian empire all collapsed in revolution.
- ★ To make matters worse, a flu epidemic spread through Europe in the winter of 1918–19. It killed around 20 million people.

This war was Germany's fault. They must be punished.
British civilians

We may have won the war, but we are nearly bankrupt. We must rebuild trade and prosperity.
British Prime Minister, Lloyd George

It's time for the USA to make the world a better place. I want to end rivalry between nations. I want small nations to rule themselves. I want a LEAGUE OF NATIONS to help to keep peace.
PRESIDENT Wilson of the USA

Germany must be crippled or we will never feel safe again.
French civilians

Fighting ended on the eleventh hour of the eleventh day of the eleventh month in 1918, with an ARMISTICE or CEASEFIRE.

The Great War was the bloodiest, costliest war that the world had ever known. The Factfile on page 55 gives you some of the raw details. What do you think people around Europe would be thinking after such an awful war?

Activity

You are one of President Wilson's political advisers. Write him a short memo beginning:

Dear Mr President
You have said you intend to make the world a better place. This may be more difficult than you think. You need to know what people in Europe are thinking at the moment. For example . . .

Parts of our country are a wasteland. The Germans must pay for what they have done.
Belgian civilians

The KAISER has left Germany. We run the country now, but it's in ruins. People are starving. They feel HUMILIATED by defeat. They are already blaming us for their problems, but what can we do about it?
German DEMOCRATIC leaders

Germany should give back all the land it took from Russia.
The Russian leader, Lenin

An armistice? I don't believe it. We should be fighting on! Germany will never be beaten. Those weak politicians at home have let us down.
A young corporal from the German army

The old Austrian empire is finished. Now we can build new nations, and rule ourselves. But how can we decide where the borders of these new countries will be?
Peoples of Eastern Europe (Serbs, Croats, Czechs)

3.2 What did the Big Three want?

Your most important aim should be to name each of the Big Three and at least one priority for each of them at the peace talks. Added bonus: list two issues that they disagreed about.

Key words **compensation; conference; ideal; justice; long term; reparations; security; self-determination; treaty**

Welcome to Paris. Actually, you are just outside Paris, at the Palace of Versailles. The leaders of the winning countries in the Great War are here. They are discussing how to put the world back together again.

The Germans are here, but they will have no say in any of the talks. They will be told to sign a peace TREATY once the Big Three have worked out the details. Germany is in no state to restart the war so it has to accept what the Big Three say.

Who are the Big Three? Have a look!

David Lloyd George, Britain

Background:
- Poor Welsh boy made good.
- Brilliant lawyer and clever talker.
- Known for being sneaky at times.

Relationship with people back home:
- People back home are saying things like: 'Squeeze Germany like a lemon.' They will only be happy with a treaty that punishes Germany.

Relationship with other two:
- He is annoyed with Wilson for saying that Britain should give freedom to its colonies.
- Clemenceau has already tried to hit him!

Priorities:
- Peace and trade: he wants peace in Europe that will last. This will allow Britain to rebuild its trade.
- The British empire: he will take some of Germany's colonies if he gets the chance.
- But he has to keep people at home happy, too.

Woodrow Wilson, the USA

Background:
- Brilliant scholar from highly respectable American family.

Relationship with people back home:
- He wants the USA to get involved in world politics as a force for good. But casualties in the war have horrified Americans. They want to be free of Europe's problems.
- His political enemies back home will take any chance to get him.

Relationship with other two:
- He thinks Lloyd George and Clemenceau are too selfish. They are just trying to get a good deal for their own countries.
- He, on the other hand, is trying to make the world a safer place.

Priorities:
- A peace treaty that will be fair. He thinks Germany should be punished but not humiliated.
- He set out his aims in January 1918 in his 'Fourteen Points', a mixture of IDEALS and practical measures. These included:
  – SELF-DETERMINATION – peoples in Austro-Hungarian empire to rule themselves in their own countries; people in colonies to have a say in their own government.
  – League of Nations – a sort of international police force to help countries to sort out disputes without going to war.

Focus task

Who wanted what at the Paris Peace Conference?

1 On the right is a list of statements that might have been made by one of the Big Three. Read them carefully. Then read about the Big Three below.
2 Decide which of the Big Three could have said which statements. You may think that some statements could have been said by more than one leader.
3 Finally, decide:
- which statements the leader would have made in open discussions (and in front of journalists)
- which statements would have been private thoughts, or voiced only at secret meetings behind the scenes.

Statements

A Germany was our number two trading partner before the war. Rebuilding Germany means jobs for our workers.

B How can I talk to a man who thinks he is the first person for 2000 years who knows anything about peace?

C I demand JUSTICE for the harm done to us. Germany must pay very large reparations.

D I want a fair peace. I do not wish to crush Germany or expand our empire.

E I want no German armed forces on my border.

F I want to see Germany broken up into smaller states.

G I want to see Germany's armed forces reduced to the very minimum.

H It is right that Germany should pay some reparations for the damage it has done.

I Lloyd George is more interested in trade than France's security.

J The French have only one thought. If we are too harsh, Germany will want revenge one day.

K The Germans will never be able to pay the reparations we are asking. But I have to demand reparations because people at home expect me to.

L We are all using words like 'right' and 'justice'. Do we really mean what we say?

M We cannot compete with Germany in the LONG TERM, but we can weaken it for many years.

N We must have a peace without winners and losers. Otherwise, the losers will want revenge one day.

O We should all reduce our armies and navies.

P We should be as harsh on Germany as it was on Russia last year – it took 40 per cent of Russia's best land.

Georges Clemenceau, France

Background:
- Journalist and politician since the 1870s.

Relationship with people back home:
- Under a lot of pressure to make France safe from German attacks in the future. For most French people, this means crippling Germany.

Relationship with other two:
- He thinks Wilson is too idealistic. He does not trust Lloyd George.
- He thinks neither of them really cares about France.

Priorities:
- Future SECURITY for France from any German attack.
- COMPENSATION from Germany (REPARATIONS) for the damage caused by the war.

3.3 The Treaty of Versailles: winners and losers

The more you know about the Treaty of Versailles, the more it will help you. Aim to remember at least three key terms of the treaty.

Key words mark; Polish corridor; union

Germany signs the treaty

After months of disputes, a treaty was finalised. On 28 June 1919, the Germans signed the Treaty of Versailles.

SOURCE 1

The excitement was tense in the extreme, as, with trembling hand, the German minister . . . took the pen and placed his signature to paper. Everyone felt the tremendous significance [importance] of the moment. Not a word was spoken, and the fall of a pin could be heard in the famous gallery. There was just the rustle of shutters of the cameras of the press photographers.

From the British newspaper, the *People*, 29 June 1919.

SOURCE 2

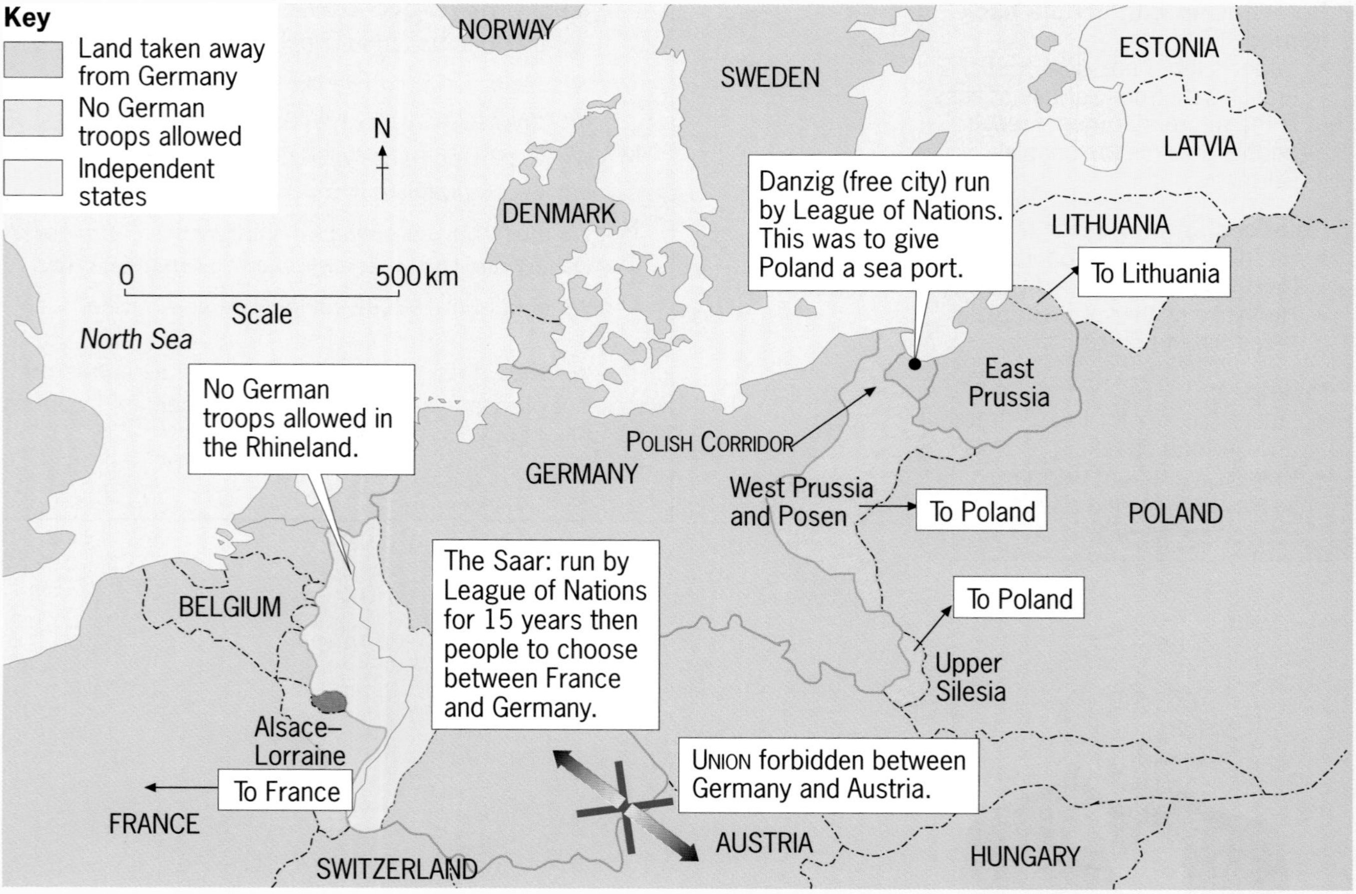
Key
Land taken away from Germany
No German troops allowed
Independent states
N
0
500 km
Scale
North Sea
NORWAY
SWEDEN
ESTONIA
LATVIA
LITHUANIA
DENMARK
Danzig (free city) run by League of Nations. This was to give Poland a sea port.
To Lithuania
East Prussia
No German troops allowed in the Rhineland.
POLISH CORRIDOR
GERMANY
West Prussia and Posen
To Poland
POLAND
BELGIUM
The Saar: run by League of Nations for 15 years then people to choose between France and Germany.
To Poland
Upper Silesia
Alsace–Lorraine
To France
FRANCE
UNION forbidden between Germany and Austria.
AUSTRIA
HUNGARY
SWITZERLAND

How the Treaty of Versailles changed German territory.

Why did the Big Three not get the treaty they wanted?

The Big Three had conflicting aims so they could not all get what they wanted. But, in fact, none of them was pleased with the treaty.

- Clemenceau wanted the treaty to be much harsher. For example, he wanted Germany broken up into smaller states. Wilson stopped this from happening.
- Wilson thought that the treaty was far too harsh and that one day Germany would seek revenge. He said that if he were a German he would not have signed it.
- Lloyd George had most reason to be pleased. He came home to a hero's welcome, but he later said that the treaty was a great pity and he predicted that it would cause another war.

Focus task

Read the terms of the Treaty of Versailles and make a table to record the main points.

- In column 1, show some of the aims of the Big Three.
- In column 2, write examples from the treaty that seem designed to achieve this aim.
- In column 3, note down which of the Big Three would approve of this aim. It might be more than one of them.

TERMS OF THE TREATY

1 Guilt for war

- Germany had to accept blame for starting the war.

2 Germany's armed forces

- The army was limited to 100,000 men.
- Conscription was banned – all servicemen had to be volunteers.
- No armoured vehicles, submarines or military aircraft were allowed.

3 Reparations

- Germany had to pay reparations to France, Belgium and Britain.
- The final figure was not agreed until 1921 – it was 6 billion MARKS (£6.6 million) – two per cent of Germany's total annual production.

To remember the terms, think **GARGLe**:

Guilt
Arms
Reparations
German territory
League of Nations

4 German territories

- Germany lost all its overseas colonies (mostly to Britain and France).
- Alsace–Lorraine and the Saar were lost.
- Union between Germany and Austria's 6.5 million Germans was forbidden.
- West Prussia and Upper Silesia went to Poland.
- Danzig became a Free City controlled by the new League of Nations.

5 League of Nations

- A League of Nations was set up as an international police force. Germany was not allowed to join until it proved it was a peaceful country.

From these two pages, work out which term upset the Germans the most.

SOURCE 3

PARIS GOES WILD WITH JOY

Paris went wild with joy last night when news of the Germans' unconditional climb-down arrived, and expressed its feelings in the traditional way – flags, processions, gun firing, illuminations [lights], cheering.

From the British newspaper, the *Star*, 24 June 1919.

SOURCE 4

THE PEACE THAT IS NO PEACE

From the British newspaper, the *Daily Herald*, 8 May 1919.

Reactions to the treaty

Let's do a quick tour of Europe to see the reactions to the treaty. Remember that the war was not technically over until the treaty was signed.

France

The treaty was greeted with enthusiasm and there were celebrations on the streets of Paris. The war was now definitely over. France had won. It looked as though the threat from Germany had ended.

Britain

Most people in Britain supported the treaty. They felt that Germany had got what it deserved. They saw Lloyd George as a hero. The King went to meet him at the train station when he returned from Paris!

However, some British people were worried. They asked whether this treaty would bring peace, and they worried about Germany's reaction to it. But most people thought the Germans were just complaining. They would soon get over it, wouldn't they?

SOURCE 5

PEACE WITH VIGILANCE

. . . though we have paralysed Germany on land, at sea and in the air, we have not destroyed totally her power for evil. Germany is still a menace.

From the British newspaper, the *Daily Mail*, 30 June 1919.

SOURCE 6

LONDON'S JOY

There were great scenes outside Buckingham Palace, where all day Londoners flocked in their thousands to cheer the King and Queen . . . The West-End was naturally the objective of all who felt the need of releasing pent-up feelings of enthusiasm, and there were carnival scenes everywhere, but no rowdiness, only boisterous merriment and noise.

From the British newspaper, the *Daily Chronicle*, 30 June 1919.

Germany

You will not be surprised to learn that the Germans were not happy about the treaty. They lost:

- 10 per cent of their land
- 12.5 per cent of their population.

Other things upset them as well.

- War guilt: they did not feel that they had started the war on their own.
- The limits on the army were humiliating.
- They had no say in the treaty. They were just told to sign it.
- Millions of Germans were now ruled by foreigners.
- East Prussia was cut off from the rest of Germany by the 'Polish corridor'.
- The German government that had to sign the treaty was not the same government that took Germany into the war. The treaty punished the wrong people.

SOURCE 7

A cartoon in the German magazine *Simplicissimus*, 1919.

SOURCE 8

THE TREATY IS ONLY A SCRAP OF PAPER!

We will seek vengeance for the shame of 1919.

From the German newspaper, *Deutsche Zeitung* (German News), 30 June 1919.

Focus task

Why did Germans object so bitterly to the Treaty of Versailles?

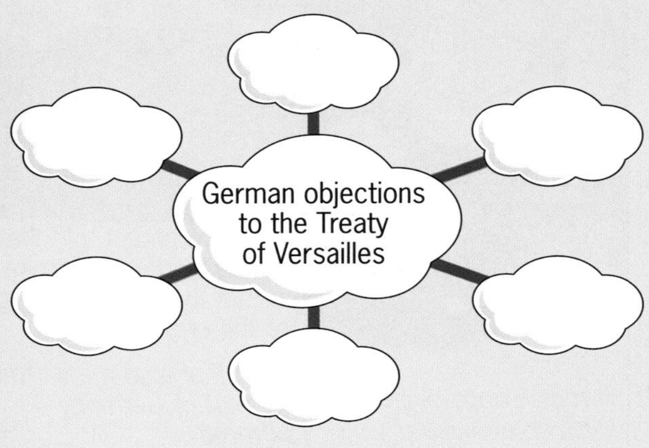
German objections to the Treaty of Versailles

1. Draw up your own version of this diagram.
2. From pages 62–65 note any features of the treaty that you think would upset the Germans. Write each one in one of the empty 'clouds'.
3. In small groups, discuss why each feature would upset them and then add the reason to your diagram.
4. As a group, discuss which term you think would upset them the most. There are no right answers to this question!
5. Now choose two German complaints. Make up a rhyme or word that will help you remember them (like GARGLe on page 63). Try more than two complaints if you can.

3.4 Was the treaty to blame for Germany's problems?

Your aim here is to remember:

- at least one problem Germany faced in the period 1919–23
- why Germans blamed the Treaty of Versailles for that problem.

Key words **Communist; crisis; hyperinflation; instalment; Nazi**

The Germans hated the Treaty of Versailles. During the years 1919–23, the country faced one CRISIS after another. Germans blamed the treaty for these crises. The story strip on these pages shows how Germans felt during these troubled years.

Focus task

Germans blamed all their post-war problems on the Treaty of Versailles, but there were other factors as well. As you read through the story strip, whenever you reach a

Problem point

ask yourself three questions.

a) What is Germany's big problem at this point?
b) What has this got to do with the Treaty of Versailles?
c) What other factor(s) are causing the problem?

Record your answers in a table. Once you have completed your table, write a paragraph to explain whether you think the Germans were right to blame the Treaty of Versailles for all their problems.

Problem point 2
I don't like signing this, but I have no choice.
May 1919: the Treaty of Versailles blamed Germany for the war, took away some of its land and ordered it to pay compensation to other countries.
The government stopped paying Helga's war pension. They blamed the Treaty.*
* But the main reason it had no money is because it had spent it all on the war.
Problem point 4
Germany paid the first INSTALMENT, then refused to pay any more. So French soldiers marched into part of Germany to take what was owed to France.*
*And the Germans could not fight back because the treaty had got rid of their army and given the French permission to do this.
They think they can do whatever they want because of that treaty.
French troops bullied German civilians
The government told the factory workers to strike so that there was nothing for the French to take.*
* But that also meant that the rest of Germany suffered.

THE HELGA EITLING STORY

Problem point 1
Helga's brothers died in the war, and her mother died in the flu epidemic of 1919.
After the war, food was so expensive that Helga had to sell her mother's precious jewellery just to eat.
What has become of our great country?
Germany was in chaos. There was street fighting between ex-soldiers and COMMUNISTS.
I can live off my savings for now. Things will be sorted out in a few years. I can earn a little extra by sewing.
Ex-soldiers blamed the new government for signing the treaty. They tried to take over the government in 1920.
It's absurd. How can we ever pay that?
Problem point 3
6 BILLION
In 1921, Germany was told how much reparations it had to pay – £6.6 million (6 billion marks!). It sounded a lot, but a much bigger problem was still debts left over from the war.
Problem point 5
Soon everyone was running out of money. Instead of trying to talk to the French, the government printed more money.
This money is worthless. I might as well burn it.
One loaf of bread. That will be 20 billion marks.
That caused HYPERINFLATION. Prices went out of control.*
*And Helga Eitling's savings of a few thousand marks were worthless.
Problem point 6
He talks a lot of sense.
Helga blamed France and the treaty for Germany's problems. So did a young NAZI called Adolf Hitler.*
* You'll find out more about him later.

3.5 Were the peacemakers 'very stupid men'?

The key point here is that people disagreed about the treaty in 1919 and they still do! Aim to remember:

- three points arguing that the treaty was unfair
- three points arguing that the treaty was fair.

Key words public opinion

Sir Harold Nicolson, a top British diplomat, was at most of the Paris Peace Conference. Source 1 gives his view of the treaty at the time.

Some historians agree with him. They say that the peacemakers made some big mistakes. The treaty was not just (fair) or wise. It stored up big problems for the future. Other historians disagree. They say that the treaty was the fairest that could have been made at the time and that the peacemakers had an impossible job. The chart below shows some of the arguments each side uses.

Historians will never agree about this. Our view of the treaty is affected by hindsight – by what we know happened next. We know that the treaty helped Hitler become leader of Germany and that, in turn, helped to lead to the Second World War.

However, try to forget that for a while. Just by looking at the period up to 1923 – from that evidence alone – is it right to call the makers of the treaty 'very stupid men'?

SOURCE 1

The historian, with every justification, will come to the conclusion that we were very stupid men. We arrived determined to get a peace of justice and wisdom. We left feeling that the terms we imposed on our enemies were neither just nor wise.

Sir Harold Nicolson, writing in his diary, 1919.

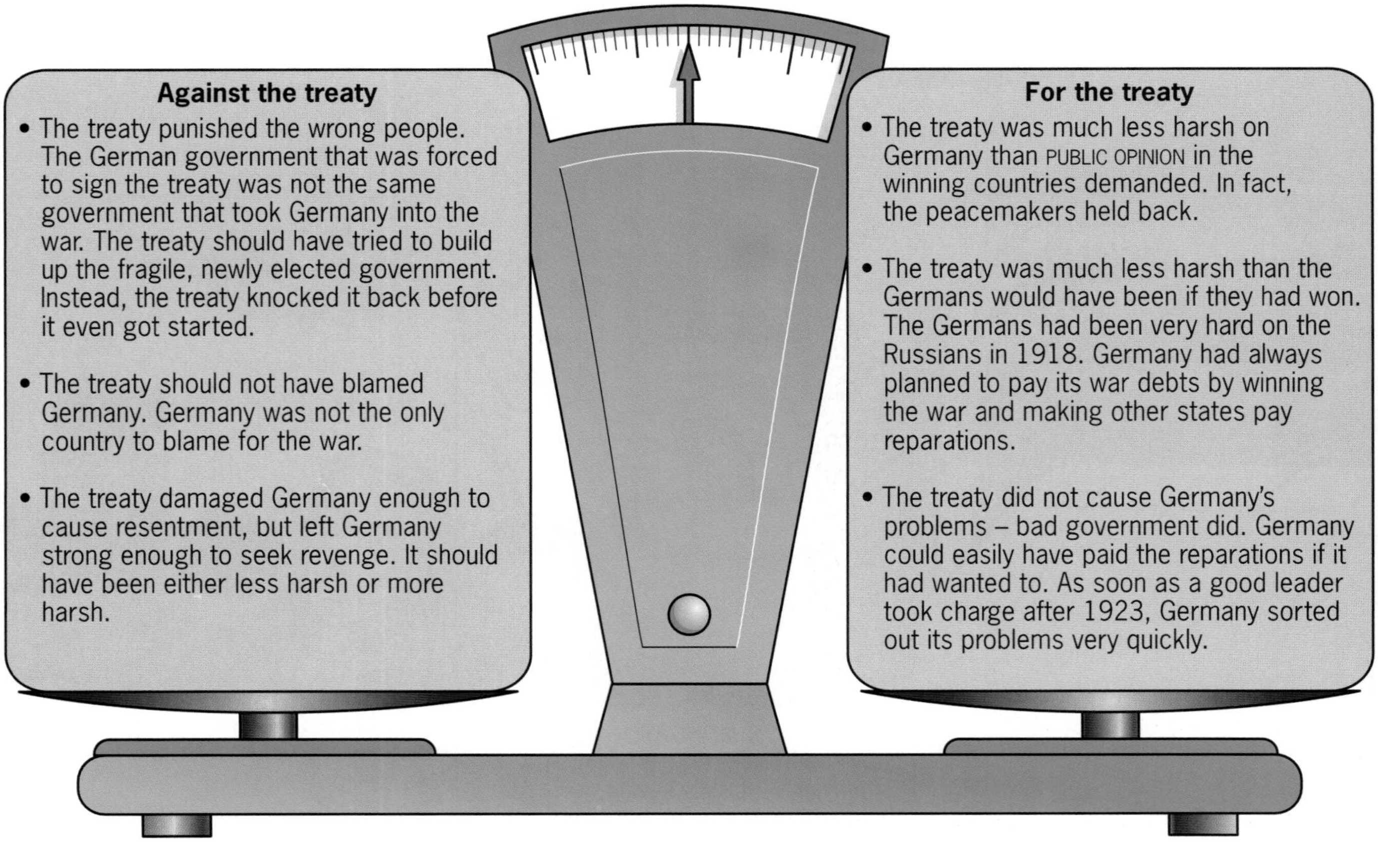
Against the treaty
• The treaty punished the wrong people. The German government that was forced to sign the treaty was not the same government that took Germany into the war. The treaty should have tried to build up the fragile, newly elected government. Instead, the treaty knocked it back before it even got started.
• The treaty should not have blamed Germany. Germany was not the only country to blame for the war.
• The treaty damaged Germany enough to cause resentment, but left Germany strong enough to seek revenge. It should have been either less harsh or more harsh.
For the treaty
• The treaty was much less harsh on Germany than PUBLIC OPINION in the winning countries demanded. In fact, the peacemakers held back.
• The treaty was much less harsh than the Germans would have been if they had won. The Germans had been very hard on the Russians in 1918. Germany had always planned to pay its war debts by winning the war and making other states pay reparations.
• The treaty did not cause Germany's problems – bad government did. Germany could easily have paid the reparations if it had wanted to. As soon as a good leader took charge after 1923, Germany sorted out its problems very quickly.

SOURCE 2

LOAN
A TRANSPARENT DODGE.
GERMANY. "HELP! HELP! I DROWN! THROW ME THE LIFE-BELT!"
MR. LLOYD GEORGE } "TRY STANDING UP ON YOUR FEET."
M. BRIAND

A British cartoon from 1920.

SOURCE 3

PEACE AND FUTURE CANNON FODDER
1940 CLASS
PEACE TREATY
The Tiger: "Curious! I seem to hear a child weeping!"

A British cartoon from 1920. The '1940 class', in the form of a weeping child, represents the children born in the 1920s who might die in a future war. 'The Tiger' was the nickname for Clemenceau.

Review task

Part 1: the case against the Treaty of Versailles

1 Look back at all your work in this chapter. Collect all the evidence that supports the view that the treaty was **not** just or wise.

Point/piece of evidence	Supports the view that the treaty was not *just* because . . .	Supports the view that the treaty was not *wise* because . . .

You could look at:
- the terms of the treaty (page 63)
- the reactions to the treaty (pages 64–65)
- the problems Germany faced because of the treaty, 1919–23 (pages 66–67).

Remember you are only looking for evidence **against** the treaty just now.

2 Choose four key points from your evidence and write them into a table like the one above. Some points could provide evidence for both columns 2 and 3.

Part 2: the case for the Treaty of Versailles

3 Now look at the arguments **for** the treaty on the scales on page 68. Look for evidence in this chapter to support each point. Write it in a table like this.

Point/piece of evidence	Supports the view that the treaty was fair because . . .	Supports the view that the peacemakers had a very hard job because . . .

4 Now write a paragraph saying which view of the treaty you hold.

Revision task

It is now time to prepare your class quiz, based on the yellow notes at the beginning of each section. Your teacher can give you a sheet to help you.

4 Keeping the peace in the 1920s

4.1 Was the League of Nations a good idea?

Your priority on this spread is to explain two aims of the League of Nations.

Key words collective security; co-operate; covenant; disarmament; international

Questions and answers about the League of Nations

Q1: What was the League of Nations?

A: The League was an INTERNATIONAL organisation. It was set up as part of the Treaty of Versailles. It was the idea of US President Woodrow Wilson – he thought the League would help to stop future wars. There were 42 countries in the League when it began in 1919.

Q2: What were the aims of the League of Nations?

A: The aims were set out in the COVENANT of the League of Nations. This document was like a 'rule book' for the League (see Source 1). The aims were:

- to be united and strong enough to discourage any nation from using force as a way to solve disputes
- to provide a place to discuss international disputes and work them out peacefully
- to encourage countries to CO-OPERATE, especially in business and trade
- to encourage DISARMAMENT by nations
- to improve living and working conditions for people around the world.

By sticking together, the nations of the world would have protection and help from each other – this was called COLLECTIVE SECURITY.

SOURCE 1

THE PARTIES [those taking part], in order to promote international co-operation and to achieve international peace and security, agree to this Covenant of the League of Nations

- *by promising not to go to war*
- *by agreeing to open, just and honourable relations between nations*
- *by agreeing that governments should act according to international law*
- *by maintaining justice and respect for all treaty obligations.*

The first words of the Covenant of the League of Nations. All members of the League signed this covenant.

SOURCE 2

The survivors
Women welcome their men back from war. One woman stands astride two silent guns holding her baby – a symbol of hope for the future.

Some of the guns are still firing but, one by one, men and women are pushing them off a precipice where they will break up and be unusable. The League tried to persuade countries to disarm.

Hand in hand
The five giants represent the five continents of the Earth. The giants are standing firm together.

At the giants' feet, leaders of all the nations are working, reading and talking together. The League's members come from all five continents. The League believed that strength came from unity.

Wall paintings by the famous Spanish artist, José Maria Sert that decorate the Assembly Chamber in the League's Headquarters in Geneva, Switzerland. They were designed to show the aims and values of the League.

Activity

Prepare a headphone commentary about the paintings in Source 2 to be used by a visitor. Make sure you point the viewer to the important details which show the aims of the League.

Your main aim on this page is to explain the difference between the League's Council and its Assembly.

Key words isolationism; moral condemnation; sanctions

Q3: How was the League organised?

A: Britain and France wanted the League to be a sort of informal club. In a crisis, the big nations would get together. There was something like this already. It was called the Council of Ambassadors. However, President Wilson did not agree. He insisted that the League should work like a kind of international government. He got his way (see Source 3).

Activity

A young secretary is arriving for his first day at the League of Nations Secretariat in the 1920s.

Prepare a bullet point briefing for him about the League. Explain the difference between the Council and the Assembly. You could also include a diagram in your briefing.

Q4: How could the League make a country do what it wanted?

A: It had three main powers. It could use:

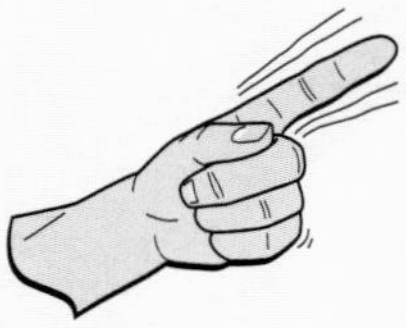

- MORAL CONDEMNATION – criticising the actions of the aggressor (the nation which was attacking another nation)

- economic SANCTIONS – cutting off important supplies like oil

- armed force – using force against the aggressor.

SOURCE 3

The Council met five times a year or when there was an emergency. It had some temporary members elected by the Assembly and four permanent members – Britain, France, Italy and Japan. The real power in the League lay with these four. Each permanent member could veto (stop) any action by the League. In any crisis, the Council took all the important decisions.

The **Assembly** was the League's parliament. It met once a year. It voted on issues such as the budget (spending) of the League, or letting in new members. Decisions had to be unanimous (every member had to agree).

The League was run by a permanent **Secretariat** (staff of office workers).

The League had a number of **commissions**, or committees, to tackle international problems such as helping refugees or improving health.

The **Court of International Justice** helped to settle disputes between countries. The court would listen to both sides and then make a decision, just like an ordinary court of law.

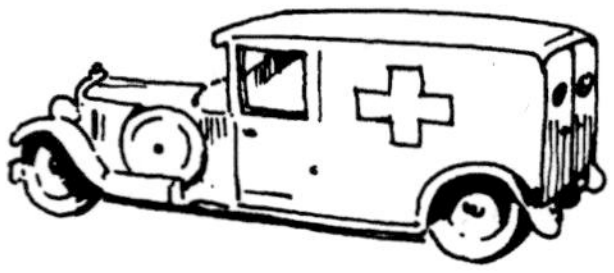

How the League of Nations was organised.

Q5: Who belonged to the League?

A: The League began with 42 nations. By 1939, there were over 50 members. But some powerful nations left the League or never joined.

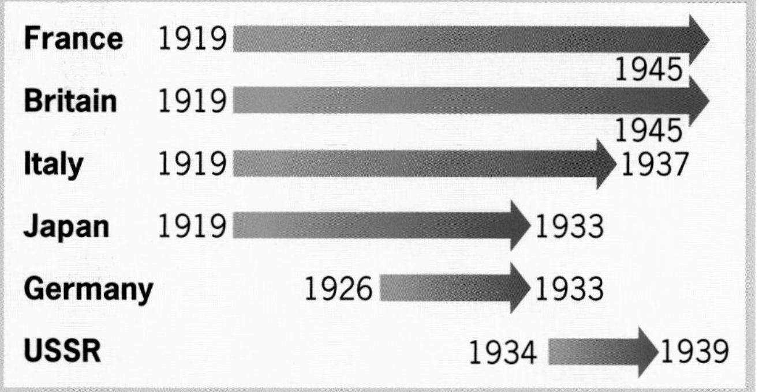
France 1919 1945
Britain 1919 1945
Italy 1919 1937
Japan 1919 1933
Germany 1926 1933
USSR 1934 1939

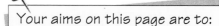

Your aims on this page are to:

- explain why it was such a blow that the USA did not join the League
- explain the attitudes of Britain and France to the League.

Q6: What about the USA?

A: The USA never joined! The League may have been President Wilson's big idea, but he could not get the rest of the USA to agree with him. The US Congress (Parliament) did not want the USA to get involved in sorting out problems in the rest of the world. This view became known as ISOLATIONISM.

This was a real setback for the League. Everybody knew that the League needed the USA's money and troops so that it could work effectively.

Q7: So was the League powerful?

A: This is a tricky question. Over the next few chapters, you will decide this for yourself!

Most people and most governments *wanted* the League to succeed. However, the League had some weaknesses right from the start.

- Its way of working – for example, the Assembly met only once a year and every vote had to be unanimous. This meant that reaching decisions could be a very slow process.
- Its membership – the USA did not join; Germany and the USSR only joined much later; Britain and France were both weakened by the First World War.
- Britain and France had their own priorities:
  - Britain wanted to protect its empire
  - France worried about another attack from Germany.

They often put these concerns ahead of the League's priorities.

Focus task

Was the League of Nations strong?

When the League was set up in 1919, people could see both its good and bad points.

Use a table like the one below to sum up the information on pages 70–73.

Key issue	Positive view	Negative view
Membership of the League	Major powers, like Britain and France, were in the League.	
How decisions were made in the League		
Powers of the League's organisations		
Attitude of Britain and France towards the League		

4.2 Did the League work well in the 1920s?

Key words facilities; interpret; plebiscite

Your core aims over these next four pages are to:

- describe one success of the League and explain why it was a success
- describe one failure of the League and explain why it was a failure.

Bonus: explain how one event was a partial success or failure.

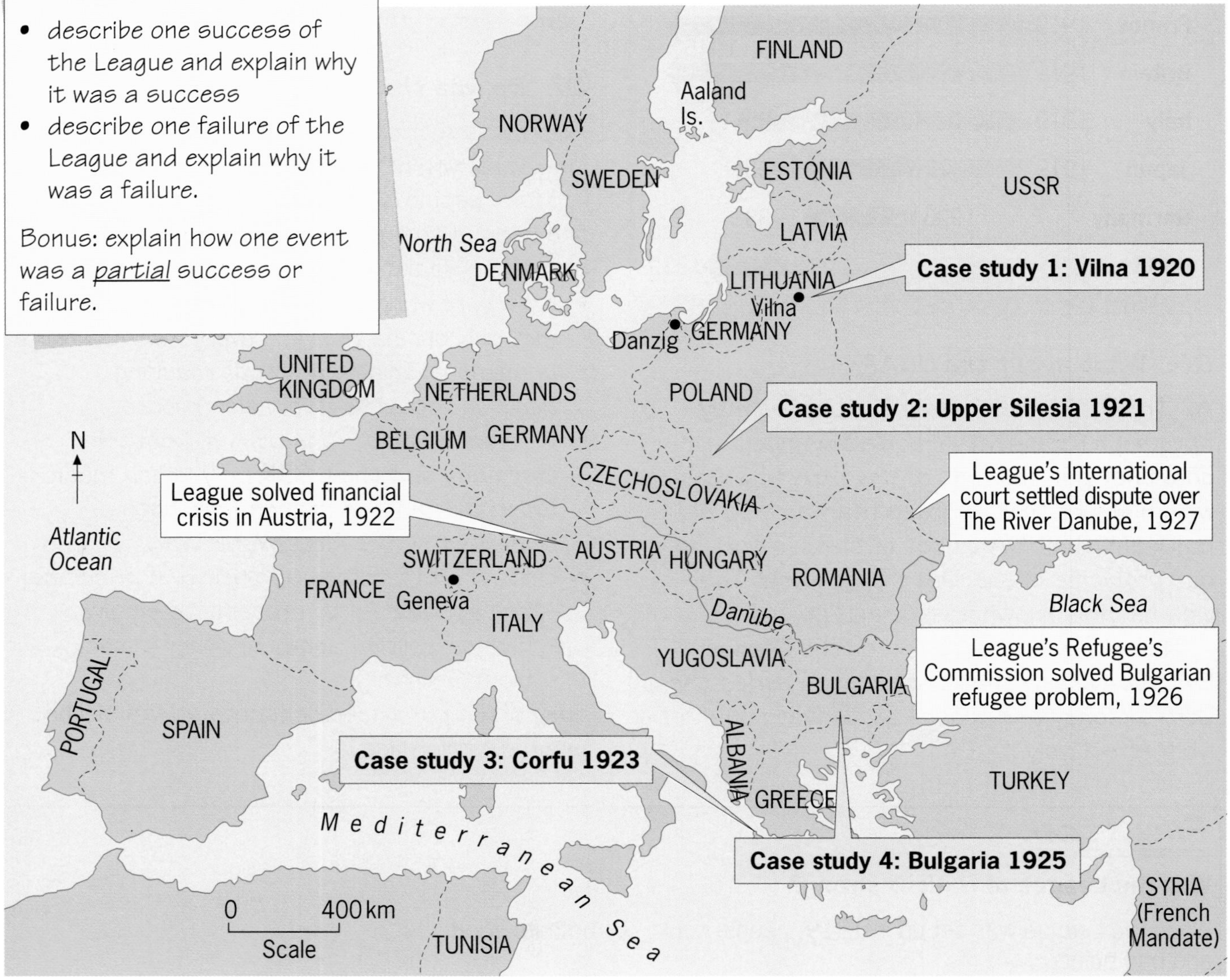

FINLAND
Aaland Is.
NORWAY
SWEDEN
ESTONIA
USSR
LATVIA
North Sea
DENMARK
LITHUANIA
Vilna
Case study 1: Vilna 1920
Danzig
GERMANY
UNITED KINGDOM
NETHERLANDS
POLAND
Case study 2: Upper Silesia 1921
N
BELGIUM
GERMANY
CZECHOSLOVAKIA
League's International court settled dispute over The River Danube, 1927
League solved financial crisis in Austria, 1922
Atlantic Ocean
SWITZERLAND
AUSTRIA
HUNGARY
ROMANIA
FRANCE
Geneva
Black Sea
ITALY
Danube
YUGOSLAVIA
League's Refugee's Commission solved Bulgarian refugee problem, 1926
BULGARIA
PORTUGAL
SPAIN
ALBANIA
Case study 3: Corfu 1923
TURKEY
GREECE
Mediterranean Sea
Case study 4: Bulgaria 1925
0 400 km
Scale
TUNISIA
SYRIA (French Mandate)

During the 1920s there were many disputes and problems in which the League played a role. The map above outlines some cases where the League helped or tried to help. On the next three pages you will look at four of them in a bit more detail and decide which were failures and which were successes.

Focus task

Many historians have studied the League in the 1920s. They have INTERPRETED events very differently. You will now look at four case studies of the League in action in the 1920s and come up with your own interpretation.

For each case study, decide:

- why you might criticise the League's actions
- why you might think the League's actions were justified or reasonable
- where you will put this event on a success scale of 0–5, where 0 is a total failure and 5 is a total success.

The two professors should help you. They have already done some of the work for case study 1!

Professor 1

I would put the League on 0 on the scale. It was useless here. It could not enforce its own rules. The French looked after their own interests. The British showed how weak they were.

Case study 1: Vilna 1920

Vilna was the capital of Lithuania, one of the new states created by peace treaties after the war. Vilna was on the border with Poland. Most of its population was Polish. In 1920, Polish troops simply moved in and took over Vilna. Lithuania asked the League of Nations for help. It was obvious that Poland had broken the League's Covenant – it was the aggressor. However, that did not make things simple.

- Most of the population of Vilna was Polish – didn't that mean the Poles had a case for moving in?
- France wanted to stay friendly with Poland. It saw Poland as a possible ally against Germany.
- Britain didn't see how it could send troops across Europe to force the Poles out of Vilna. Not many British people cared enough about Vilna to support that kind of action.

The League did nothing in the end. The Poles kept control of Vilna.

Where would **you** put this event on the scale?

Professor 2

Now be fair. I would put the League on at least 3 on the scale. They were right to do nothing. Vilna was very Polish so the Poles had a point. Also, how could Britain and France march troops across Europe?

Case study 2: Upper Silesia 1921

Upper Silesia was on the border between Poland and Germany. Poles and Germans lived there. The area also contained a valuable steel industry. Germany and Poland both wanted to control the area. The League organised a PLEBISCITE. British and French troops kept order during the voting. The vote was divided, so the League divided Upper Silesia between Germany and Poland. The League also made sure that the division did not disrupt railway lines, power supplies or other FACILITIES. Germany and Poland both accepted the League's decision.

How do you think Professor 1 would criticise the League?

Where would **you** put this event on the success scale from page 74?

How do you think Professor 2 would defend the League?

Key words boundary; Refugees Commission; trafficking

Case study 3: Corfu 1923

This started off as another BOUNDARY dispute. In 1923, an Italian army unit was mapping the border between Greece and Albania. The soldiers were attacked, but it was not clear who attacked them. The Italian general, Tellini, was killed. Italy's leader, Benito Mussolini, blamed the Greeks. He demanded that the Greeks hand over the murderers. He also demanded compensation. In August 1923, he invaded the Greek island of Corfu.

The Greeks appealed to the League. Early in September, the League condemned Mussolini's actions. It was clear that he had broken the League's Covenant. However, Mussolini got to work behind the scenes. He put pressure on the members of the League's Council to support Italy instead of Greece. By the end of September, things had turned around. The Council began to put pressure on the Greeks. The Greeks had to apologise to Mussolini and pay compensation for the murder of Tellini.

How do you think this professor would criticise the League?

Where would **you** put this event on the success scale?

How do you think this professor would defend the League?

Case study 4: Bulgaria 1925

In October 1925, Greek and Bulgarian forces clashed on the border between the two states. Bulgaria claimed that Greece was to blame. Greece appealed to the League. The League decided that the Greeks were at fault. They had to pull back their troops and pay compensation to Bulgaria. The Greeks obeyed the League's orders. However, they also complained that the League had not treated Italy in the same way as it had treated Greece (see case study 3). Did the power of the League only apply to small states like Greece?

How do you think this professor would criticise the League?

Where would **you** put this event on the success scale?

How do you think this professor would defend the League?

Other developments in the 1920s

The League's commissions did some tremendous work. For example, the REFUGEES COMMISSION helped 400,000 prisoners of war to return home after the Great War. The Health Committee helped to fight deadly diseases such as malaria and leprosy. The League also fought against drug TRAFFICKING and slavery. It freed 200,000 slaves in Sierra Leone.

The League also helped its members to agree some important treaties. In 1925, Germany signed the Locarno Treaty. This meant it accepted the borders of Germany set out in the Treaty of Versailles. In 1928, 65 states signed the Kellogg-Briand Pact. They promised not to use force to settle disputes.

There were still problems, of course. And one big failure was that the League failed to make any progress on disarmament. Nevertheless, by early 1929, the world was more peaceful and stable than it had been for many years.

Revision task

It is now time to prepare your class quiz, based on the yellow notes at the beginning of each section. Your teacher can give you a sheet to help you.

Focus task

End of decade report on the League of Nations

It is the end of the 1920s. You have to write a report on the League.

This will be a bit like a school report. You have to grade the League on the areas in the table below and add a comment on its progress, achievements and weaknesses. The section on disarmament has been filled in to give you an example of how to complete the report.

Area of performance	Overall grade for 1920s (A–E)	Comments (including examples of achievements or weaknesses)
To be united and strong enough to discourage any nation from using force as a way to solve disputes.		
To provide a place to discuss international disputes and work them out peacefully.		
To encourage countries to co-operate, especially in business and trade.		
To encourage nations to disarm.	E	I'm afraid the League has made little progress in disarmament in this decade. The League needs to work harder in the years to come.
To improve living and working conditions for people around the world.		

5 Weimar and Nazi Germany 1918–45

Part A The Weimar Republic

5.1 How did things look for the Weimar Republic in 1919?

The next three pages give you background information to help you understand what happened to Germany after the Great War. Aim to:

- remember two problems facing the Weimar Republic in 1919
- explain why these issues were important.

Key words **abdicate; economy; industrialist; malnutrition; republic; scarce**

Before the First World War, Germany had been a proud country with a strong army, an overseas empire and powerful industry.

The war destroyed that old Germany. There was a revolution in 1918. The Kaiser ABDICATED and fled the country. In January 1919, the Germans elected a new president, Friedrich Ebert. He faced a big challenge.

Imagine you are Ebert at the start of your term as President.

Here's THE GOOD NEWS for you

- Germany is now a democratic REPUBLIC. You have wanted this for your entire political career.
- You lead the Socialist Party. Yours is now the single most popular party in Germany. The majority of German people support you – they want you to succeed.
- You are the President of the new republic. That's not bad for an ordinary working man, the son of a saddle-maker.

Focus task

Outlook for the Weimar Republic

Look at the six pieces of bad news for Ebert. Which do you think is the worst? Work in pairs or small groups to tackle this task.

1 Summarise each problem on a separate card.
2 Put the cards in order according to how serious the problem is.
3 Write a sentence for each problem card to explain its rank.
4 Add two or three sentences to explain how some of the problems are connected to each other.
5 Add a final sentence to explain whether you think Ebert's new government will last. You could give a percentage chance of survival with a short explanation of your decision – 0 per cent chance would mean no chance of surviving; 100 per cent would mean that it was sure to survive.

Now here's THE BAD NEWS!

- **Germany lost the war,** but the German people don't believe this. The Kaiser and the army never told bad news to the people. You will have to break the news to the German people that they really lost the war. You need to make clear that Germany cannot restart the war and win.
- **Germany's ECONOMY is a disaster.** The state has debts of 150 billion marks because of the war. You can't even afford to pay war pensions to 600,000 families whose fathers or sons have been killed in the war.
- **People are starving.** Food is SCARCE and expensive. Possibly 300,000 Germans have suffered the effects of MALNUTRITION.

- **Germany is more divided than ever.** Some wealthy INDUSTRIALISTS got rich from the war while poor families had to sell their possessions just to buy food.
- **Most Germans don't know how democracy works.** Germany has never been a democracy. In the old days, the Kaiser made decisions with his top ministers. So no-one today knows what it is like to ask ordinary Germans how they want their country to be run.
- **Berlin is dangerous – some Germans don't want democracy.** Armed gangs of former soldiers are fighting in the streets with police, troops and each other. Many of these gangs are totally opposed to democracy. Berlin (the capital city) is so dangerous that your new government has to meet in the small town of Weimar instead.

The democratic politicians had been given power at just the time when things were going badly wrong.

A
Run along. We'll take the important decisions. We know what's best for Germany.
PROUD COUNTRY
STRONG ARMY
GREAT EMPIRE
STRONG INDUSTRY
1914

B
DEFEAT
ECONOMIC DISASTER
SHORTAGES
DIVIDED SOCIETY
We feel that it is important you share in these crucial decisions.
1918

What might Ebert be thinking? Write a thought bubble explaining his thoughts in each cartoon.

■ *5.2* How well did the Weimar Republic do from 1919 to 1923?

There is a lot going on in the next five pages. Set yourself the target of being able to describe:

- one challenge the Republic handled successfully (and why)
- one challenge the Republic did not handle well (and why).

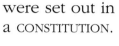

Key words **Chancellor; constitution; proportional representation; Reichstag**

CHALLENGE 1 *Setting up a democratic government*

Germany got a new system of government. The rules for it were set out in a CONSTITUTION.

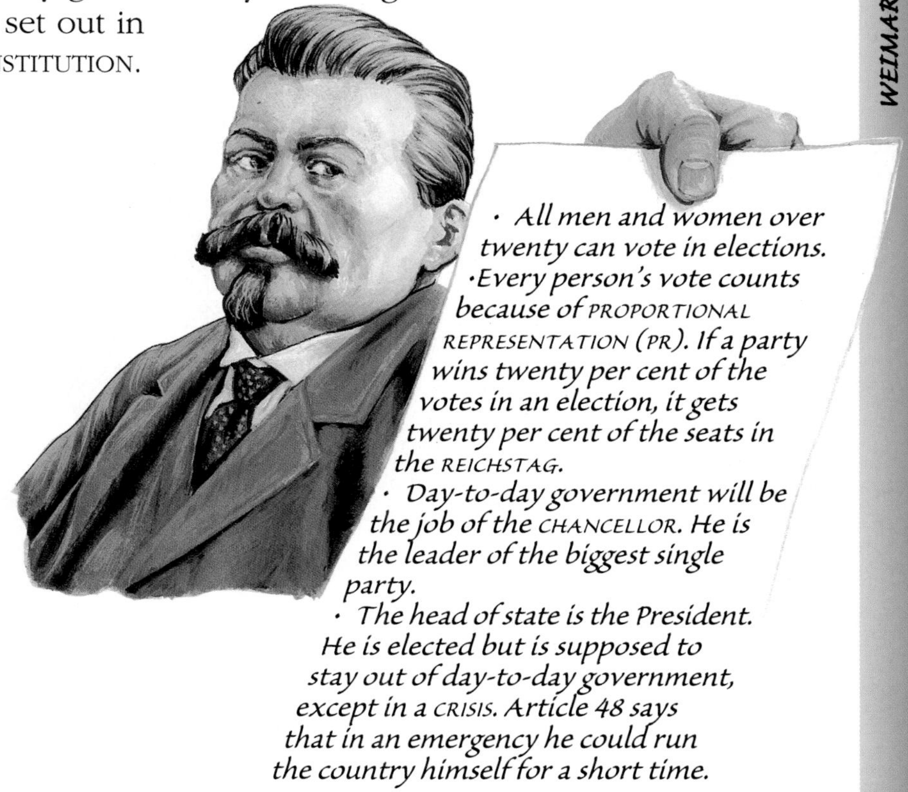
· All men and women over twenty can vote in elections.
· Every person's vote counts because of PROPORTIONAL REPRESENTATION (PR). If a party wins twenty per cent of the votes in an election, it gets twenty per cent of the seats in the REICHSTAG.
· Day-to-day government will be the job of the CHANCELLOR. He is the leader of the biggest single party.
· The head of state is the President. He is elected but is supposed to stay out of day-to-day government, except in a CRISIS. Article 48 says that in an emergency he could run the country himself for a short time.

Civil servants, judges, military leaders, university professors and owners of big industries.

It was a very democratic constitution but these people did not like it. They did not think democracy was the right system for Germany. They longed for the good old days when the Kaiser ruled Germany. They did their best to hold on to power and to stop the new government from doing well.

CHALLENGE 2 *Dealing with extremists*

Ebert faced EXTREMISTS on both sides.

Key words extremist; Freikorps; putsch; revolt

On the left wing – Communists

Communists wanted Germany to have a Communist revolution like Russia. They wanted workers to take over factories, farms and the government.

In the middle – Ebert

On the right wing – Freikorps

FREIKORPS were ex-soldiers who wanted Germany to be run by the army, as it was in the old days. They hated the Communists, but they did not like democracy either.

SOURCE 1

German Communists in 1919.

SOURCE 2

Freikorps troops in action.

Don't get hung up too much about the exact aims of the Communists and the Freikorps. The important point is that both left-wing and right-wing groups disliked the idea of democracy. They also hated each other.

In January 1919, the Communists started a REVOLT. This is known as the Spartacist revolt. Ebert asked his opponents on the right to deal with his opponents on the left. The army and the Freikorps arrested and killed the Communist leaders. The revolt was soon over. The German people were shocked by the violence. However, people accepted Ebert's actions because many Germans were very afraid of Communism.

In March 1920, it was the turn of the Freikorps. Freikorp leader Wolfgang Kapp tried to take over Berlin. This is known as Kapp's PUTSCH. This time, Ebert appealed to the ordinary people of Berlin for help. They went on strike to show their opposition to Kapp. Berlin's roads, railways, power, water and sewage services were all brought to a standstill. Kapp gave up and fled the country.

1 Look closely at Sources 1 and 2 on page 82. Make four short lists:
- What the sources **definitely tell** you about the Communists
- What the sources **definitely tell** you about the Freikorps
- What the sources **suggest** about the Communists
- What the sources **suggest** about the Freikorps.

Focus task

Copy and complete a chart like the one below. Fill out the first two rows for the first two challenges you have looked at on pages 81–83. You can get a 'statement bank' from your teacher to help you.

Challenge	How did the government try to deal with this challenge?	Who supported and who opposed the action?	How effective do you think the government was on a scale of 1 (success) to 5 (failure)?
1: Setting up a democratic government			
2: Dealing with extremists			
3:			
4:			

Key words inherited; passive resistance

CHALLENGE 3 *Coping with the Treaty of Versailles*

Germans were outraged by the Treaty of Versailles. Germany had to accept blame for starting the war. It lost 10 per cent of its land and 12.5 per cent of its population. It also lost most of its army. Germany had to pay £6.6 million of reparations.

SOURCE 3

Wir Auslandsdeutschen
protestieren
gegen den Gewaltfrieden und
gegen den
Raub unseres Privateigentums
Wir Auslandsdeutschen
protestieren
gegen den Gewaltfrieden und
gegen den
Raub unseres Privateigentums

Germans demonstrating against the Treaty of Versailles.

Ebert was not involved in drawing up the treaty. In fact, no Germans were. Some Germans said that Ebert should have refused to sign such an unfair treaty. Ebert felt he had no choice. If he had not signed, the Allies would have restarted the war and Germany would have been badly defeated. All the work that had been done to set up a new republic would have been destroyed.

But, from then on, Germans blamed Ebert and the Weimar Republic for the treaty. When opponents wanted to harm Ebert's government, all they had to say was, 'look at that treaty he signed – he is weak and useless', and many Germans would instantly agree.

Focus task

How well did the Weimar Republic do?

Look back at your table from page 83. Fill out the next rows for challenges 3 and 4. You can also use Chapter 3 to help you.

CHALLENGE 4 *Sorting out the money problems*

The Weimar Republic INHERITED war debts of 150 billion marks. These were the Kaiser's debts but the Weimar Republic had to deal with them. Added to that, the Treaty of Versailles forced Germany to pay reparations of six billion marks.

In January 1923, Ebert's government refused to pay reparations. French troops moved in to take what was owed (see page 66). Ebert called for PASSIVE RESISTANCE. The workers supported the President. They went on strike and refused to co-operate with the French. Over one hundred German workers were killed in demonstrations.

To help to solve the reparations problem, Ebert's government simply printed more money. It paid off billions of marks' worth of war debts by doing this. But this caused hyperinflation. The price of everything went sky high. In 1921, one pound was worth 500 marks. In November 1923, one pound was worth 14 billion marks! Middle-class Germans who had savings lost everything. Many of them blamed Ebert and his government for the economic chaos.

In early 1924, Germany got a new Chancellor, Gustav Stresemann. He persuaded Ebert to use his emergency powers. Ebert and Stresemann scrapped the worthless mark and introduced new money called the rentenmark. At this point, the USA also came to Germany's rescue with money to pay its debts and to get its industry going again.

1 Look at Source 4. The caption has seven words. Write a more helpful caption to explain the picture to a GCSE student. Aim to write about 30 words.

You could mention:
- who is in the picture
- what they are doing
- when the picture was taken
- why it was taken
- what the background suggests about the people.

SOURCE 4

Children playing with bundles of worthless banknotes.

Focus task

Here are two interpretations of the achievements of the Weimar Republic 1919–23:

a) The events of 1919–23 show that the Weimar Republic was doomed. It faced powerful threats and the German people did not support it.

b) The events of 1919–23 show that the Weimar Republic was strong. It overcame some major challenges and people supported it.

Use your completed table to write three paragraphs to explain:
- **Paragraph 1:** what evidence suggests view **a)** is right.
- **Paragraph 2:** what evidence suggests view **b)** is right.
- **Paragraph 3:** which view *you* think is right!

5.3 Was the Weimar Republic a success 1924–29?

Your main aim on the next four pages is balance. You need to be able to balance Weimar achievements and problems 1924–29. Aim to remember:

- two ways in which the Weimar Republic was stable 1924–29
- two threats to the Republic's STABILITY 1924–29.

Key words civil service; coalition; judiciary; stability

Focus task

It is 1929. An inspector from the League of Nations has been sent to Germany to judge how it is doing. As you read through pages 87–89, help him by filling in a chart like the one below.

LEAGUE OF NATIONS REPORT

League of Nations Inspector's report
Date: 1929
Country: Germany

Question	Grade A–E	Explanation
Is democracy working?		
Is the economy stable?		
Is Germany working peacefully with other countries?		

Question 1: is democracy working?

There were no more riots, revolutions or political crises between 1924 and 1929. In fact, quite the opposite.

- There were several peaceful elections in this period. Most Germans voted for parties that supported the Weimar Republic (see Source 1).
- The army, CIVIL SERVICE, JUDICIARY and other officials all co-operated with the government.
- Gustav Stresemann was a leading member of every government during this period. He was opposed to the Republic at first, but then changed his views and became a strong supporter. He convinced many other Germans to do the same.
- In 1925, there were elections for the post of President. The winner was Paul von Hindenburg. He was a hero of the Great War. The fact that a great military leader was prepared to be part of the Weimar Republic encouraged more Germans to support it.

However . . .

Proportional representation (PR) was causing problems. One aim of PR was that no political party would dominate the Reichstag. Parties would have to form COALITION governments and co-operate with each other.

The parties did form coalitions, but were not very keen to co-operate. The governments broke down. The longest government lasted for only two years. People got fed up with so many elections and squabbling politicians. This damaged their faith in democracy as a system.

SOURCE 1

Left wing → Right wing	Communist Party (KPD) – Wanted to overthrow the Republic	Social Democratic Party (SPD) – Loyal to the Republic	Democratic Party (DDP) – Loyal to the Republic	Centre and Catholic parties – Loyal to the Republic	Conservatives (DVP) – Supported by industrialists	Nationalists (DNVP) – Supported by landowners	Nazis (NSDAP) – Wanted to overthrow the Republic
1919	0	187	75	91	19	44	0
1920	4	186	39	64	65	71	0
May 1924	62	100	28	65	45	95	32
Dec 1924	45	131	32	69	51	103	14
1928	54	153	25	62	45	73	12

Seats won by parties in Reichstag elections 1919–28.

1. Look at Source 1. Explain why these figures would be encouraging for supporters of the Weimar Republic.
2. Some historians have said that the Republic's PR system was 'too democratic'.
   - **a)** Explain what this comment means.
   - **b)** Do you agree that a system can be too democratic?

Key words foreign affairs; negotiate; traitor

Question 2: is the economy stable?

In the late 1920s, if you walked down the streets of Berlin there was much to see. Cafés were full. Shops and theatres were doing good business. Architects were creating exciting new buildings. Film-makers were producing successful new films. The economy was clearly recovering from the crisis of 1923.

In 1924, Germany was helped by the USA. The Dawes Plan gave Germany huge loans (800 million marks). The USA also reorganised Germany's reparations payments. This gave Germany economic stability. Wages for workers rose. Industrial production went up. Big businesses, like chemicals and steel, did well. So did the big cities where these industries were based.

However . . .

- Germany's recovery was totally dependent on American loans. These loans were for a short period only. The American banks could demand their money back at very short notice if they wanted.
- Farmers found it hard to sell their goods at a decent price.
- Small businesses (such as local shops) suffered from competition from big businesses (for example, department stores).
- The wages of people working in public services did not go up as fast as wages for industrial workers. As a result, many people in these sections of society felt bitter towards the Weimar Republic.

SOURCE 2A

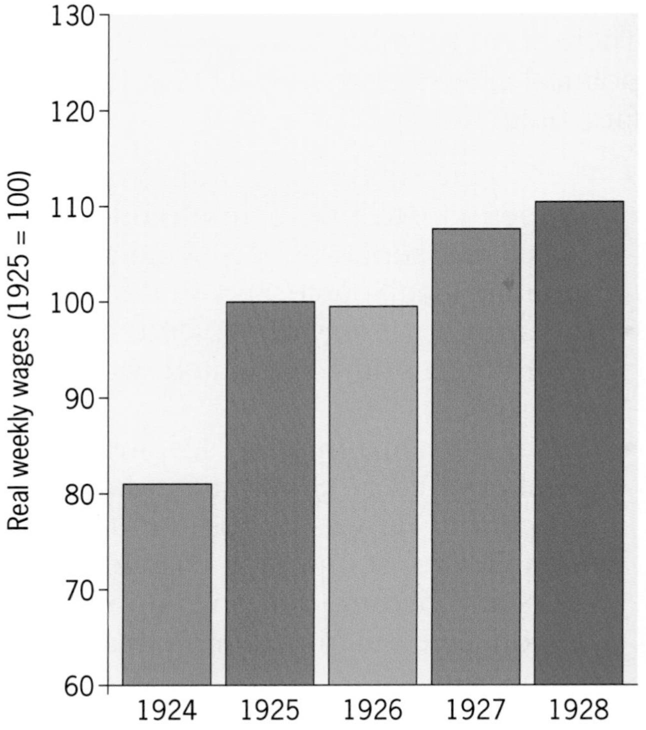
Real weekly wages (1925 = 100)
130
120
110
100
90
80
70
60
1924
1925
1926
1927
1928

Real weekly wages in the 1920s. This graph shows the buying power of workers' wages.

SOURCE 2B

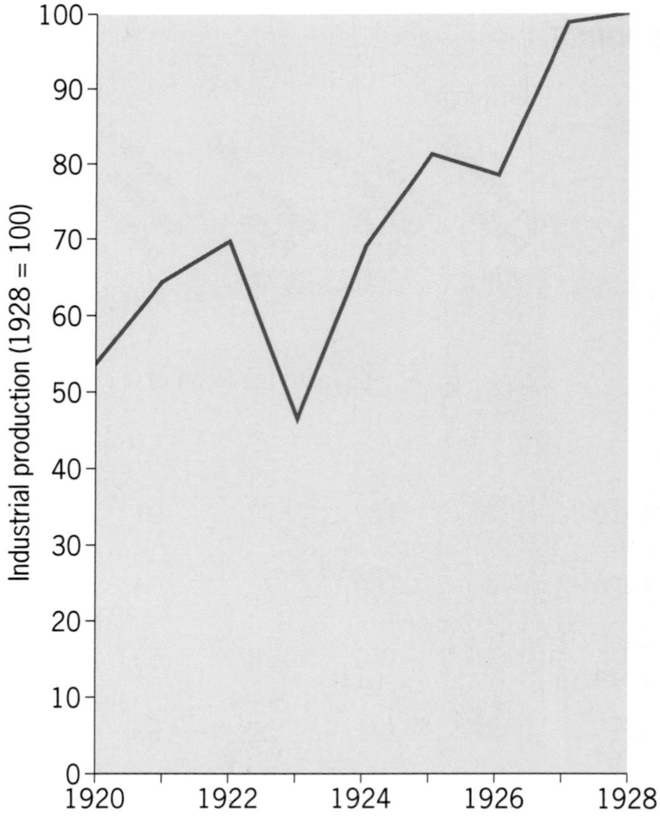
Industrial production (1928 = 100)
100
90
80
70
60
50
40
30
20
10
0
1920
1922
1924
1926
1928

Industrial production in Germany in the 1920s.

Question 3: is Germany working peacefully with other countries?

- Stresemann was a FOREIGN AFFAIRS expert.
- He built good relations with Germany's former enemies.
- In 1925, Stresemann signed the Locarno Treaty. This meant that Germany agreed to accept the borders between Germany, France and Belgium, which had been set out in the Treaty of Versailles.
- The Locarno Treaty improved Germany's relations with France, Britain and the USA.
- The Locarno Treaty left Poland and Czechoslovakia feeling a bit nervous. It did not say anything about **their** borders with Germany.
- In 1926, Germany was invited to join the League of Nations.
- Being invited to join the League of Nations showed that Germany was accepted by the rest of the world again.
- Being part of the League of Nations helped Stresemann to NEGOTIATE some of the other terms of the Treaty of Versailles.
- Stresemann agreed the Young Plan with the USA. This reduced Germany's reparations payments and spread out the payments to make them easier to afford.
- Some groups of extremists (including Adolf Hitler's Nazi Party) accused Stresemann of being a TRAITOR for co-operating with Britain, France and the USA.

Activity

This section on foreign affairs is not organised into plus points and 'howevers' like the previous two sections.

a) Rearrange the ten bullet points so that they are divided into 'plus points' and 'howevers'.
b) Shorten each bullet point to a single word or phrase so you can remember it.

SOURCE 3

A FOR ARBITRATION
D
GERMANY
WEST FRONTIER
EAST FRONTIER
LEAGUE OF NATIONS
ENGLAND
FRANCE
POLAND
ITALY
LOW

"PLEASSE, MISS, I HAF LEARNT DER LESSON. MAY I GET DOWN ?"

A British cartoon from March 1925 commenting on Germany's attitude to the League of Nations. Arbitration means working out problems by negotiation. The person on the stool represents Germany.

Part B From Weimar Republic to Nazi dictatorship

■ 5.4 How did Germans feel about the Nazis in the 1920s?

Key words **Aryan; master race; racist; rally; SA; Slav; trial**

A good way to get a feel for the story of the Nazis in the 1920s is to look at source material from the time.

The main issue to understand in this section is how strong the Nazis were in the 1920s. You need to be able to explain:

- three main beliefs of the Nazis
- two reasons why they gained little support.

1 The Nazi Party was founded in Bavaria in 1919 by Anton Drexler. Adolf Hitler joined the party because he liked its ideas. Here is his membership card, number 55.

SOURCE 1

If you think this looks wrong you're right – check out the task on the next page.

2 Hitler soon took control of the party from Drexler. He organised young Nazi supporters into the SA storm troopers. They acted as guards at Nazi meetings and also attacked other parties' meetings. Hitler had tremendous energy and passion. Before long, the Nazis were gaining attention. Look at Source 2.

SOURCE 2

3 Hitler was a RACIST. He said that Germans were part of a MASTER RACE of humans – ARYANS. He believed that Aryans were threatened by what he called 'inferior' humans such as Jews and SLAVS (people like Russians or Poles).

He thought that Germany had lost the war because it had been 'stabbed in the back' by weak leaders. The Weimar politicians who had signed the Treaty of Versailles were traitors. Hitler believed that Socialists, Communists and Jews had all betrayed Germany. He promised a strong Germany with strong industries, strong armies and a strong leader – himself!

Hitler did not believe in democracy. In November 1923, he and his supporters marched into a government meeting in Munich, Bavaria. He announced he was taking over the government of Bavaria, as Source 3 says.

SOURCE 3

Focus task

Evidence and sources

We had a bit of a disaster on this page! This story of the Nazis in the 1920s was supposed to have sources in it. Unfortunately, we've ended up with spaces, while all the sources are on page 92 AND they're in the wrong order!

Sort out which of Sources A–F on page 92 should go where on this page. Your teacher can give you a sheet to help you.

4 Unfortunately for Hitler, the Munich Putsch was a disaster. The army did not join him and the police opened fire on his supporters. He ran away and was arrested soon afterwards. He was sent to prison for five years. Look at Source 4.

SOURCE 4

5 However, the putsch helped Hitler in one way. The judge at his TRIAL supported some of his ideas, so the judge let him use the trial to get his ideas across to the German people. His trial speech was reported in all the newspapers (see Source 5). He was sent to a very comfortable prison.

SOURCE 5

6 While he was in prison, Hitler changed his policy. He decided he could not seize power in a revolution. He would have to take power by being elected. Hitler served only nine months of his five-year sentence before he was released. When he came out of prison, he totally reorganised the Nazi Party.

- He divided the country into districts, or Gau.
- He set up a network of local branches in each Gau.
- The branches held RALLIES and meetings and handed out leaflets.
- They also ran Hitler Youth organisations, which aimed to encourage young people into Nazism.
- There was lots of training for Nazi speakers.
- There was a big propaganda organisation under Josef Goebbels. Goebbels was brilliant at setting out the Nazi message clearly (see Source 6).

SOURCE 6

Hitler also gave up trying to attract workers. Instead he aimed at farmers and the middle classes. He tried to play on people's fear of Communism. He also stirred up feelings against the Jews.

This new approach brought in new members. By 1928, party membership was over 100,000 although this was still not nearly enough to win an election. In the 1928 election, the Nazis had less than three per cent of the vote.

SOURCE A

Deutsche Arbeiter-Partei (D. A. P.)
Ortsgruppe München Abteilung:
Mitgliedskarte
für Herrn Adolf Hitler
München, den 1. Jan. 1920.
Nr. [redacted] Für den Arbeitsausschuß:
Drexler
Schriftwart
Diese Karte gilt als Ausweis bei geschlossenen Versammlungen

Hitler's Nazi Party membership card. Nazi was short for National Socialist German Workers' Party (NSDAP in German). Hitler was actually member 55, but the Nazis started numbering from 500.

SOURCE B

A wonderful ferment was working in Germany . . . most Germans one met struck you as being democratic, liberal, even pacifist [peace loving]. One scarcely even heard of Hitler or the Nazis except as jokes.

From American journalist, William Shirer. He was in Germany in the 1920s, but was writing in the 1960s.

SOURCE C

We demand:

- *a struggle against the shame of the Versailles Treaty*
- *work and a decent living for every working German*
- *homes for German soldiers and workers. If there is not enough money to build them, drive the foreigners out so that Germans can live on German soil*
- *land on which to grow the grain that will feed our children*
- *a government of statesmen who are men and whose aim is the creation of a German state.*

Every four years Germans elect a new set of torturers, and everything stays the same. Therefore we demand the annihilation [total destruction] of the democratic system. Germany for the Germans!

From 'We Demand', a Nazi propaganda leaflet written and published by Goebbels in 1927. It set out what the Nazis stood for.

SOURCE D

The Bavarian Ministry is removed. The government of the November Criminals and the Reich president are declared to be removed . . . I propose that the policy of the National Government of Germany be taken over by me . . .

Hitler declares the revolution, 8 November 1923.

SOURCE E

The most active political force in Bavaria at the present time is the National Socialist Party . . . Adolf Hitler from the very first has been the dominating force and has undoubtedly been one of the most important factors contributing to its success . . . His ability to influence a popular assembly is uncanny.

From an American intelligence report on political activities in Germany, 1922.

SOURCE F

By the time his trial ended, Hitler had turned defeat into triumph. He impressed the German people with his speaking ability and his passion, and got his name on the front pages of the world.

From the American journalist, William Shirer.

Focus task

The Nazis in the 1920s

Tackle this task once you have sorted out the sources on page 92.

Historians can use sources to support or challenge ideas about the past. Here are some statements about the Nazis in the 1920s. Decide if the evidence supports or challenges each statement.

Statement	Do you think it is true or false?	Are you 100 per cent sure or less? (Say what per cent)	Explain why you have reached this decision
Hitler founded the Nazi Party.			
The Nazis were a small party.			
Jews could join the Nazi Party.			
The Nazis were a moderate political party.			
The Nazis believed anyone who wanted to live in Germany should be able to do so.			
Hitler was the dominant force in the Nazi Party.			
Hitler was a reasonable speaker.			
The Munich Putsch was a complete disaster for Hitler.			
Nazis did not really go in for propaganda posters and leaflets.			
The Nazis were going nowhere by the end of the 1920s.			

Doing an exercise like this makes you read the information and sum it up. This helps you to remember it. When you come to revise, you will be glad you did this exercise.

Extension

Source E on page 92 is an intelligence report on the Nazis in 1922. Write an update on this report set in the year 1928. Your aim is to use the evidence to sum up:

- what the Nazi movement stands for
- how it is organised
- its strengths
- its weaknesses
- any important events linked to it
- whether you think it is a threat to the Weimar Republic in 1928.

5.5 How did Hitler become Chancellor in 1933?

The key here is to cut down the story to basics. Try to remember:

- two ways in which the DEPRESSION helped Hitler
- one piece of evidence to support your two choices.

Key words **Depression; nationalisation; SS**

In the 1920s, the Nazis decided that the best way to achieve power was to campaign in elections. In 1928, less than three per cent of Germans voted for them. Five years later, the Nazis were the biggest party in the Reichstag and Hitler was Chancellor of Germany. How did this happen?

A number of factors helped, as you will see on pages 94–97.

Factor 1: the Depression

The Depression was bad news all around the world, but in Germany it was disastrous. US banks forced German businesses to repay the money they had loaned to them during the 1920s. The results were:

- businesses went bankrupt
- there was huge unemployment – by late 1932 it was at six million (one in three workers)
- demand for farm goods collapsed, and farmers lost their farms
- some German banks collapsed, and some middle-class Germans lost their savings
- the Weimar government made matters worse. It tried to save money by cutting welfare payments. Some unemployed people had no money coming in at all. They were forced to live in shanty towns and beg for food.

The Depression was very bad news for Germany, but it was just what the Nazis needed. People ignored the Nazis in the 1920s because they were so extreme. Now Germans were looking for extreme answers to their problems. The Nazis had plenty of those!

SOURCE 1

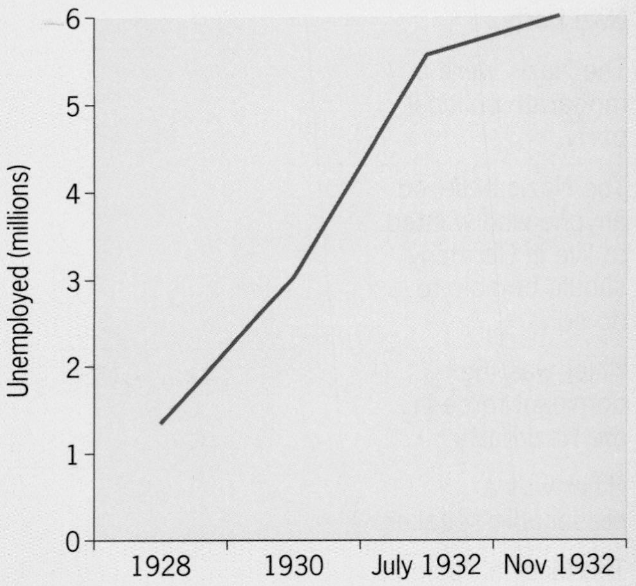

Unemployed (millions)
0
1
2
3
4
5
6
1928
1930
July 1932
Nov 1932

Unemployment in Germany 1928–32.

Are you worried about unemployment? I say put the unemployed people into the army, or get them building roads. We can make Germany great again.

Factor 2: disillusion with Weimar democracy

As the Depression ruined people's lives, the Weimar politicians seemed to spend more time arguing with each other than trying to help ordinary Germans. When an election was called in 1930, millions of people voted for parties like the Nazis. These parties planned to get rid of democracy altogether, but now people listened to them. The Nazis increased their vote from three to eighteen per cent.

These Weimar politicians are weak and useless. Germany needs strong leaders. I'll be your strong leader.

SOURCE 2

	Number of seats in Reichstag	
	Nazis	Communists
1928	12	54
1930	107	77
July 1932	230	89
Nov 1932	196	100

The growing vote for the Nazis and Communists, 1928–32.

Factor 3: fear of Communism

Ever since the Russian Revolution, ordinary Germans had been frightened of a Communist revolution in their own country. They knew what would happen:

- Communists wanted NATIONALISATION (state control) of all major industries. This alarmed businessmen.
- Communists believed in state control of the land. This alarmed farmers and landowners.
- Communists didn't believe in religion. This alarmed German churchgoers.

Are you frightened of the Communists? We'll crush the Communists. We're the only ones who really know how to deal with them.

In the 1930s, the Communists were getting stronger. Communist gangs called the Red Fighting League attacked the meetings of other parties. The only group that seemed able to deal with the Communists were the Nazis. The Nazis sent their own gangs (the SA and SS) to deal with the Red Fighting League. Many people who would not normally vote for the Nazis decided to support them because they seemed able to deal with the Communist threat.

1 Explain how the Communists helped the Nazis without meaning to. You might find it helpful to draw a diagram as part of your answer.

Factor 4: Nazi election plans

The Depression gave the Nazis their chance and they took it. Most historians agree that the Nazi campaign (push for votes) was very good.

- Nazi messages were simple. They talked about going back to the good old days. People liked this idea.
- The Nazis criticised Weimar politicians for signing the Treaty of Versailles. They also attacked Communists, who, they said, wanted to take over Germany. This meant that the Nazis gave people someone to blame.
- The Nazis used the press and radio well. Hitler travelled around by plane. This all showed that the Nazis were a modern party in touch with modern technology and ideas.
- Germans wanted order and strong government. Nazi meetings and rallies were huge and well organised. The SA and SS looked good in their smart uniforms. To many people, the Nazis looked like the right party.
- Most of all, the Nazis had Hitler. He was a wonderful speaker. People felt that he truly understood them. Germans were looking for a leader.

SOURCE 3

Deutschland
erwacht!
Wählt
Liste:
2
Nationalsozialisten

A Nazi election poster from 1932. The caption says 'Germany Awake!'

These Nazis are well organised and disciplined. They will bring order and strong leadership back to Germany.

SOURCE 4

A Nazi Party rally in Frankfurt, 1932.

SOURCE 5

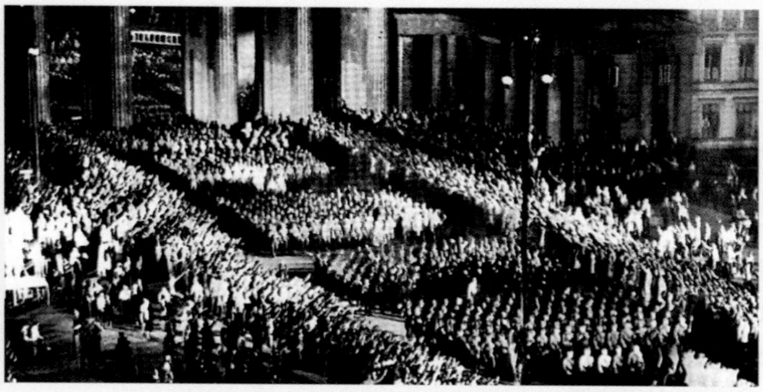

The Nazis celebrating Hitler's appointment as Chancellor in January 1933.

Late in 1932, President Hindenburg and some other powerful politicians decided to do a deal with Hitler. Hitler became Chancellor. Hindenburg and his friends thought they would be able to control Hitler. What a mistake they made!

Focus task

How did Hitler become Chancellor in 1933?

Prepare a presentation on this question. There are three possible diagrams you could use in your presentation.

1 Choose one of the diagram options.
2 Plan and prepare a presentation to go with that diagram. The most important point is that you explain to the audience:
- at least two factors that helped Hitler become Chancellor
- how each factor helped him
- the evidence that supports this view.

Diagram option 1

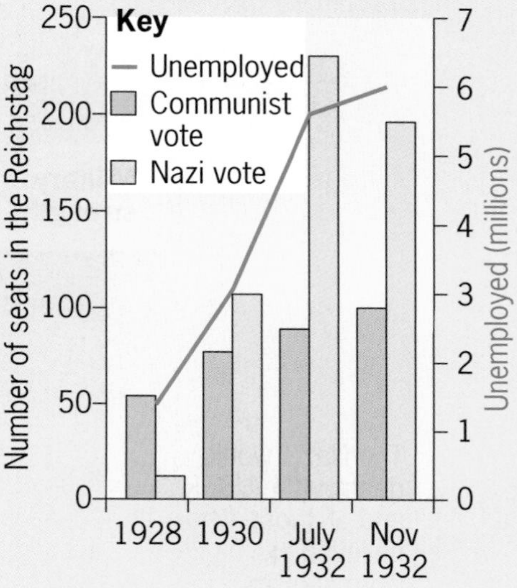
Key
Unemployed
Communist vote
Nazi vote
Number of seats in the Reichstag
Unemployed (millions)
0
50
100
150
200
250
0
1
2
3
4
5
6
7
1928
1930
July 1932
Nov 1932

Diagram option 2

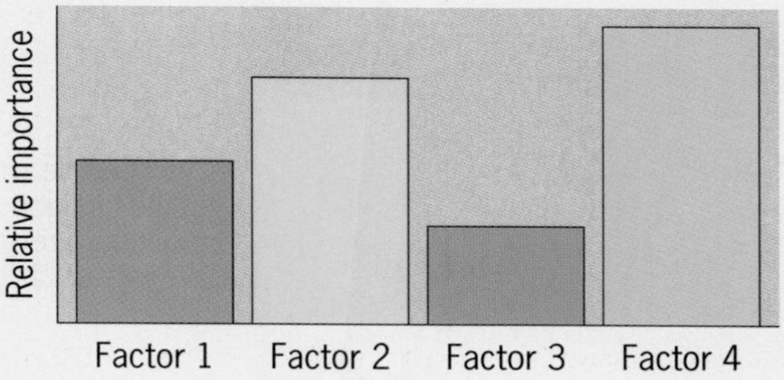
Relative importance
Factor 1
Factor 2
Factor 3
Factor 4

Diagram option 3

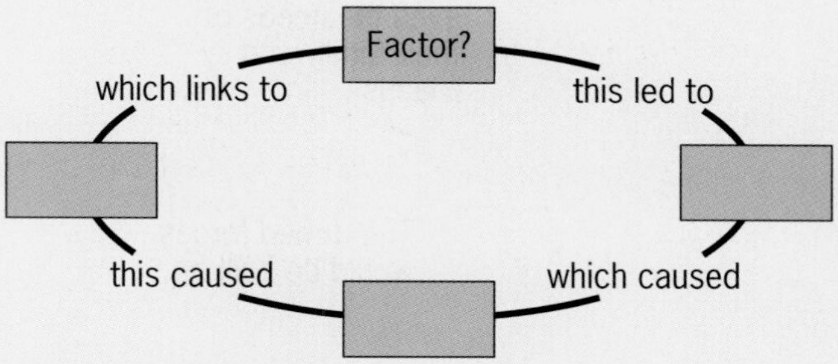
Factor?
this led to
which caused
this caused
which links to

(You choose the factors to be shown in diagram options 2 and 3.)

If you want to go further

3 Explain whether you think particular factors were more important than others.
4 Explain how your two factors are different (for example, short term, long term).
5 Explain how your factors affected each other.

5.6 What was Hitler's vision for Germany?

From this section, you need to be able to explain:

- two of Hitler's broad aims that German people would have supported
- two detailed points of Hitler's aims that they would not have supported.

Key words **Führer; *Lebensraum*; National Community; racial purity; regime; terror**

Most Germans voted for the Nazis because they thought they would bring economic recovery and strong, stable government. They probably did not take too much notice of other Nazi plans for Germany. The diagram below summarises the Nazi vision.

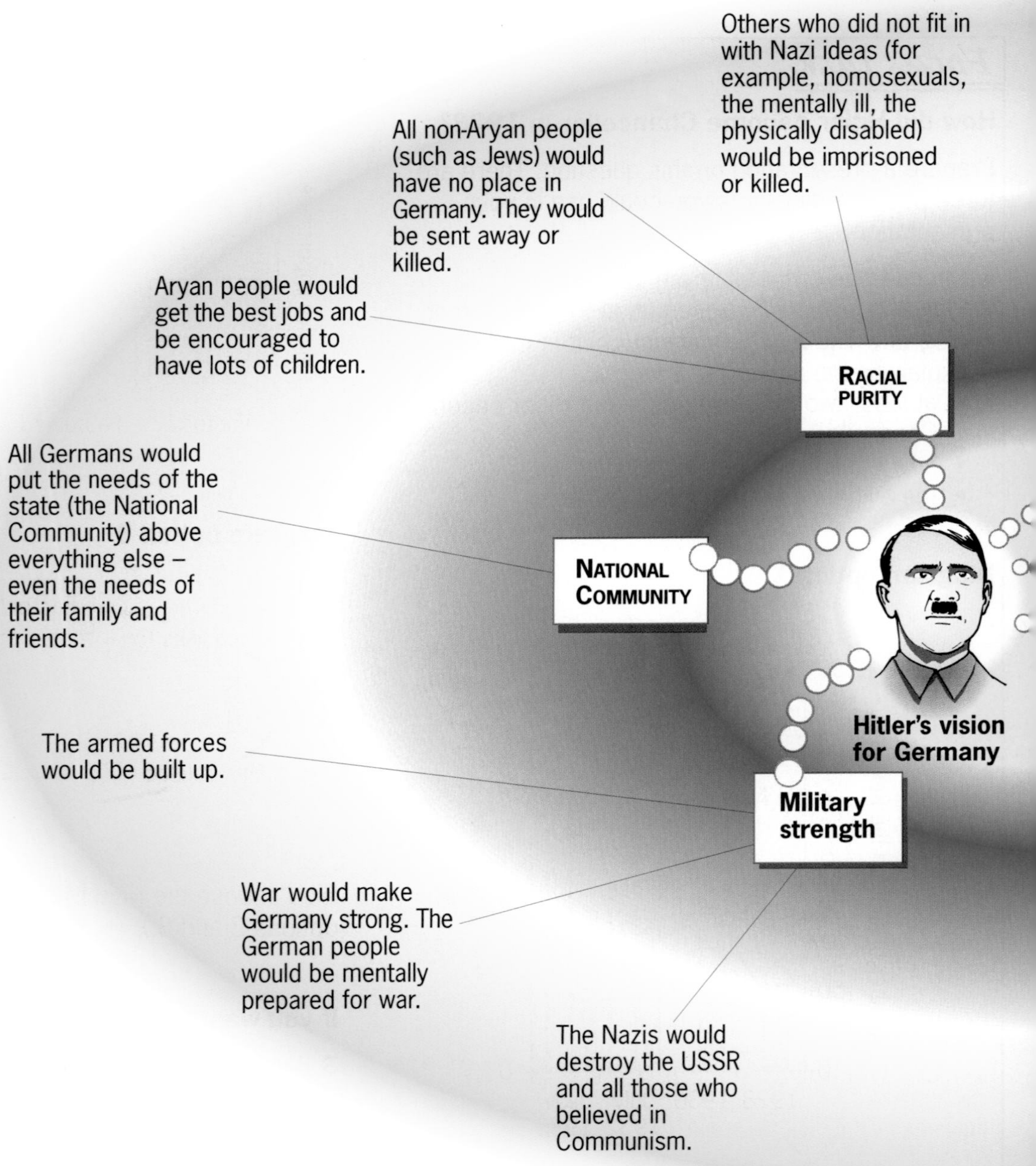
Others who did not fit in with Nazi ideas (for example, homosexuals, the mentally ill, the physically disabled) would be imprisoned or killed.
All non-Aryan people (such as Jews) would have no place in Germany. They would be sent away or killed.
Aryan people would get the best jobs and be encouraged to have lots of children.
RACIAL PURITY
All Germans would put the needs of the state (the National Community) above everything else – even the needs of their family and friends.
NATIONAL COMMUNITY
The armed forces would be built up.
Military strength
War would make Germany strong. The German people would be mentally prepared for war.
The Nazis would destroy the USSR and all those who believed in Communism.
Hitler's vision for Germany

Activity

This diagram was put together in 2001, using sources from the 1930s, other textbooks, TV programmes and interviews. It shows a complete summary of Hitler's vision.

In pairs or small groups, look at Hitler's plans and aims. Take each one in turn. Decide whether you think each aim would gain Hitler support or put off most Germans. Remember most Germans wanted:

- national pride
- economic recovery
- strong, stable government.

After you have worked through the rest of this chapter, see if you were right.

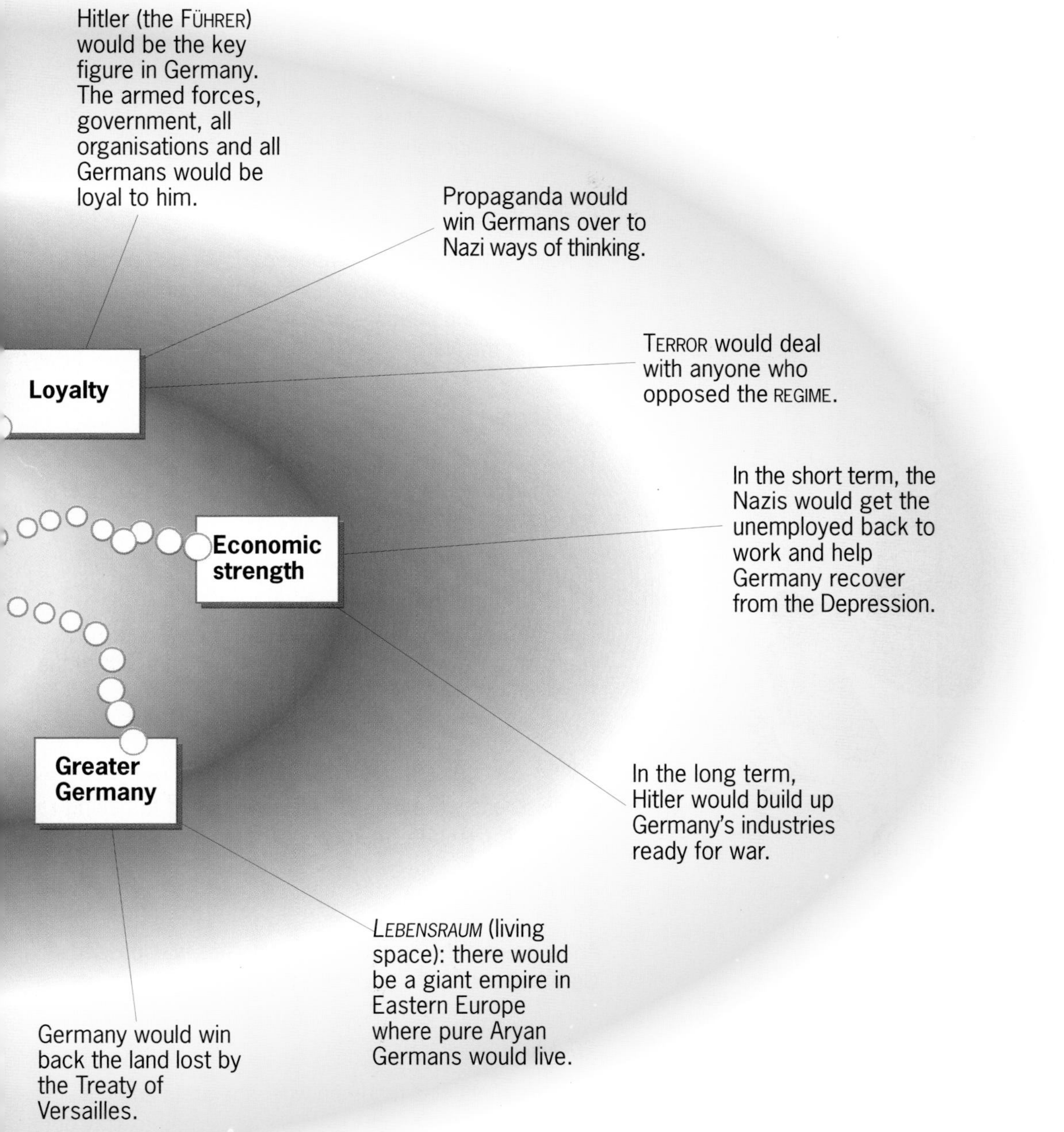
Hitler (the FÜHRER) would be the key figure in Germany. The armed forces, government, all organisations and all Germans would be loyal to him.
Propaganda would win Germans over to Nazi ways of thinking.
Loyalty
TERROR would deal with anyone who opposed the REGIME.
In the short term, the Nazis would get the unemployed back to work and help Germany recover from the Depression.
Economic strength
In the long term, Hitler would build up Germany's industries ready for war.
Greater Germany
LEBENSRAUM (living space): there would be a giant empire in Eastern Europe where pure Aryan Germans would live.
Germany would win back the land lost by the Treaty of Versailles.

5.7 How did Hitler take control of Germany?

The key point to understand in this section is the range of Hitler's methods. Aim to be able to explain:

- two examples of Hitler **using force** to take control of Germany
- two examples of him **doing deals** to take control of Germany.

Key words **concentration camp; dictator; elite; emergency powers; hard labour**

Hitler was delighted to be Chancellor. But he was not really in control. Most Chancellors had not lasted very long in the Weimar Republic.

Hitler was determined to be different.

To get control of Germany, he used a mixture of methods, as you can see from the timeline below.

SOURCE 1

Auch wenn man warm sitzt, sitzt man oft ungemütlich. .!
„Der Wahre Jacob", Berlin,
den 4. März 1933

A cartoon from 1933. The people below the chair represent the German ELITE.

1933

30 January

Hitler became Chancellor. He co-operated closely with President Hindenburg and other important people.

Early February

CONCENTRATION CAMPS were opened. Political opponents (mainly Communists) were taken to the camps. They got HARD LABOUR and beatings until they agreed to stop opposing the Nazis.

27 February

The Reichstag building burnt down. Hitler said it was a Communist plot and had 4000 Communists and other opponents arrested.

24 March

The Enabling Act gave Hitler EMERGENCY POWERS for four years and allowed him to pass laws without going to the President. It made Hitler a DICTATOR in law.

2 May

Trade unions were banned. All workers had to belong to the new Nazi-run German Labour Front (DAF).

14 July

A law against the start-up of new parties was passed. Germany became a one-party (Nazi) state.

20 July

An agreement was made between the state and the Roman Catholic Church. The Church agreed to stay out of politics, and the government left the Church alone.

SOURCE 2

HITLER'S UNKEPT PROMISES
LOW

A British cartoon commenting on the Night of the Long Knives, 1934. Its title was 'They salute with both hands now'.

1934

Spring

The SA leader, Ernst Röhm, wanted Hitler to join the army and the SA under Röhm's command. Hitler had to choose whether to go with army leaders or to stick with his friend Röhm. By the summer, Hitler had decided.

30 June

Night of the Long Knives:
SS troopers used trucks and arms supplied by the army to arrest about 400 SA leaders. Anyone else seen as a threat was also arrested. Around 90 of those arrested (including Ernst Röhm) were murdered. Hitler spoke on radio the next day to defend his actions.

August

Hindenburg died, and Hitler took over his role as President. He declared himself Führer (leader) of Germany.

German armed forces swore an oath of loyalty to Hitler in return for getting rid of the SA.

Focus task

How did Hitler take control of Germany 1933–34?

Make your own copy of the table below. Use it to work through pages 100–101 and note down how Hitler dealt with various groups in Germany 1933–34. You may want to work in pairs or small groups.

Group	Example of Hitler doing a deal or working with them	Example of Hitler using force or threats	Example of other method
Germany's elite (for example, army leaders; industrialists)			
Communists			
Trade unions			
Other political parties			
Churches			
Other powerful people in the Nazi movement			

Part C Life in Nazi Germany

5.8 How did the Nazis keep control in Germany?

These two pages are straightforward. Make sure you can explain two examples of Nazi terror methods.

Key words **agent; conforming; Gestapo; inform on; lawyer; persecute; protective custody; re-education; torture**

The Nazis faced very little opposition in Germany in the 1930s. What did they do to make sure of this?

Focus task

The Nazis used a range of methods to control Germany. Your task over the next six pages is to explain this cartoon. Add notes to your own copy of the cartoon to explain each of the three elements – the stick, the carrot and the notice in front of the donkey's eyes.

In the Activity on page 107 you will think about examples of each of these methods in action.

I'LL TELL YOU WHAT TO THINK

SOURCE 1

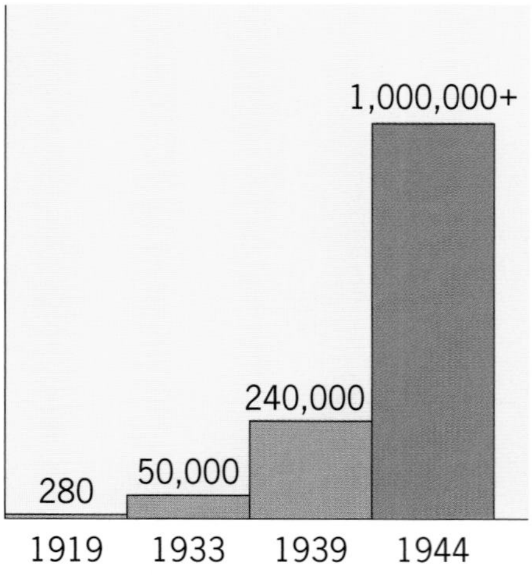
1,000,000+
240,000
50,000
280
1919
1933
1939
1944

The growth of the SS.

Method 1: the stick – terror

After the Reichstag fire, the Nazis rounded up many opponents and killed or TORTURED them in concentration camps.

Police and courts

Early in 1933, the Nazis took control of the police and courts. Later they controlled judges and LAWYERS. This meant that opponents of the regime could not expect a fair trial.

The SS (leader: Heinrich Himmler)

The SS began life as Hitler's personal bodyguard (created from the best members of the SA). After the SA was destroyed in 1934, the SS grew into a huge organisation under Heinrich Himmler. The SS had many sub-divisions (for example, the Death's Head Units which ran the concentration camps). As its power increased, the SS began to use its own courts. These sentenced 200,000 Germans to be sent to concentration camps.

SOURCE 2

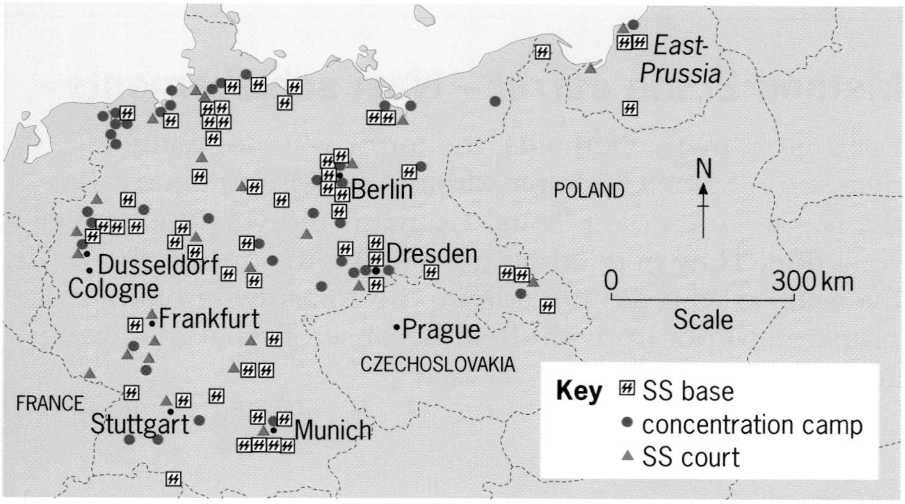
East-Prussia
Berlin
POLAND
N
Dusseldorf
Cologne
Dresden
0
300 km
Scale
Frankfurt
Prague
CZECHOSLOVAKIA
FRANCE
Stuttgart
Munich
Key
SS base
concentration camp
SS court

The power of the SS, 1933–37.

The GESTAPO (leader: Reinhard Heydrich)

The Gestapo's role was to root out possible enemies of Nazism, such as:

- a teacher who taught his pupils to see through Nazi propaganda
- a grocer who told anti-Nazi jokes to his customers
- a worker who refused to give the 'Heil Hitler' salute.

SOURCE 3

Type of case	% of cases
Belonging to banned organisations	30.0
Non-CONFORMING behaviour (e.g. criticising the Nazis)	29.0
Possessing banned printed materials	4.5
Listening to foreign radio	2.3
Not interested in politics	0.9
Non-political criminal activity	12.0

The work of the Gestapo in the Dusseldorf region 1933–45.

Germans feared that Gestapo AGENTS were everywhere. They INFORMED ON each other because of this fear. When war broke out in 1939, the Gestapo rounded up 162,000 people into 'PROTECTIVE CUSTODY'.

The terror organisations gave the Nazis power, but they did not always have to use it. Fear made people conform.

PERSECUTING minorities

Terror tactics were used against other groups in society that the Nazis did not like. Jews, homosexuals, Gypsies, Jehovah's Witnesses, tramps and alcoholics were also taken to concentration camps for 'RE-EDUCATION'.

SOURCE 4

It is clear that the majority of the people have two faces; one which they show to close friends and family; and the other for the authorities. The private face criticises everything; the official one beams with optimism and contentment.

From a report written by an agent of the Socialist Party living in Germany, August 1937.

These are two more simple pages. Make sure you can explain two reasons why German people approved of Nazi rule.

Key words boom; guaranteed; Reich; resistance

Method 2: the carrot – Nazi achievements

For a great many Germans, the terror was not really necessary. Some Germans admired Hitler and liked what the Nazis were doing. Many Germans did very well out of Nazi rule. They needed no persuading to support the Nazis. Even those who did not admire the Nazis were often prepared to put up with them because of what they were achieving in Germany.

BENEFITS OF NAZI RULE

The economy

- Re-arming Germany created an economic BOOM and increased national pride.
- Huge government spending on roads, housing, etc. created jobs and brought unemployment down.

Big business

- Big jobs working for the government were available.
- There were no trade unions to make trouble.

Industrial workers

Middle classes

- The threat of Communism was removed.
- People had pride in Germany after Hitler overturned the terms of the Treaty of Versailles.

Farming communities

- The Reich Entailed Farm Law protected farms from being closed by banks.

The Nazis helped farming communities with measures like the Reich Entailed Farm Laws. The government promised to buy farmers' produce. It also stopped banks from taking land from farmers who were in debt. However, not all farmers gained from Nazi policies. Even so, many country people left the land to work in the factories, where they earned higher wages.

Industrial workers also gained. They got work. They also got better working conditions from the Beauty of Labour Movement. And they got leisure activities organised by the Strength Through Joy labour movement.

Life for industrial workers had its down sides as well. In 1933, the working week was 43 hours, but it had risen to 47 hours by 1939. The value of wages did not get back to 1928 levels until 1938.

Overall, workers accepted the benefits and kept their heads down. They may not have liked Nazi rule, but they were prepared to put up with it.

The Strength Through Joy organisation provided leisure opportunities (for example, sports clubs and holidays).

The Beauty of Labour organisation improved working conditions in industries (for example, canteens and washrooms).

The REICH Food Estate gave farmers GUARANTEED markets and prices for their goods.

SOURCE 5

I have just returned from a visit to Germany. I have now seen the famous German leader and also something of the great change he has achieved. Whatever his methods, there can be no doubt that he has achieved a marvellous transformation in the spirit of the people and in their social and economic outlook.

From an article by David Lloyd George in the *Daily Express*, November 1936. Lloyd George was a former British Prime Minister.

SOURCE 6

There was no resistance movement and there couldn't be. Nowhere in the world can develop a resistance movement when people feel better from day to day. We were stones in a torrent and the water crashed over us.

Emmi Bonhoffer, sister of RESISTANCE leader Dietrich Bonhoffer, interviewed in 1989.

SOURCE 7

November 1933: *Millions of Germans are indeed won by Hitler. I hear of some actions by the Communists . . . But what good do such pinpricks do? Less than none, because all Germany prefers Hitler to the Communists.*
September 1937: *I believe ever more strongly that Hitler really does embody the soul of the German people, that he really stands for Germany and that he will consequently keep his position.*

From the diaries of Victor Klemperer, a Jewish university lecturer in Germany.

At the end of these two pages, aim to:

- list two ways in which the Nazis controlled the media
- explain one way in which propaganda was effective.

Key words culture; glorify; transmitter; warden

Method 3: control by propaganda

A vast propaganda effort supported both the 'stick' and the 'carrot'. Both Hitler and Goebbels were experts in propaganda. They believed that all the mass media had to be carefully controlled. They thought that people had to be told what to think. This diagram shows how the Nazis controlled the mass media.

SOURCE 8

A scene from the film, *Triumph of the Will*, 1934. It was a great success, with huge queues to see it.

The Reich Ministry for Popular Enlightenment and Propaganda (set up in March 1933 and headed by Josef Goebbels)

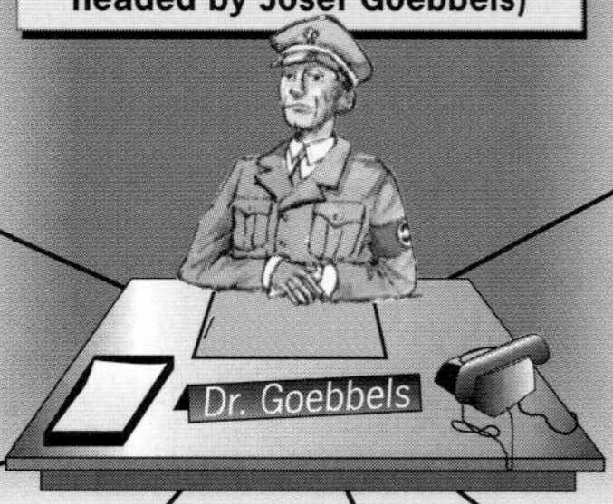
Dr. Goebbels

Radio

- The Ministry controlled radio stations and TRANSMITTERS.
- Cheap radio sets were made. Germany had more radios per head than the USA (but radios could only pick up programmes from Germany).
- Special WARDENS made sure people listened to the radio.

Press

- The Ministry closed down about two-thirds of Germany's newspapers.
- It also controlled information supplied to the remaining newspapers.

Special events

- Goebbels staged impessive rallies, meetings and processions.
- The most spectacular success was the 1936 Olympic Games in Berlin. Germany won the most medals and Goebbels commissioned a special film called *Olympia*. It was a box office smash.

Art and culture

- The Reich Chamber of CULTURE was set up in September 1933 and headed by Goebbels.
- Anyone who worked in journalism, radio, film, literature, theatre, music or the arts had to belong to the Chamber. Otherwise, they could not get a role in a play, publish a book, sell a painting, etc. Members had to be approved by Goebbels so that there was virtually no need for censorship.

Film

- There were some major propaganda films made by Nazi-approved film-makers, such as *Triumph of the Will* (about the 1934 Nuremberg Rally) and *The Eternal Jew*, 1940 (a vicious anti-Jewish film).

The environment

- The Nazis built huge new buildings, especially in Berlin. Nazi-approved artists made massive sculptures showing idealised bodies.
- Posters and photographs were everywhere, especially ones GLORIFYING Hitler.

Propaganda and terror together

- Propaganda made terror more effective. The Nazis made sure people knew what happened to their opponents. So, people *thought* the Gestapo had an agent on every street corner. *In fact*, they did not. For example, in Wurzburg there were only 28 Gestapo agents to one million Germans.
- Terror made propaganda more effective. The SS and the Gestapo rounded up anyone who tried to show a banned film or sell a banned book. So, opponents of the Nazis found it hard to spread their anti-Nazi ideas.

Propaganda and achievement together

- Propaganda reminded German people how successful Nazi Germany was. So they were constantly told about Germany's booming economy, or Hitler's successes in getting land for Germany.
- Propaganda reminded people of Hitler's vision for Germany (see pages 98–99). Germans were regularly told to beware of Jews. They were reminded of how they hated the Treaty of Versailles.

Activity

Here are a number of real-life situations. Would you say each person is being controlled by:

- the stick
- the carrot
- propaganda
- a combination of them all?

1 Pastor Paul Schneider is sent to a concentration camp because he preaches an anti-Nazi sermon.
2 Gertrude Weber joins the Nazi Party because she is very moved by one of Hitler's speeches.
3 The Northeim Nazi newspaper reports that the homes of twelve Northeimers have been ransacked in a search for anti-Nazi literature.
4 Jewish professor, Victor Klemperer, puts out a Nazi flag, just like everyone else, even though he hates the Nazis – he would be in danger if he did otherwise.
5 Herman Schulze gives up Socialism because he needs a job and Socialists can't get jobs.
6 The government appoints radio wardens to make sure that everyone listens to official radio broadcasts.
7 Jochen Klepper is forced to resign from his job as a radio scriptwriter because his wife is Jewish.
8 Book stalls in Berlin railway stations are visited by the SS and told to stop selling foreign newspapers.
9 Writer Bertholdt Brecht flees to the USA because he refuses to have his songs and plays censored by the Nazis.

Focus task

How did the Nazis control Germany?

Here are the three main ways that the Nazis controlled Germany:

- terror
- achievements
- propaganda.

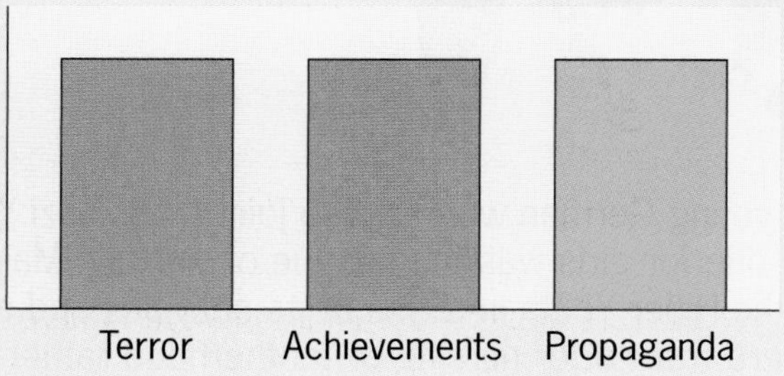
Terror
Achievements
Propaganda

1 At the moment they are shown as equally important on the graph. Draw your own graph and represent each factor at a size that shows how important it was.
2 Now turn your graph into words:
I think the biggest bar should be . . .
The next biggest is . . .
The third biggest is . . .
3 Now turn these words into a piece of extended writing:
The most important way the Nazis controlled Germany was . . .
This made the opposition fail because . . .
Another important factor was . . .
This made the opposition fail because . . .
A final factor was . . .
This also made it difficult for the opposition because . . .

5.9 How did young people react to the Nazis?

At the end of these two pages, check that you are clear about two ways in which the Nazis won over young people.

SOURCE 1

I liked it in the Hitler Youth. I thought the uniform was smashing, the dark brown, the black, the swastika [the Nazi symbol], all the shiny leather. Before we didn't even have a decent football to play with. Now the Hitler Youth provided us with sports equipment. Never in my life had I been on a real holiday, now under Hitler I could go to lovely camps in the mountains. I liked the comradeship, the marching, the sport and the war games. We were brought up to love our Führer, who was to me like a second God. I was convinced that because of the German blood in my veins I was superior.

From *Through Hell for Hitler* by Henrik Metelmann, published in 1990.

Henrik Metelmann loved the Hitler Youth so much that he often argued with his own father, who hated the Nazis. Henrik chose to be in the Hitler Youth. There was no law that made people join, but only one member of Henrik's class did not join.

When Henrik left school, he became an engineer. The first question his employers asked him was whether he was in the Hitler Youth.

Henrik joined the army when war broke out. He fought against the USSR along with millions of other young men.

SOURCE 2

Millions of young German women also joined the Nazi Youth organisations. The main one for girls was the League of German Maidens (BDM). It was similar to the Hitler Youth in terms of its activities and aims. However, the girls were trained for nursing or motherhood rather than war. This photograph shows a hike organised by the BDM.

Activity

Imagine you are Henrik Metelmann or a BDM member trying to convince a friend to join the Hitler Youth or BDM. What would you say?

Why were the Nazis so successful in winning over the young people of Germany? In many ways, it is not that surprising.

They controlled the schools. By the mid-1930s, most teachers were either Nazi supporters or were forced to teach the curriculum the Nazis created. You can probably guess what this curriculum was like. It involved lots of physical exercise to make young people fit and tough. It also featured lots of German history which stressed Germany's glorious military past. This history also warned young people that Jews and Communists had ruined Germany and that Adolf Hitler was the saviour of Germany. Even maths and science were used to get across the Nazi messages of racial hatred and the glory of war.

The Nazi youth organisations were attractive. They provided holidays, sports equipment and comradeship. Many young people enjoyed the opportunity to get away from their parents and be with their friends. They enjoyed the practical activities, like map reading, and it was quite exciting for a teenage boy to handle a rifle and clean it like a proper soldier.

The Nazi propaganda deliberately targeted young people. Most Hitler Youth meetings contained a short lecture on Nazis ideas. Posters, radio programmes and even games tried to establish Nazi ideas (see Source 4).

SOURCE 4

Deutsches Mädel
Als zukünftige Trägerin der Nation ist es Deine Pflicht, auf sorgfältige Gesundheits- und Körperpflege zu achten.

An advertisement for the German pharmaceutical industry. It reads: 'German Girl. As the future bearer of the nation it is your duty to take care of your health and beauty.'

SOURCE 3

All subjects – German language, History, Geography, Chemistry and Mathematics – must concentrate on military subjects, the glorification of military service and of German heroes and leaders, and the strength of a rebuilt Germany. Chemistry will develop a knowledge of chemical warfare, explosives etc., while mathematics will help the young to understand guns and artillery.

From the German newspaper *Der Angriff*, October 1939.

Activity

Have a look at your current school or college timetable. Suggest at least five ways that the Nazis would change it. Think about:

- subjects they would get rid of
- new subjects they might introduce
- ways they would change the existing subjects
- whether they would give more or less time to particular subjects.

Aim to remember two examples of young people resisting the Nazis.

Key words corrupt; executed

Did all young people support the Nazis?

Henrik Metelmann adored the Führer – he says so in Source 1 (on page 108). But is it possible that some of his friends joined the Hitler Youth just for the football and the holidays? There are many accounts from members of the Hitler Youth and BDM that suggest so. These people talk about the fun. They also say that when the lectures about Nazi ideas began, they mentally switched off. However, other young people were much firmer in opposing the Nazis.

The Swing Movement

Swing groups were anti everything in a way. While some members were in the Hitler Youth, the Swing Movement resented the way the Nazis controlled people's lives. They showed their discontent through their interest in banned music. They were heavily into American music such as jazz and swing. They hung out in nightclubs and bars, and danced American dances. They even opposed the Nazis directly.

The Swing Movement was only a tiny minority of young people, who generally came from better-off families. Nevertheless, they irritated the Nazis. The Nazis did not like the fact that they did not conform. They also saw their interest in jazz as CORRUPT. The Nazis acted against them by closing the bars they went to. Some Swing Movement members were arrested (see Source 5).

SOURCE 5

Suddenly Radio Hamburg came on air again . . . the British soldiers who had taken over the station had five or six Glenn Miller records with them and the first one they played was In The Mood. *It was the happiest day of my life! The Nazis had gone and I had such a feeling of freedom!*

Uwe Storjohann describing his feelings when the Nazis were defeated in 1945. He had been arrested several times for playing Swing Music and ordered to stop. He was imprisoned from 1941 to 1945 for refusing to give up.

1. Write your own 30-word definition of the Swing Movement for a historical dictionary of Nazi Germany.
2. Look at Source 5. What does it tell historians about
   a) Uwe Storjohann
   b) the Swing Movement
   c) Nazi attitudes to the movement?

The Edelweiss Pirates

This was a name given to many small groups of young people from many different parts of Germany. They wore the edelweiss flower (and other emblems) as a symbol of their resistance to the Nazis. The earliest groups appeared in 1934. By 1939, there were an estimated 2000 Edelweiss Pirate groups. Some Pirate groups were like the Swing groups. They just opposed Nazi control of their lives. Others, like the group in Cologne, opposed Nazi political ideas. They made fun of Hitler Youth groups or even violently attacked them.

When war started in 1939, the Pirates stepped up their activities. Some groups were involved in spreading anti-Nazi propaganda and even in helping enemy air crews who had been shot down. The Nazis began to clamp down on the groups. In December 1942, 739 Pirates in Cologne were sent to labour camps. In 1944, the Nazis hanged the leaders of the Cologne Edelweiss Pirates.

SOURCE 6

Edelweiss Pirate leaders being hanged in 1944.

3 Write your own definition of the Edelweiss Pirates for a historical dictionary of Nazi Germany. Do you think this definition should be longer than the Swing Movement definition?

Students

Students like Sophie Scholl (see Source 7) joined the White Rose. This was a student movement that published anti-Nazi material. The White Rose activists were brave, but they were always a small movement.

SOURCE 7

We have written and said what is in the minds of all of you, but you lack the courage to say it aloud.

The last words of Sophie Scholl of the White Rose before she was EXECUTED in 1943.

Focus task

What would you have done?

Here are the options that were open to young people during the Nazi period:

A Whole-hearted membership of Nazi Youth organisations
B Membership of the Nazi Youth organisations – but only for the activities
C Not belonging to any organisation at all
D Swing Movement
E Edelweiss Pirates.

1 The great majority of young people would have belonged in categories A and B. Write a short paragraph to explain why this was the case. Mention at least one of these factors:

- education
- the attractions of Nazi Youth organisations
- pressure to join (for example, from the Nazis, from other young people).

2 What would you have done if you had been a young person in Nazi Germany? Think about this question honestly. For example:

- Do you have strong political or moral views?
- Do you have interests that the Nazis would have disapproved of?
- Would you have liked the activities the Hitler Youth provided?
- If you had doubts about the Nazis, would you have stood up for your ideas or kept you head down?

5.10 How did the Nazis treat women and families?

Make sure you can explain:

- two ways in which women lost out under Nazi rule
- two ways in which women gained from Nazi rule.

Key words grant; honours system; housekeeping; traditional values

What were Nazi policies towards women and the family?

SOURCE 1

A painting showing the ideal Nazi family.

1 Look closely at Source 2 on page 113. Make a list of the ways in which it is similar and different to Source 1.
2 Would you say that Sources 1–3 provide historians with all the information they need about Nazi policies towards women and the family? Explain your answer.

Source 1 is a propaganda painting showing the ideal Nazi family. The man is the strong protector of the family. The woman is also strong, but in a motherly sort of way. She is busy breastfeeding the baby. The young boy is active. He is playing a 'manly' game by digging in the sandpit. The daughters are preparing to be mothers – notice the older daughter watching and learning from her mother. The younger daughter has a doll.

In Nazi Germany, hundreds of posters like this, as well as pamphlets, radio programmes and films, spelled out the same message about the role of women in the Nazi state. It was a very important role. German women were expected to be proud to serve Germany by being mothers and producing as many healthy, racially pure (Aryan) babies as possible.

The Nazis supported this message with actions. As soon as they came to power, they forced many professional women to quit their jobs. Women were banned from civil service jobs in 1933 and from working as lawyers in 1936. In the League of German Maidens (BDM) and at school, girls were taught about health and HOUSEKEEPING skills. Women were offered cheap loans and GRANTS if they were married and had children. An HONOURS SYSTEM was set up – a couple with eight children got the highest Gold Cross award. These measures worked to some extent. The birth rate in Germany increased from 15 per 1000 in 1933 to 20 per 1000 in 1939.

These policies were popular with many Germans (even those who were not Nazi supporters).

- Many unemployed men felt that women should give up work and let men have their jobs.
- In many small towns and rural areas, TRADITIONAL VALUES about women and the family were very strong. Working women, especially young working women, were seen as immoral or corrupt.
- Many older women agreed with the view that women should be wives and mothers.
- The churches generally supported the idea of women as homemakers, wives and mothers.
- There is also evidence that many women found the Nazi women's organisations very rewarding. They got to meet new people and to travel around the country. Hitler was particularly popular among women.

SOURCE 2

A painting of an Aryan farm family in Kahelenberg by the Nazi artist Adolph Wissel, 1939.

But as with so many aspects of Nazi Germany these policies ended in chaos and the Nazis had to change track. In 1936, Germany's economy was recovering. Unemployment was falling and the armed forces were growing. By 1938, Germany was short of workers. Guess who took the new jobs? The women. By 1939, there were 1.4 million more working women than there had been in 1933 (but mostly in low grade jobs with low wages).

There were also some very well known women in Nazi Germany. Magda Goebbels, the wife of propaganda boss Josef Goebbels, often appeared in news films. She talked and wrote about health, beauty and fashion. Sources 4 and 5 on page 114 show two more famous women. But these were exceptions. Source 3 sums up Hitler's attitude to the role of women.

SOURCE 3

I hate women who dabble in politics. And if their dabbling extends to military matters it becomes unbearable. In no local section of the Party has a woman the right to hold even the smallest post. It has therefore often been said that we are a party who hate women, who regard women only as a machine for making children. That's far from the truth. Everything that involves war is exclusively men's business. There are so many other fields in which one must rely upon women. Organising a house, for example . . .

A report of comments made by Hitler in a conversation in January 1942.

Focus task

What does the evidence suggest about life for women in Nazi Germany?

SOURCE 4

Film-maker Leni Riefenstahl, who made some of the most famous films of the Nazi period.

SOURCE 5

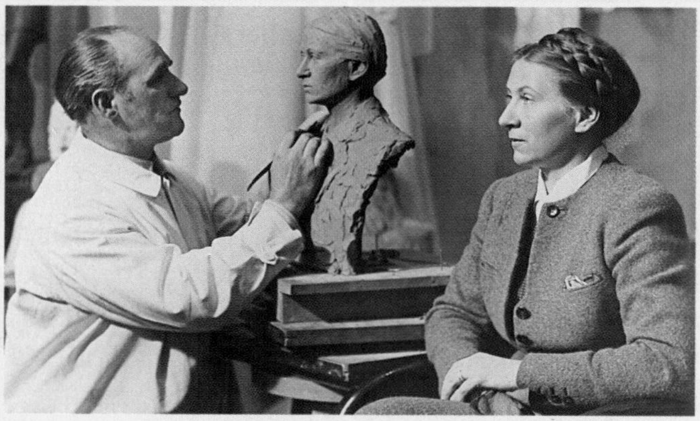

Nazi women's leader, Gertrude Scholz Klink, posing for a sculpture. She was head of the Nazi Women's Bureau and the only female member of the Nazi government. She was tall, blond, racially pure, had four children and was a true Nazi. Even Klink found that senior Nazis ignored her views.

You are doing some research on Nazi Germany using the internet. You come across a site that tells people how well women did in Nazi Germany. There are only two sources on the site. The sources are Sources 4 and 5.

1 Write an e-mail to the website author. Explain why these two sources do not give a complete picture of life for women in Nazi Germany. Start by explaining what impression people get if they only look at these two sources.

Then explain why there is more to this story. You could mention:

- Nazi policies on women and work
- Nazi attitudes to the family
- what evidence suggests this.

2 Design your own web page to tell the real story. Unfortunately, space is limited. You can only have:

- one visual source
- one text source
- 50 words of your own writing.

Extension

3 Explain what the poster in Source 6 is saying.

4 Do you think the Socialists' prediction was right? Explain your answer.

SOURCE 6

FRAUEN,
so geht's euch im »Dritten Reich«!
»Die Frau muß wieder Magd und Dienerin werden« sagt der Naziführer Feder. Deshalb ist auch in der Hakenkreuzfraktion keine Frau vertreten.
K.
Eure Antwort:
Kampf den Nazi – –
für die Sozialdemokratie!

A Socialist Party poster from December 1930. The caption says 'Women, this is what it will be like in the Third Reich (Nazi Germany)'.

5.11 Why did the Nazis persecute minorities?

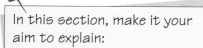

In this section, make it your aim to explain:

- why the Germans persecuted ASOCIALS and racial groups
- how persecution of the Jews got worse when the Second World War started.

Key words asocial; boycott; Einsatz; euthanasia; fatherland; Final Solution; gas chamber; ghetto; Nuremberg Laws; slave labour; sterilised; transported

The Nazis used terror tactics against their political opponents, such as Communists. But they also ran terror campaigns against other groups that did not appear to be a threat to their power at all.

Why did the Nazis persecute racial groups?

The Nazis believed that the ideal German was an Aryan (a white person with blond hair). They believed that Aryans were the master race and were superior to other racial groups. Hitler feared that Aryans would mix with inferior races. So the Nazis persecuted, and later murdered, members of what they called racially inferior groups. Gypsies and Jews suffered most. It is estimated that about 500,000 Gypsies died in death camps such as Auschwitz.

Why did the Nazis persecute 'undesirables'?

The Nazis also persecuted anyone who did not fit their idea of an ideal German. They called these people 'asocials' or 'undesirables'. The Nazis thought that Germany wasted money looking after them and that their presence 'polluted' the country. Hitler said that getting rid of some of the weakest Germans would strengthen Germany.

- Ideal Germans were **socially useful** – they worked hard and served the FATHERLAND. So the Nazis persecuted tramps, beggars, alcoholics and anyone who refused to work. Around 500,000 tramps and beggars were sent to concentration camps in 1933.
- Ideal Germans pledged **total loyalty** to Hitler – so the Nazis persecuted anyone who refused to do this. For example, Jehovah's Witnesses refused to offer total loyalty to anyone other than God, so one-third of them in Germany were sent to concentration camps.
- Ideal Germans **married, had children and created stable families** – so the Nazis persecuted homosexuals, prostitutes and problem families.
- Ideal Germans were **strong and powerful** – so the Nazis persecuted mentally handicapped people and those with inherited diseases. About 350,000 were STERILISED. Later, the Nazis started a EUTHANASIA campaign. About 200,000 people were killed in nursing homes.

SOURCE 1

The Hashude camp for problem families was a bit like a concentration camp, but not as harsh. Inmates were locked up and forced to work.

The Holocaust

The group that suffered most under the Nazis was the Jews. No-one knows for sure why Hitler hated the Jews so deeply, but in speeches and in his book *Mein Kampf (My Struggle;* see page 126), Hitler blamed the Jews for many of Germany's problems.

Other Nazis realised that one way of impressing Hitler was to suggest new methods of persecuting the Jews. From 1933 onwards, Jews in Germany were treated more and more badly, as you can see from the timeline below.

SOURCE 2

The construction of the new Holocaust memorial in Berlin, on the site where some of the headquarters of the Nazi regime stood. The memorial will be made up of 2700 concrete stones.

1933

- The Nazis came to power.
- The SA and SS organised a BOYCOTT to stop people using Jewish shops.
- Laws made it difficult for Jews to work in the civil service, media and education.

1935

The NUREMBERG LAWS made marriages and relationships between Jews and Germans illegal.

1938

- *Kristallnacht* (Night of the Broken Glass), November 1938 – after a Jewish student killed two Nazi officials in Paris, Goebbels planned a big pay-back in Germany. Jewish properties were smashed and synagogues were burned down. Over 100 Jews were killed and 30,000 were arrested. Many ended up in concentration camps.
- German Jews had to register their names and addresses with the Nazi authorities.

1939

The start of the Second World War. Hitler's invasion of Poland brought about one million more Jews under Nazi control. They were rounded up and forced to live in GHETTOS. Thousands died from starvation and disease.

1941

- The German invasion of the USSR brought yet more Jews under Nazi control. Special units of SS troops called EINSATZ began rounding up and shooting Jews.
- All Jews still living in Germany were forced to wear the Star of David.

1942–45

Senior Nazis met together in January 1942. They came up with what they called the 'FINAL SOLUTION to the Jewish problem'. All Jews in Nazi-ruled lands were rounded up. They were TRANSPORTED to camps in Germany and Poland. Some were murdered in GAS CHAMBERS as soon as they arrived. Others were forced to work as SLAVE LABOUR, making materials that Germany needed for its war effort. When they were too old, ill or weak to work anymore, they were murdered. Bodies were stripped of hair, gold fillings and anything else of value. They were then burned in ovens.

SOURCE 3

This is what Gad Beck said about the old memorial:

On this spot was the first old people's home of the Jewish community in Berlin. In 1942, the SS transformed it into an assembly camp for Jewish citizens. Fifty-five thousand Berlin Jews, ranging from infants to the aged, were taken forcibly to Auschwitz and other concentration camps and bestially murdered. Don't ever let this be forgotten.

SOURCE 3

Jewish resistance fighters operated throughout the Nazi period. They helped Jews to escape Germany. We also know of at least one unsuccessful Jewish plan to kill Hitler in 1935.

Focus task

Did most people benefit from Nazi rule?

Look closely at Source 5 on page 105. It is 55 words long. It gives a very incomplete picture of life for German people in the 1930s. Use information from pages 102–117 to write a more complete summary of life in Nazi Germany. Aim to do this in 50 words. If you find this too difficult, aim for 150 words.

Be sure to mention:

- how bad things were in Germany 1929–32
- at least two examples of people or groups who gained something from Nazi rule in the 1930s
- at least two balancing examples that show ways in which life was not so great for others.

Focus task

Why did the Nazis persecute certain groups in German society?

On pages 115–16 you will find five factors that led the Nazis to persecute minorities.

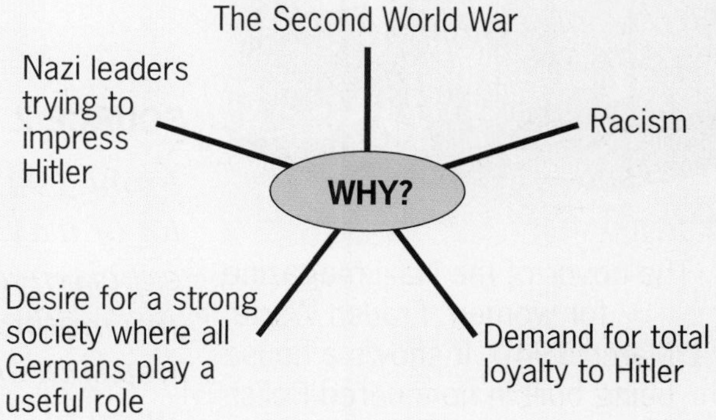

The Second World War
Nazi leaders trying to impress Hitler
Racism
WHY?
Desire for a strong society where all Germans play a useful role
Demand for total loyalty to Hitler

1. Copy this diagram.
2. For each factor, add an example of how it either caused persecution or made existing persecution worse.

5.12 How did Nazi Germany cope with the demands of war?

Test your understanding by making sure you can:

- remember at least two effects of the war on ordinary Germans (with examples)
- explain two factors that hampered Germany's war effort.

Key words armament; conquer; loot; raw materials; resources; territory

The early stages of the war

Hitler's vision for Germany involved a great war to prove Germany's strength. However, most Germans did not share Hitler's enthusiasm. When war broke out in September 1939, it took many Germans by surprise. They had got used to Hitler gaining TERRITORIES for Germany without having to go to war (see page 127).

Germans soon felt the impact of the war. Food rationing began in September 1939. From November 1939, clothes were rationed. On the other hand, the news from the war was good. German forces won one great battle after another (see page 137).

There were other benefits to war as well. The SS under Heinrich Himmler LOOTED the countries the Nazis invaded. Food, RAW MATERIALS and other RESOURCES were sent back to Germany. Pure Aryan Germans were encouraged to settle in the new territories that had been CONQUERED.

The tide turns

Hitler turned his forces on the USSR in 1941. The attack went well at first, but in the long run it was a terrible mistake. By 1943, the USSR's forces were beginning to drive the Germans back. The fighting was vicious and the cost was appalling. The strain of war began to tell at home.

SOURCE 1

NS
Frauen Warte
die einzige parteiamtliche Frauenzeitschrift
Deutschland baut auf im Osten

The cover of the Nazi magazine for women, *Frauen Warte*, 1 March 1940. It shows a house being built in conquered Polish territory. The caption says 'Germany is building in the East'.

SOURCE 2

From 1942 to 1943 we, as children, were visibly aware of a lot of ways in which the war affected families. I myself experienced how two of my father's brothers and also two of my mother's brothers fell. The 'Deaths' column in the newspapers increased noticeably from 1943, and grew even more in 1944.

From an interview in 1994 with a citizen of the German town of Warstein.

The Nazi war effort

As the war went on, the state began to control life and work even more closely than before. The Gestapo kept a close watch for people who did not support the war effort. The SS became increasingly powerful. It developed its own armed forces and even its own ARMAMENTS industries.

In 1942, Hitler put Albert Speer in charge of German industry. It became much more efficient but:

- Allied bombing destroyed factories and transport links (see pages 144–45)
- rivalry between leading Nazis made it difficult for Speer to get things done.

Germans were bombarded by propaganda. Sometimes they were told how well the war was going. Sometimes they were encouraged to support the war effort. Sometimes the propaganda just tried to keep people's spirits up.

However, not even Goebbels could hide the effects of war, especially in the cities. From 1942 onwards, there were serious food shortages. An even bigger problem was the housing shortage caused by bombing (see pages 144–45).

The July bomb plot

For most of the Nazi period, almost all of the army supported Hitler. However, in July 1944, with the war going very badly indeed, some army officers tried to kill Hitler and take over Germany. Colonel Claus von Stauffenberg planted a bomb under the table where Hitler was meeting with other Nazi leaders. The bomb exploded, but failed to kill Hitler. The planned take-over flopped. Stauffenberg and around 5000 others were executed in the Nazi revenge for the attack.

Defeat

By 1945, it was clear to most Germans that they were losing the war. In 1945, Goebbels was put in charge of the German Home Defence Force. He had to organise teenagers and old men to fight the invading Soviet, American and British forces. It was hopeless.

In April, with Soviet, British and American troops closing in on each side, Hitler killed himself, Germany surrendered and the Nazi Reich (empire) was over. Germany was left to count the cost of Hitler's vision.

Focus task

Draw a cloud diagram (see page 65) to sum up the ways in which the war affected Germany and the German people. Your teacher can give you a sheet to help you.

SOURCE 3

Deutsche Erfinder
wachsen heran
für die Zukunft Europas!
Während tapfere Männer auf den Schlachtfeldern den Sieg erkämpfen, dessen Krönung das geeinte Europa kommender glücklicher Jahre sein wird — arbeitet die deutsche Heimatfront schon heute an den Planungen und Konstruktionen, die dann den befreiten Völkern zugute kommen sollen. Und auch die deutsche Jugend bereitet sich zielbewußt auf die großen, schönen Aufgaben vor, die ihr diese Friedens- und Aufbauarbeit stellen wird. Da wird gebastelt und modelliert — aus Spiel und Zeitvertreib wird zielstrebiges, schöpferisches Lernen. Ob im handwerklichen Unterricht der Schulen, ob abends daheim oder in den Arbeitsstunden der Jugend-Organisationen — überall ist dabei UHU, der von der deutschen Kunststoff-Chemie entwickelte Spezial-Leim, ein begehrter, zuverlässiger Helfer!
UHU
DER ALLESKLEBER
UHUWERK H. u. M. FISCHER
BÜHL-BADEN

An advertisement for UHU glue published in 1944. It says: 'German inventors are working for the future of Europe!' German industry was fully involved in all aspects of the German war effort.

Revision task

It is now time to prepare your class quiz, based on the yellow notes at the beginning of each section. Your teacher can give you a sheet to help you.

6 The road to war 1929–39

6.1 The road to the Second World War – a summary

*These two pages outline the main events that you will study in Chapter 6. You will find it useful to refer to them throughout the chapter. For revision, try to describe in your own words **how** each event helped cause the war.*

1929–33 Economic depression

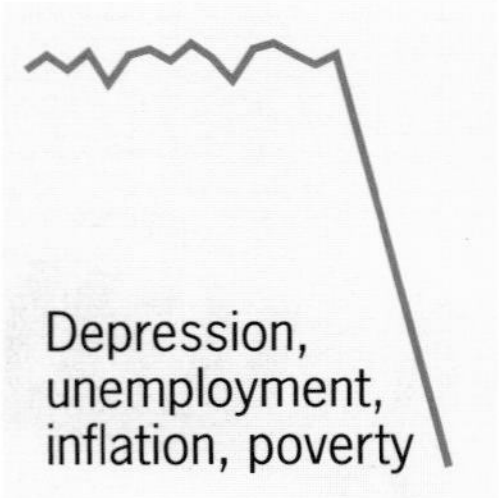

Depression,
unemployment,
inflation, poverty

The Depression led to unemployment and poverty in many countries. Before the Depression, many countries helped each other. After the Depression, they acted in self-interest.

1931–33 Manchurian crisis

Manchuria
JAPAN
CHINA

Japan invaded a part of China called Manchuria. The League of Nations took a year to decide how to respond. In the end, it did nothing! This made other countries think that they could do what they wanted. The League appeared weak.

1934–36 Abyssinian crisis

Italy's leader Mussolini wanted an empire in Africa. He invaded Abyssinia (Ethiopia). The League of Nations did not protect Abyssinia. Mussolini got away with it. From this time on, no one took the League of Nations seriously.

1936–38 Hitler ignores the Treaty of Versailles

German leader Adolf Hitler moved German troops into the Rhineland. Then he united Austria with Germany. The Treaty of Versailles did not allow these actions. France and Britain were worried, but they did nothing to stop him.

Focus task

This task will help you to plant the information on this spread firmly in your mind.

1. Write the dates on one set of cards and the events on a separate set of cards. Then match them up without looking in this book.
2. Check in this book that you have matched the cards correctly. Then paste the cards on a sheet of paper in the correct order to make a timeline.
3. As you work through this chapter, make notes about how each event helped lead to war. These notes will be very useful when you get to the task on page 135.
4. Look back at the work you did on pages 4–7. Can you find any similarities between the causes of the Second World War and the causes of the First World War?

1938 The Munich Agreement

Hitler invaded a part of Czechoslovakia called the Sudetenland. Britain and France let him do this as long as he promised not to invade the rest of Czechoslovakia. Hitler promised. This was called the Munich Agreement.

1939 Hitler invades the rest of Czechoslovakia

Despite his promise, Hitler took over the rest of Czechoslovakia. Britain and France said that they would declare war if he invaded any more countries.

August 1939 Nazi–Soviet Pact

POLA
ND

Hitler wanted to invade Poland. He worried that the USSR might try to stop him so he did a deal with his great enemy, Stalin. Hitler and Stalin divided Poland between them.

1939 Hitler invades Poland

IT'S WAR!

In September 1939, Hitler invaded Poland. Britain and France declared war on Germany.

6.2 What were the effects of the Depression?

The key idea to grasp here is that the Depression created problems in various countries, **which led** to political problems later.

These two pages will help you to:

- *describe how the Depression affected Germany and Japan*
- *think about how the Depression created conditions that led to war.*

Key words manufactured goods; tariff

Economic depression

In the 1920s, world trade depended on the USA. It was the richest country in the world. It lent money to other countries, and it bought goods from other countries. Trade was good for international peace. All the experts said that countries were less likely to fight if they were trading with one another.

In 1929, a depression began in the USA.

- Farms, banks and businesses went bust.
- Millions of workers lost their jobs.
- The Americans bought less (for example, they bought less silk from Japan).
- The USA wanted to protect its own industries so it put TARIFFS on all goods coming into the USA.
- American banks were in trouble so they wanted all the loans they had made to Germany in the 1920s repaid.

Focus task

Here is a basic diagram. Add examples so that it tells a fuller story.

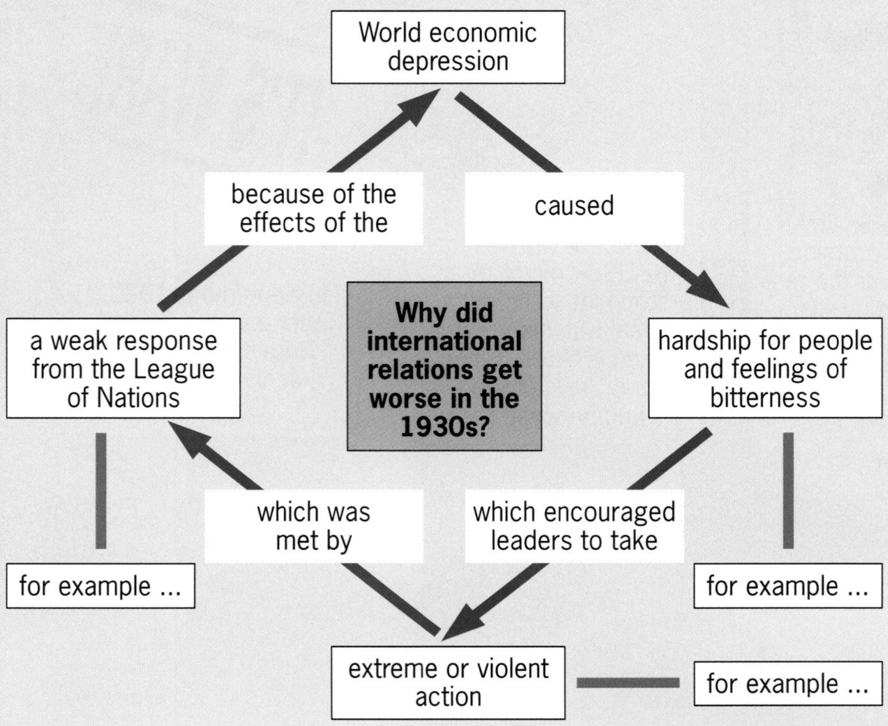
World economic depression
caused
hardship for people and feelings of bitterness
for example ...
which encouraged leaders to take
extreme or violent action
for example ...
which was met by
a weak response from the League of Nations
for example ...
because of the effects of the
Why did international relations get worse in the 1930s?

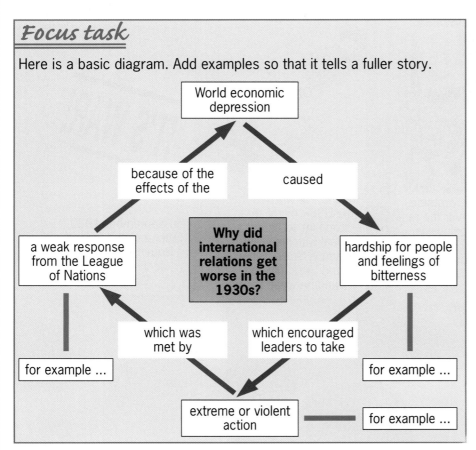

Some historians think that this economic depression was an important cause of the Second World War. You might find this hard to understand. After all, how can businesses going bust in the USA cause a war? The answer lies in **the links between events**. The Depression in the USA did not start the war. However, it created conditions that made war more likely. Examples of these links are explained in the diagram in the Focus task (left).

The USA

One way that the League of Nations could stop one country invading another was to use economic sanctions. But the Depression made the USA unwilling to help in this because economic sanctions would make its own economy even worse.

Top priority – sort out US economy.
Low priority – help sort out international disputes.

Britain

Britain was one of the leaders of the League of Nations. But, like the USA, it was unwilling to help sort out international disputes while its economy was bad. For example, when Japan invaded Manchuria it did nothing – it did not support economic sanctions against Japan and did not send troops to protect Manchuria.

Top priority – sort out British economy.
Low priority – help sort out international disputes.

Japan

The Depression threatened to bankrupt Japan. Its main export was silk to the USA, but the USA was buying less silk. So Japan had less money to buy food and raw materials. Its leaders were all army generals. They decided to build an empire by taking over weaker countries that had the food and raw materials Japan needed. They started by invading Manchuria (part of China) in 1931.

Plans for Japanese empire

Germany

The Depression hit Germany badly. There was unemployment, poverty and chaos. Germany's weak leaders seemed unable to do anything.
As a result, Germans elected Adolf Hitler to lead them. He was not good news for international peace. He openly planned to invade Germany's neighbours and to win back land that Germany had lost in the Great War.

He'll make Germany great again.

Activity

In which country might you have heard statements A–F during the Depression? Match each statement to one of the following countries:

- the USA
- Japan
- Germany
- Britain

A

I have been unemployed since last year.

B

We must ban foreign MANUFACTURED GOODS, then people will buy home-produced goods.

C

If we had our own empire, we would have all the resources we need.

D

Our leaders are weak. We need a strong leader to sort this out.

E

The bank has closed. We've lost everything.

F

The USA wants the loan back. We must close our business.

You might have heard some of the statements in more than one country. Explain the choices you have made.

6.3 Why did the League of Nations fail in the 1930s?

Aim to remember at least two weaknesses of the League of Nations and how these affected Abyssinia.

Key word **Fascist**

The League of Nations was set up to help solve problems such as Japan's invasion of Manchuria (see page 120). But in the 1930s, it failed. The Manchurian crisis showed how weak and indecisive the League was. However, it was the Abyssinian crisis that really finished off the League. You are now going to look at this crisis in detail.

Case study: Italy and the Abyssinian crisis

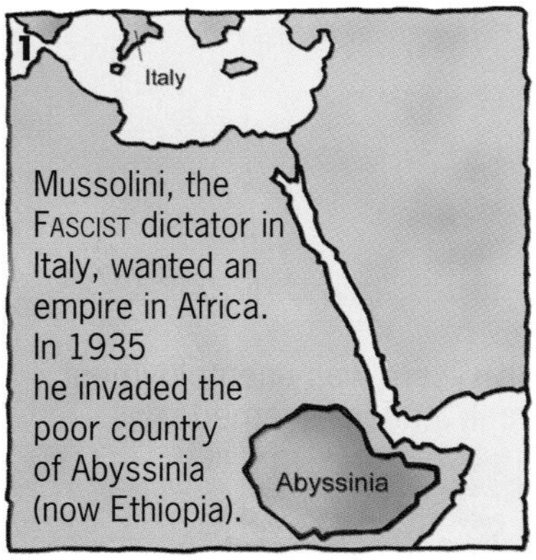
1
Italy
Mussolini, the FASCIST dictator in Italy, wanted an empire in Africa. In 1935 he invaded the poor country of Abyssinia (now Ethiopia).
Abyssinia

2
Stop trading with Italy?
Send soldiers to protect Abyssinia?
Throw Italy out of the League?

Italy and Abyssinia were both members of the League of Nations. Abyssinia asked the League for help. The League took months to decide what to do. In the end it tried sanctions, but didn't ban the only thing that really mattered – oil – because it knew the USA would supply oil to Italy if League members did not.

3

Meanwhile, Britain and France privately offered to let Mussolini have Abyssinia in return for his support against Hitler! When this news leaked out, there was uproar.

4

While the League was thinking about Abyssinia, Hitler sent his troops into the Rhineland. Abyssinia was forgotten.

5
While Britain and France worried about the Rhineland, Italy took Abyssinia. Mussolini had got what he wanted.

6

A big country took over a little country and the League's two leading members, Britain and France, did little to stop it. The message to Hitler was clear. Strong countries could do as they wanted. The League would do nothing in Europe.

Focus task

Why did the League of Nations fail in the 1930s?

Here is a diagram summarising the failure of the League of Nations. Complete the diagram to explain how each weakness affected Manchuria and Abyssinia. We have filled in one point for you. There is one weakness that you will not be able to write about – you will find out about it on page 126.

The memory aid FAILURe should help you remember this for an exam.

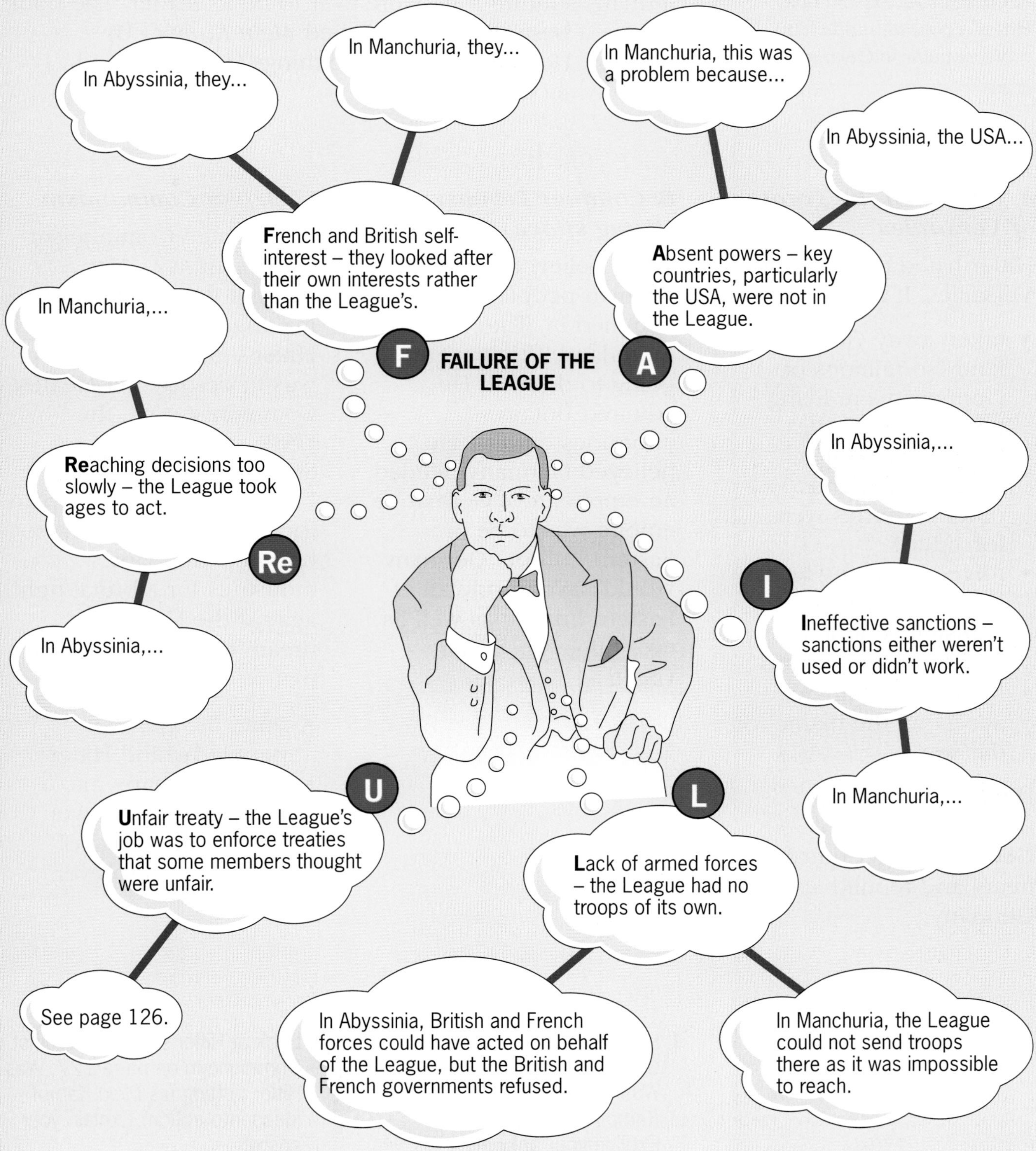

In Abyssinia, they...
In Manchuria, they...
In Manchuria, this was a problem because...
In Abyssinia, the USA...
French and British self-interest – they looked after their own interests rather than the League's.
Absent powers – key countries, particularly the USA, were not in the League.
In Manchuria,...
F
FAILURE OF THE LEAGUE
A
Reaching decisions too slowly – the League took ages to act.
Re
In Abyssinia,...
In Abyssinia,...
I
Ineffective sanctions – sanctions either weren't used or didn't work.
U
Unfair treaty – the League's job was to enforce treaties that some members thought were unfair.
L
In Manchuria,...
Lack of armed forces – the League had no troops of its own.
See page 126.
In Abyssinia, British and French forces could have acted on behalf of the League, but the British and French governments refused.
In Manchuria, the League could not send troops there as it was impossible to reach.

6.4 Hitler's words, Hitler's actions

From these two pages remember at least one of Hitler's aims and one action he took to achieve it.

Added bonus: explain how Hitler's policies made him more popular in Germany.

Key words **Bolshevism; destiny; pact; rearmament**

Mein Kampf – Hitler's words

In the 1920s, Hitler wrote a book setting out his views on Germany's future if he were ever to be its leader. The book became a bestseller. It was called *Mein Kampf* (*My Struggle*). Here are some of the things Hitler believed Germany should do.

A. Get rid of the Treaty of Versailles

Hitler hated the Treaty of Versailles. It had:

- taken away German land (so millions of Germans were living under foreign rule)
- forced Germany to disarm (when no other countries were forced to)
- forced Germany to pay huge reparations (causing economic problems in Germany)
- forced Germany to accept all the blame for the war.

Hitler said it was his DESTINY as leader of Germany to get rid of the treaty and rebuild Germany.

B. Conquer Lebensraum (living space)

Hitler believed that the German people were hemmed in. They needed more land if they were going to do well. He admired Britain's enormous empire. He believed Germany needed an empire, too. Germany's empire was to be in Eastern Europe. Germany would have to rule all of Eastern Europe as well as take huge bits of the USSR.

C. Defeat Communism

Hitler hated Communism (or BOLSHEVISM). He thought it was a poison, making Germany weak. Hitler's greatest ambition was to destroy the greatest Communist state, the USSR, and its dictator, Stalin.

In 1936, he wrote a plan for the next eight years to build up Germany's industries for a brutal fight against the USSR. His dream was a gigantic war that would:

- unite the German people behind Hitler
- make Germany into a leading world power
- destroy the threat of Communism forever.

1 Look at Hitler's actions on German territory on page 127. Was Hitler putting his *Mein Kampf* ideas into action? Explain your answer.

2 Look at Hitler's actions against Communism on page 127. Was Hitler putting his *Mein Kampf* ideas into action? Explain your answer.

Hitler's actions 1933–36

A. Rearmament

Almost as soon as he took power in 1933, Hitler left the League of Nations' Disarmament Conference. He started to build new weapons secretly. Then in 1935, he announced a massive REARMAMENT programme for Germany.

Over the next six years, Germany built 8000 tanks, warships and military aircraft. By 1939, the German army had 950,000 men (the Treaty of Versailles allowed only 100,000).

Hitler told other European powers that, because they had not disarmed, Germany had every right to rearm. The German people loved seeing Hitler stand up to the nation's old enemies. Rearmament made Germans feel proud and it also created work for the unemployed.

B. German territory

In 1935, 90 per cent of the people of the Saar region (see page 62) voted to become part of Germany. Under the Treaty of Versailles they had a choice between France and Germany. It was a great victory for Hitler.

In 1936, Hitler took his biggest gamble. While France and Britain were watching Abyssinia (see page 124), he moved German troops into the Rhineland. This was totally against the terms of the Treaty of Versailles. The French were horrified but Britain did not object. The French would not take on the Germans without British support. Hitler later admitted that if Britain or France had resisted, he would simply have withdrawn his troops. The Germans did not even have enough ammunition!

C. Anti-Communism

Hitler still hated Communism. In 1933, he banned the Communist Party and arrested any Communists who did not escape the country.

In 1936–37, he brought Italy, Japan and Germany together in the Anti-Comintern PACT (Comintern was short for **Intern**ational **Com**munism). The three countries agreed to fight Communism wherever they found it. The real target of this alliance was, of course, the USSR.

Focus task

The year is 1936. You are a reporter for a British newspaper. Write a 150-word article about Hitler's actions from 1933 to 1936.

Your article needs to:

- sum up Hitler's main aims
- describe the actions he has taken 1933–36
- explain why he has taken those actions
- comment on how people in Germany have reacted
- explain whether you feel Hitler is a threat to Britain
- say whether you think Hitler is a threat to any other countries.

Remember, it is only 1936. You do not know what is going to happen in the next few years. You have to base your article on what was known then.

Swap reports with a partner. Search your partner's report for anything not known in 1936.

6.5 Was appeasement a good idea?

Make sure you can explain:

- what APPEASEMENT was
- how the Munich Agreement shows appeasement in action.

Key words ***Anschluss*; appeasement; compromise; demonstration; mineral resources; war footing**

If you had been the British prime minister, would you have stopped Hitler between 1933 and 1936? In 1937, Britain had a new prime minister, Neville Chamberlain. He soon faced some very difficult decisions about Hitler.

SOURCE 1

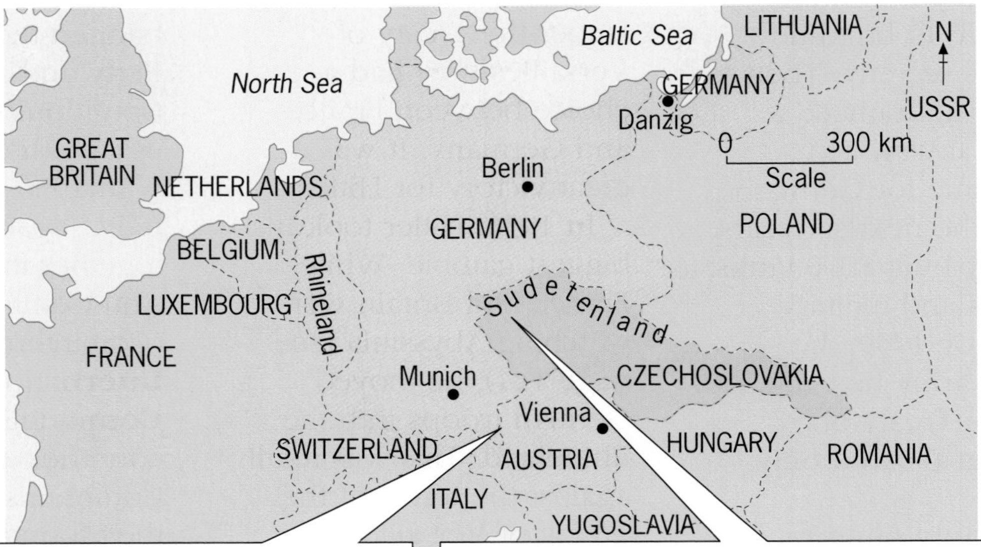

Baltic Sea
LITHUANIA
N
North Sea
GERMANY
Danzig
USSR
0
300 km
Scale
GREAT BRITAIN
NETHERLANDS
Berlin
GERMANY
POLAND
BELGIUM
Rhineland
LUXEMBOURG
Sudetenland
FRANCE
Munich
CZECHOSLOVAKIA
Vienna
SWITZERLAND
AUSTRIA
HUNGARY
ROMANIA
ITALY
YUGOSLAVIA

Decision 1: March 1938 – should Chamberlain object to the *Anschluss*?

Chamberlain's first test came in 1938. On 11 March 1938, Hitler moved his army into Austria. He then asked the Austrian people to vote on whether they wanted *Anschluss* (union with Germany). Most voted for *Anschluss*, although the figure of 99.75 per cent in favour was a bit suspicious.

Union between Austria and Germany was forbidden by the Treaty of Versailles. Chamberlain had to decide what to do next. He could:

- forbid *Anschluss*, declare war on Hitler and send troops to remove the Nazis from Austria
- let Hitler get away with it.

Chamberlain decided that the Austrians should be allowed to join Hitler's Germany. He felt that people in Britain didn't want to fight Germany over this issue. Even if they did, he thought that Britain was not strong enough to win. France and Czechoslovakia were concerned about the situation, but they did nothing to stop Hitler either.

So Hitler had challenged another part of the Treaty of Versailles and got away with it.

Decision 2: September 1938 – should Chamberlain go to war over the Sudetenland?

After *Anschluss*, Hitler felt very confident. It seemed as if other countries were not prepared to risk war to stop him getting what he wanted.

In April 1938, Hitler called for the Sudetenland to become part of Germany. The population was mainly German. Hitler said the Czechs were mistreating the Sudeten Germans. He threatened to invade if the area was not handed over.

The Czech leader Eduard Beneš refused. If he had the armed support of Britain and France, he was ready to fight to defend the Sudetenland against Germany. In the 1920s, Britain, France and the USSR had all signed treaties promising to support Czechoslovakia if it was threatened.

Beneš knew how important the Sudetenland was. It contained vital MINERAL RESOURCES and industries. Both sides argued throughout the summer. By September, it looked as if there would be war. Air-raid protection was prepared in Britain. In the last two weeks of September, the crisis came to a head, as you can see from the story strip opposite.

Central Europe in the late 1930s.

The Munich Crisis

I only want the parts of the Sudetenland where more than half the people are German.

15 September
Chamberlain met Hitler and got him to cut back his demands.

You must sign! The peace of Europe depends on it!

19–21 September
Britain and France pushed Czech leader Beneš to accept this COMPROMISE.

I want the whole of the Sudetenland – German parts and non-German parts!

22–26 September
Chamberlain met Hitler again. Hitler now rejected the compromise.

You all have my word that once this Sudeten German question is settled, that is the end of Germany's territorial claims in Europe.
Can I trust him?

WHAT SHOULD CHAMBERLAIN DO NOW?

However much we may feel sorry for Czechoslovakia, we cannot involve the whole British empire in war simply on her account. If we have to fight, it must be on larger issues than that. I am a man of peace . . .

27 September
Chamberlain made a radio broadcast to the British people explaining his view of the situation.

Meanwhile, Britain went on to a WAR FOOTING. Chamberlain ordered quicker rearmament. Local authorities started digging air-raid shelters.

29 September
Chamberlain flew to a Four Power Conference (Britain, Germany, Italy and France) in Munich. On 30 September, they signed the Munich Agreement. Hitler was given the Sudetenland. The Czechs had no say. Hitler promised not to take over any more land in Europe.

Here is the piece of paper that bears Hitler's name as well as mine, which means peace in our time . . .

War was prevented. Hitler was appeased. Chamberlain got a hero's welcome back in Britain.

1 October onwards
The Munich Agreement gave Hitler everything he wanted. The Czechs had to accept the loss of Sudetenland or fight Germany on their own. So they left the Sudetenland and Hitler marched in.

Some of this material is quite tough. But be sure you can describe:

- one reason why Chamberlain followed the policy of appeasement
- one reason people criticised the policy.

Key words aggressive; naïve

How did people react to the Munich Agreement?

Chamberlain's policy of giving in to Hitler to prevent war is called appeasement. Chamberlain himself was convinced he was right. Some people at the time agreed with him – others did not.

SOURCE 2

I will be good
(SIGNED)
Adolf Hitler

A cartoon by David Low for the Evening Standard, 4 October 1938.

SOURCE 3

The hour of need has found the man. Since he took office, Mr Chamberlain has never wavered in his determination to establish peace in Europe. At a time when the dark clouds of war hung most menacingly over the world, the Prime Minister took a wise and bold decision. Well may we call him Chamberlain the peacemaker. Three cheers for Chamberlain.

A commentary from a British news film, 21 September 1938.

SOURCE 4

My Dear Prime Minister

. . . I am fully prepared to take my share in defending the Munich Agreement but I cannot conceal from myself that the last few days have disclosed between you and me a considerable difference of view.

I am afraid that I remain profoundly sceptical [untrusting] of Nazi promises and shall do so until I see peaceful words accompanied by pacific [peace-loving] deeds. I can therefore only regard the present situation not as 'peace in our time' but as an uneasy truce.

A private letter from Trade Minister, Oliver Stanley, to Prime Minister, Neville Chamberlain, 3 October 1938. Stanley was a member of Chamberlain's Cabinet.

SOURCE 5

God bless you, Mr Chamberlain,
We're all mighty proud of you,
You look swell, holding your umbrella,
All the world, loves a wonderful fella.
So carry on Mr Chamberlain,
You know we're all with you,
And when we shout 'God Bless You Mr Chamberlain'
Our hats go off to you.

A popular song from October 1938.

1 Study Sources 2–5. Which are in favour of Chamberlain's policy? Which are against it? Explain your choice.

The end of appeasement

The Munich Agreement prevented war, but only for six months. In March 1939, Hitler did what the critics of appeasement expected all along. He broke his promise and invaded the rest of Czechoslovakia. Six months later, he invaded Poland and the Second World War began – with all the terrible consequences and human suffering that you will investigate in Chapter 7.

People have argued about appeasement ever since. Some wonder how Chamberlain could have been so stupid as to trust Hitler in 1938. Others believe that Chamberlain had very good reasons for following a policy of appeasement in 1938.

Focus task

Arguments for and against appeasement

These are the main arguments on either side:

Britain did not have allies who were prepared to fight with her against Germany in 1938.

A strong Germany was not such a bad idea because Hitler was ready to fight Communism.

Appeasement gave Britain time to rearm. In 1938, Britain's army was small and its weapons were old.

Appeasement worried other countries in Eastern Europe. If Britain and France were not prepared to defend Czechoslovakia, then would they defend other countries?

Peace was very precious. After the horrors of the First World War, Chamberlain was right to do anything he could to avoid another war.

Appeasement was NAÏVE. Hitler had always said he intended to conquer Eastern Europe.

Chamberlain was weak. He was unwilling to make tough decisions.

British people did not want war in 1938. They supported Chamberlain's policy.

Appeasement did not prevent war. It just put it off.

Hitler's demands were not unreasonable. He was simply putting right unfair parts of the Treaty of Versailles. If the Sudeten Germans wanted to join Germany, Britain should not risk war to stop them.

Appeasement gave Germany time to build more weapons.

Appeasement encouraged Hitler to be AGGRESSIVE because it made him think Britain would do anything to avoid war.

Appeasement made Germany stronger. In taking over land, Germany got the factories and raw materials it needed.

The arguments above are mixed up.

1 Your teacher can give you a set of cards with these arguments on. Sort the cards into arguments for and against appeasement. Which is the bigger pile?

2 Discuss the following questions with a partner:

a) Is 'the bigger pile' the same thing as 'the better argument'?

b) Which are the strongest arguments?

c) Are any of the arguments connected to any of the others? For example, can you produce a set of arguments under the heading 'Britain was not ready'?

3 Now reach your own conclusions. Do you think the policy of appeasement was a wise policy or a cowardly cop-out?

a) Write a paragraph to explain your choice.

b) Write a second paragraph to explain why you reject the other option.

Make sure you include at least two arguments and two pieces of evidence in each paragraph.

6.6 Shock horror! The Nazi–Soviet Pact 1939

You should try to get clear at least:

- one reason why Hitler needed to make a deal with Stalin
- one reason why Stalin agreed to a deal with Hitler.

Key words **border post; neutral**

Here is a reminder of the story so far. By April 1939, Hitler had:

- introduced rearmament to Germany (1933 onwards)
- moved his troops back into the Rhineland (1936)
- taken over Austria (1938)
- taken over the Sudetenland (1938)
- taken over the rest of Czechoslovakia (1939).

But he did not want to stop there. Hitler now wanted to reclaim the (mainly German) city of Danzig. He also wanted to join German East Prussia to the rest of Germany. The problem was Poland. If Hitler attacked Poland, he would come face to face with the USSR. He was not ready for that conflict . . . **yet** (see Source 1).

To Britain and her allies, this seemed like good news. If Hitler was not ready to fight the Soviet Union, then he would not dare invade Poland, so there would be no need for war. But on 23 August 1939 that illusion was shattered.

Stalin (the leader of the Soviet Union) and Ribbentrop, Hitler's Foreign Minister, announced the Nazi–Soviet Non-Aggression Pact to a stunned world. (You can see the terms in Source 2.) The two sworn enemies had done a deal. It was an agreement that both sides knew would be broken at some point. It was dishonest.

SOURCE 1

DANZIG

A British cartoon from 1939. The Danzig star is the Pole Star, which travellers use to find their directions; the bear is the symbol of Russia.

1 Look at Source 1. The cartoonist was trying to say that Hitler wanted Danzig, but was not sure whether he could take it. Explain how the cartoonist shows this as though you were writing to a friend who knows nothing about the events of the 1930s.

SOURCE 2

The public parts of the pact:

- *Germany and the USSR agreed not to attack each other.*
- *Each country would remain* NEUTRAL *if the other was attacked by another state.*

The secret parts of the pact:

- *Germany and Russia agreed to divide Poland between them.*
- *They also set out which states would be part of Germany or in the power of the USSR.*
- *Under further agreements, the USSR supplied Germany with grain, oil and metal ores in return for industrial and military technology.*

Terms of the Nazi–Soviet Non-Aggression Pact, August 1939.

Helpful to Stalin

For Stalin, the pact was not perfect but it was the **best option** available. Stalin was sure that Hitler would attack the USSR one day. In 1939, he had tried to get Britain and France to make an alliance with him against Hitler, but they had refused. After the appeasement of 1938, Stalin did not trust Britain and France to stand up to Hitler. He hoped the pact would buy him time to build up his armed forces for when Hitler would eventually invade the USSR.

Perfect for Hitler

For Hitler, the pact was **perfect**. It gave him the breathing space he needed to attack Poland. From Poland he could also get resources, like oil, which Germany was short of.

Disaster for everyone else

For the rest of the world, especially for the Poles, it was a **disaster**. On 1 September, Hitler staged a fake attack by Polish troops on a German BORDER POST. He used this as an excuse to invade Poland. By the middle of September, Poland was utterly defeated as the USSR invaded from the East. Poland ceased to exist.

On 2 September, Britain and France declared war on Germany. The Second World War had begun.

Activity

Look closely at Source 3 and the background information on the pact. If there were thought bubbles in this photograph, what might each man be thinking?

SOURCE 3

A photograph showing German Foreign Minister, Ribbentrop, shaking hands with Stalin over the Non-Aggression Pact in 1939.

SOURCE 4

Why did Britain and France help Hitler to achieve his aims? By rejecting the idea of an alliance proposed by the USSR, they helped Hitler. They appeased him by giving him Czech lands. They wanted to direct German aggression towards the USSR.

In 1939 the USSR stood alone against the German threat. The USSR had to make a treaty of non-aggression with Germany. Some British historians tried to prove that this treaty helped to start the Second World War. The truth is it gave the USSR time to strengthen its defences.

Kukushkin (a group of Soviet cartoonists) writing in 1981 about the Nazi–Soviet Pact.

2 Source 4 is a Soviet view of the Nazi–Soviet Pact. Which parts of it do you:
a) agree with
b) disagree with?

6.7 Hitler's war?

When you go into the exam, you should be confident that you can explain:

- at least two ways in which Hitler was responsible for the war
- at least two other factors that also played a part in causing the war.

Key words **defence; prosecution; war-mongering**

Hitler killed himself in the ruins of Berlin in 1945. Let's imagine for a moment that he didn't. Instead, imagine he was put on trial for starting the war. We are near the end of the trial. The lawyers are summing up their cases for and against Hitler.

Men and women of the jury, the charge against Adolf Hitler is very serious, but it is also very simple. This was Hitler's war. He planned it; he started it; he caused it. He should bear full and sole responsibility for it.
Let me summarise my evidence:
• Hitler's own words condemn him.
• Hitler's attitude to the Treaty of Versailles condemns him.
• His dishonest treaties with other countries condemn him.
• His WAR-MONGERING invasions condemn him.

Activity A

You are the PROSECUTION lawyer. How can you support the points above with evidence? Fill out your own copy of this table. The facts opposite will help you. Look up the page references if you want to find out more. You can add extra points of your own or more rows to your table if you want.

Your points against Hitler	**Supporting evidence**
Hitler's words	
Attitude to the Treaty of Versailles	
His dishonest treaties	
His invasions	

- In speeches, he told the world of his plans for a German empire (page 126).
- In *Mein Kampf*, he wrote about his plans to destroy the USSR (page 126).
- He told the German people that a war would be a good thing that would strengthen the German nation (page 126).
- He invaded Poland in 1939 although he knew this would mean the start of a war (page 133).
- He repeatedly broke the Treaty of Versailles. He did not care if this started a war (page 127).
- He made a dishonest treaty with the USSR just to allow him to invade Poland (pages 132–33).
- He made promises then broke them, just to get his own way (page 131).
- He rearmed Germany to prepare it for war (page 127).

Men and women of the jury, it is not that simple. Hitler must bear some blame, we know that, but not the sole blame. Standing there in the dock alongside him should be all the others whose mistakes, foolishness, misjudgements, weaknesses and lack of care for Germany in its hour of need, played into Hitler's hands. They helped to create Hitler and they should bear their share of the blame.

Let me summarise my evidence in Hitler's defence:

- The bankers of the USA helped to cause the war by . . .
- The weak leaders of the League of Nations helped to cause the war by . . .
- The writers of the Treaty of Versailles helped to cause the war by . . .
- The British Prime Minister Chamberlain helped to cause the war by . . .
- Stalin helped to cause the war by . . .

Activity B

You are the DEFENCE lawyer. How can you support your five points with evidence? Fill out your own copy of this table. In the first column, put the five points from above. In the second column, write the evidence. The facts below the table will help you. Look up the page references if you want to find out more. You can add extra points of your own if you want.

Your points defending Hitler	Supporting evidence
The bankers of the USA helped to cause the war	

- American bankers wanted their loans back, which plunged Germany into Depression and brought Hitler to power (page 122).
- The unfair Treaty of Versailles created resentment in Germany, which drove Germany to try to undo these injustices (page 126).
- When a strong reaction to Hitler was required, Britain and France lacked the will to resist him – appeasement helped to cause the war (pages 128–29).
- The League of Nations failed to stand up to dictators (pages 124–25).
- Stalin signed the Non-Aggression Pact and so paved the way for Hitler to start the war (pages 132–33).

Focus task

Was the Second World War Hitler's war?

In your examination, you are not expected to find the definite answer to this question. Historians at universities are still arguing about it! However, the examiner will expect you to understand that there are two viewpoints and that the evidence is unclear.

Work in pairs. Look back over the evidence you came across in the trial. Write two paragraphs:

- Paragraph 1 must give at least two pieces of evidence that make the case against Hitler. It could start like this:
  Some evidence definitely suggests Hitler was responsible for the Second World War.
- Paragraph 2 must give at least two pieces of evidence that make the case that other factors were responsible. It could start like this:
  Some evidence definitely suggests other factors, apart from Hitler, were responsible for the Second World War.

Here are some connecting phrases that will help you to build your paragraphs using the evidence you have selected:

On balance, . . . probably shows that . . .
. . . definitely proves that . . .
. . . strongly suggests that . . .
. . . might indicate that . . .
. . . seems to show that . . .
. . . could be used as evidence against Hitler because . . .
. . . could be used as evidence that other factors played a role because . . .

Revision task

It is now time to prepare your class quiz, based on the yellow notes at the beginning of each section. Your teacher can give you a sheet to help you.

7 Britain in the Second World War

Part A Britain at war 1939–45

7.1 Why couldn't Britain stop Hitler 1939–40?

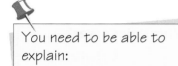

You need to be able to explain:

- at least two German strengths

Key words ***Blitzkrieg*; Expeditionary; mine; phoney; tactics**

SOURCE 1

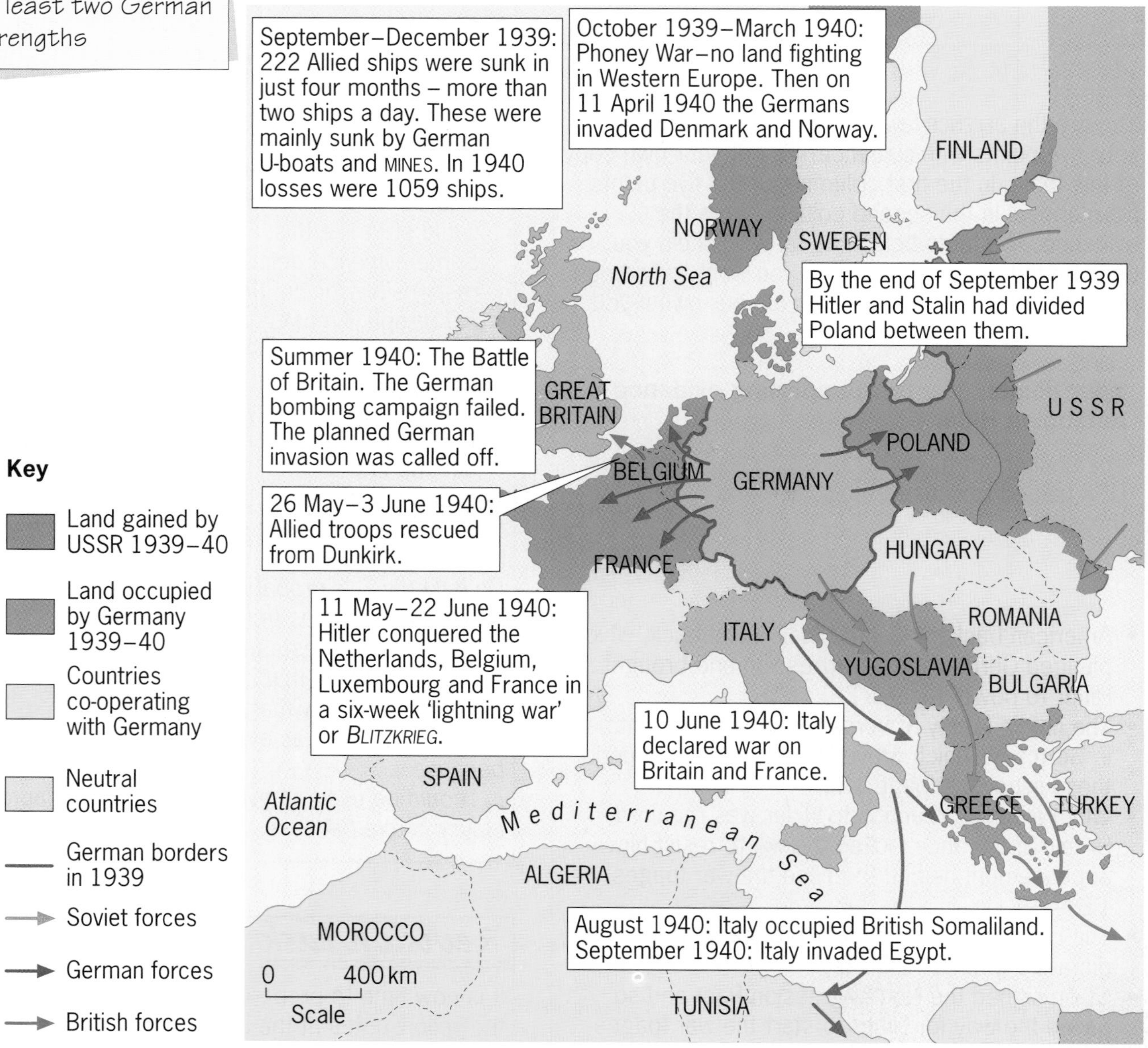

September–December 1939: 222 Allied ships were sunk in just four months – more than two ships a day. These were mainly sunk by German U-boats and MINES. In 1940 losses were 1059 ships.
October 1939–March 1940: Phoney War–no land fighting in Western Europe. Then on 11 April 1940 the Germans invaded Denmark and Norway.
FINLAND
NORWAY
SWEDEN
North Sea
By the end of September 1939 Hitler and Stalin had divided Poland between them.
Summer 1940: The Battle of Britain. The German bombing campaign failed. The planned German invasion was called off.
GREAT BRITAIN
USSR
POLAND
BELGIUM
GERMANY
26 May–3 June 1940: Allied troops rescued from Dunkirk.
FRANCE
HUNGARY
11 May–22 June 1940: Hitler conquered the Netherlands, Belgium, Luxembourg and France in a six-week 'lightning war' or BLITZKRIEG.
ITALY
ROMANIA
YUGOSLAVIA
BULGARIA
10 June 1940: Italy declared war on Britain and France.
SPAIN
Atlantic Ocean
Mediterranean Sea
GREECE
TURKEY
ALGERIA
MOROCCO
August 1940: Italy occupied British Somaliland. September 1940: Italy invaded Egypt.
0 400 km
Scale
TUNISIA
Key
Land gained by USSR 1939–40
Land occupied by Germany 1939–40
Countries co-operating with Germany
Neutral countries
German borders in 1939
Soviet forces
German forces
British forces

The war in Europe 1939–40.

'The Phoney War'

Hitler conquered Poland by the end of September 1939. After that, there was a period known as the 'PHONEY War' – war had been declared but there was very little fighting.

The British sent their British EXPEDITIONARY Force (BEF) to France to support French forces in case of German attack.

Blitzkrieg

In April 1940, the Phoney War ended. Hitler invaded Denmark and then Norway.

In May 1940, he invaded the Netherlands, Belgium, Luxembourg and then France. The Germans used TACTICS known as '*Blitzkrieg*', which means 'lightning war' (see Source 2).

On 10 June, Italy joined the war on Hitler's side. France was now threatened from the north and the south. On 22 June, France surrendered. Hitler toured Paris in an open-topped car. It had taken just six weeks to achieve what the German army had failed to do in four years of the Great War. You can imagine how Hitler must have felt.

Focus task

Why couldn't Britain stop Hitler?

Write a report from the BEF in France to the Prime Minister, Winston Churchill, in London. List at least three reasons why the Germans have been so successful. Source 2 will help you.

SOURCE 2

modern aircraft
attacks behind enemy lines
BLITZKRIEG = LIGHTNING WAR
forces co-ordinated by radio messages in code
powerful weapons, fast motor vehicles and tanks

Blitzkrieg tactics.

7.2 How important were Dunkirk and the Battle of Britain?

Make sure you can make a balanced case about Dunkirk. Aim to identify:

- two reasons for seeing Dunkirk as a success
- two reasons for seeing it as a failure.

Key words evacuation; intact

Dunkirk: 'a miracle of deliverance'?

As the Germans advanced through France, the British and French retreated. By 24 May, the BEF and about 10,000 French troops had been driven back to Dunkirk on the coast. At this point, Hitler hesitated. This provided some vital time.

Between 26 May and 4 June, the entire BEF (plus 10,000 French troops) were taken back to Britain by a fleet of large and small boats. At the time, this EVACUATION was called Operation Dynamo, but it is now simply referred to as 'Dunkirk'.

A victory or a defeat?

By evacuating their troops, the British were admitting defeat. They were retreating in the face of superior forces. However, Dunkirk was presented to the public as a dramatic story of success against the odds. The headline of the *Daily Mirror* – one of Britain's best-selling newspapers – said simply: 'Bloody Marvellous!' The newspapers focused on the hundreds of private ship owners who risked everything to sail to Dunkirk to rescue small groups of soldiers. Many people in Britain thought that Dunkirk demonstrated the true British character that would defeat Nazism in the end.

Britain's new Prime Minister, Winston Churchill, was more realistic. He called the events in France 'a colossal military disaster'.

However, Churchill could also see the propaganda value of the evacuation. He came out of the crisis as a truly great leader who could speak honestly and realistically about the war, but at the same time inspire confidence in the British people. He vowed that they would 'fight on the beaches, in the fields, in the streets and in the hills' to defend Britain.

SOURCE 1

Dunkirk was a military disaster – and took the British public by surprise . . . But almost at once, victory was being plucked from defeat and the newspapers began to manufacture the Dunkirk myth . . . The government encouraged it to flourish – and allowed nothing to be published which might damage morale. Dunkirk was a military defeat but a propaganda victory.

A BBC media correspondent commenting in 2000 on how the government and media handled Dunkirk.

SOURCE 2

Dunkirk has been a miracle of deliverance [escape]. But we must be very careful not to assign to this deliverance the attributes [characteristics] of a victory. Wars are not won by evacuations.

Winston Churchill, 4 June 1940.

SOURCE 3

A painting of the Dunkirk evacuation by the official British war artist, Charles Cundall.

1 In what ways do Sources 3 and 4 give a different impression of the events at Dunkirk?
2 Using Source 1, explain whether you think Source 4 was ever published in Britain.

SOURCE 4

The beach at Dunkirk, 1940.

Focus task

Look at this list of facts about Dunkirk.

1 Sort the facts into two categories – facts that suggest Dunkirk was a success and facts that suggest it was a failure.
2 Choose your top two successes (the strongest evidence that it was a success) and top two failures (the strongest evidence that it was a failure). Use these to help you answer question 3.
3 Do you agree with Source 1 that Dunkirk was just a propaganda victory? Explain your answer in paragraphs. You need to consider:
   - the evidence that Dunkirk was a military success
   - the evidence that Dunkirk was a military disaster
   - the effects of Dunkirk on Britain's morale.

FACTS ABOUT DUNKIRK

- 34,000 troops were left behind in France. They spent the entire war as prisoners.
- Hundreds of ordinary British people helped out by sailing small boats across the Channel to bring back a few soldiers at a time. They carried about 80,000 men between them.
- Most of the army's heavy equipment, such as tanks, was left behind.
- Almost 340,000 soldiers, 71 heavy guns and 595 vehicles were rescued.
- RAF fighter planes over Dunkirk shot down three German planes for every plane they lost.
- Dunkirk inspired British civilians to make sacrifices and do their bit for the war effort.
- The British abandoned the French army and France was soon defeated.
- The efficiency of the operation showed how powerful and effective the Royal Navy was.
- The media co-operated fully and effectively with the government. They kept the start of the operation secret, but when the small boats were needed they spread the word quickly.
- Britain's navy and air force remained INTACT.
- Churchill came through as a powerful war leader who could unite the country behind him.

At the end of this section, check that you can state:

- two reasons why the Battle of Britain was an important event.

The Battle of Britain: 'a turning point in the war'?

Key words **bail out; decisive; intercept; morale; radar; staging post; strategic**

Hitler danced for joy when France surrendered in June 1940! But he still had not conquered Britain. To do this he would have to:

- get past the Royal Navy
- defeat the Royal Air Force.

The Germans gathered a huge force of troops and invasion barges in French ports. First of all though, Hitler ordered his air force (the Luftwaffe) to destroy the RAF. What followed has become known as the Battle of Britain. From July to September 1940, Luftwaffe bombers attacked RAF air fields and aircraft factories. British planes were sent to INTERCEPT them and shoot them down.

SOURCE 5

The gratitude of every home in our island, in our empire and indeed throughout the free world, goes out to the British airmen who, undaunted [not put off] by odds, unwearied in their constant challenge and mortal danger, are turning the tide of war by their prowess [skill and bravery] and by their devotion [commitment]. Never in the field of human conflict was so much owed by so many to so few.

From a speech by Winston Churchill on BBC radio, 19 August 1940.

SOURCE 6

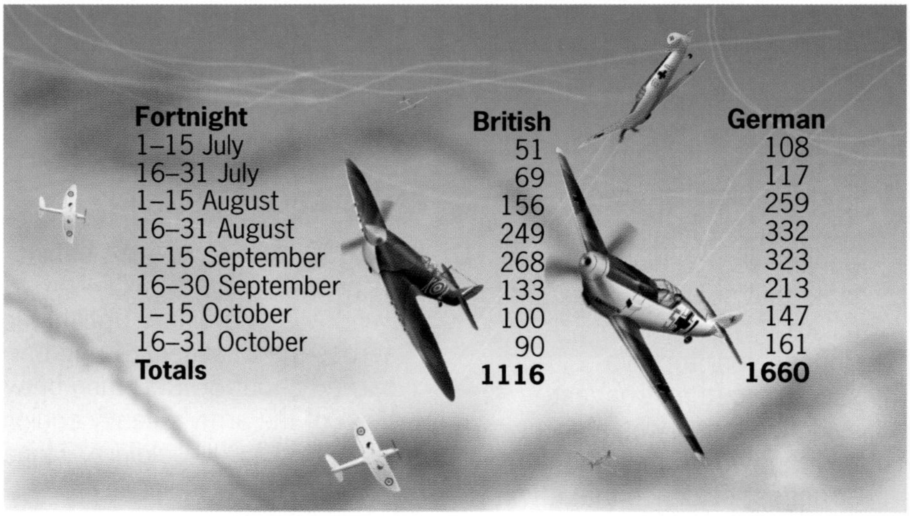

Fortnight	British	German
1–15 July	51	108
16–31 July	69	117
1–15 August	156	259
16–31 August	249	332
1–15 September	268	323
16–30 September	133	213
1–15 October	100	147
16–31 October	90	161
Totals	**1116**	**1660**

British and German aircraft destroyed, 1 July–31 October 1940.

Casualties were high – thousands of pilots and planes were lost on both sides (see Source 6). But throughout the battle, British pilots shot down more planes than they lost. Also, British factories built planes faster than they were losing them and they had better RADAR technology. Most of all, they had the home advantage. If a British pilot was shot down and he BAILED OUT he could fight again the next day. Any German who was shot down became a prisoner of war.

Hitler's tactics were not working. In September, he scrapped his plan to invade Britain and concentrated on bombing British cities instead (see pages 150–51).

1 Read Source 5 carefully. Rewrite it as though you were explaining it to one of your friends. Make sure you explain each of the five phrases that are underlined.

Importance of the Battle of Britain

Compared with other fighting in the Second World War, this battle was small. It involved only a few thousand pilots on either side. But some people argue that it was a DECISIVE event in the war.

It was Hitler's first real set-back. Psychologically, this was very important. It highlighted German weaknesses. This was good for British MORALE and bad for German morale.

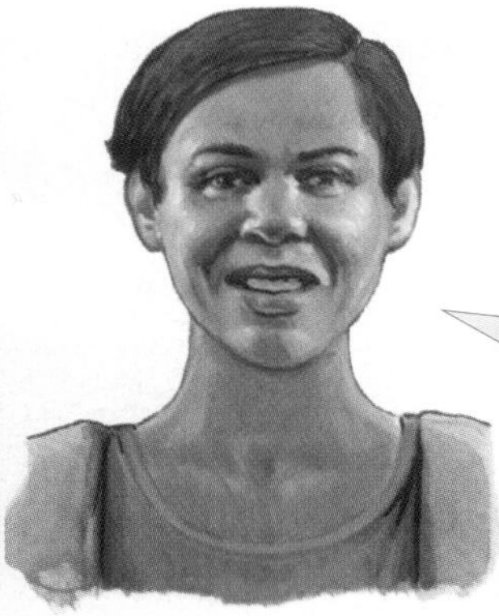

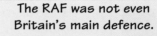

It protected the USA. If Hitler had been able to invade Britain, then he would have had even easier access to the North Atlantic and eventually to the USA.

Britain survived to launch a counter-attack. STRATEGICALLY, this was very important. For the next five years, aircraft from Britain launched successful bombing campaigns against German targets (see pages 144–45). Britain and Northern Ireland were the STAGING POSTS for the re-taking of Western Europe by Allied forces in the D-Day landings of 1944 (see page 147). This would have been impossible if Britain had been invaded.

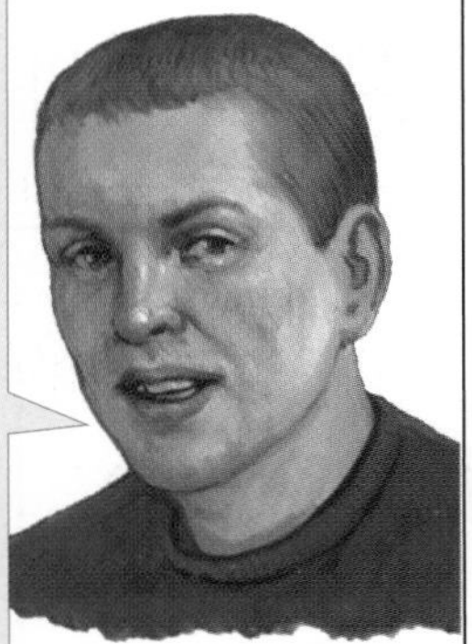

On the other hand, there are people who say the battle is over-rated.

It was not a victory. All it did was stop an invasion. It did not defeat Hitler.

The RAF was not even Britain's main defence. Britain's navy was much more important. If the RAF had lost, the navy could still have held off Hitler's invasion.

Other countries could have fought on without Britain. Britain was not the only or the most important country fighting Hitler. Even if Britain had been invaded, there would still have been the British empire, and eventually the USA, to fight back.

Focus task

How important was the Battle of Britain?

A local museum is setting up an exhibition about the Second World War. Unfortunately, the museum is short of space. It needs to cut:

- **either** the feature on the Dunkirk evacuation
- **or** the feature on the Battle of Britain.

Write a letter to the museum explaining what it should do. Explain **one** of the following:

- why Dunkirk should go
- why the Battle of Britain should go
- why they are both vital and neither must go. (If you choose this option, you must suggest how much of the total space should go to each event).

7.3 Why did the Battle of the Atlantic frighten Churchill?

Make it your goal to explain:

- two reasons why the Allies won the Battle of the Atlantic
- two reasons why the Battle of the Atlantic was important.

Key words **depth charges; imports; liberate; lifeline; merchant seamen; secret code**

After the war, Churchill said that the Battle of the Atlantic was the only thing that ever really frightened him. His advisers said that the first thing he wanted to know each morning was news of the war at sea. He would leap out of bed if the news was good. If it was bad, he would sit and brood. To understand why this was so important to him, let's look at the war at sea from his point of view.

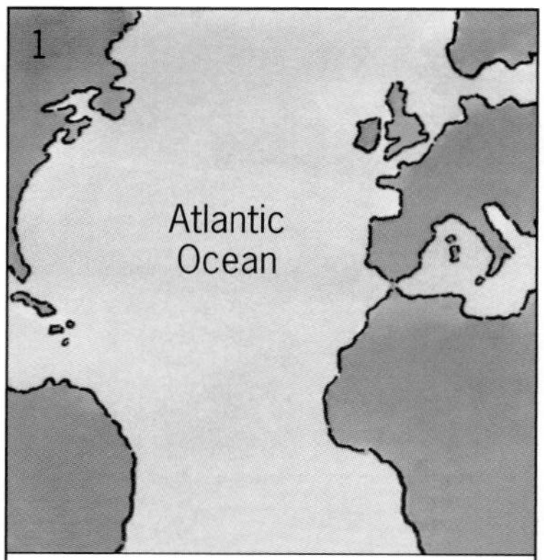
1
Atlantic Ocean

When the war started, everyone knew that the Atlantic was vital. It was the LIFELINE that brought food, raw materials, equipment and troops to Britain from the USA and Canada.

2
Come up with a plan to destroy the British economy.
But Germany has only eighteen submarines in the Atlantic!

When war broke out in 1939, even the Germans thought Britain's trade was safe. This is a real conversation that took place between Hitler and a navy commander in November 1939.

3

However by mid-1940, Churchill was worried. Working from their bases in Norway and France, German bombers and U-boats had sunk 25 per cent of Britain's shipping.

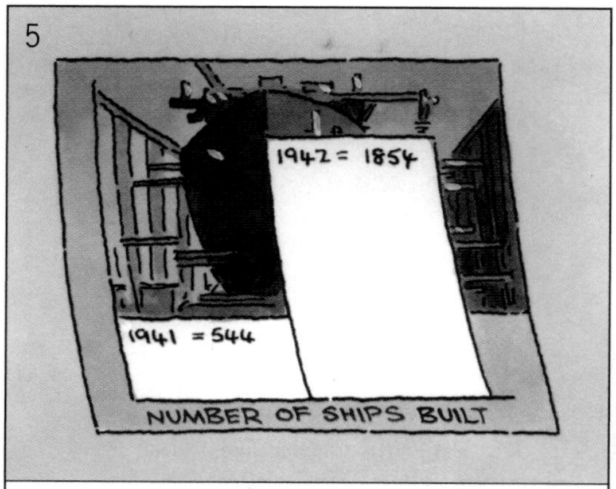
5
1942 = 1854
1941 = 544
NUMBER OF SHIPS BUILT

Churchill was happier in December 1941. The USA entered the war against Germany. American shipyards built hundreds of new ships. The US navy co-operated with the Royal Navy to protect Atlantic ships. Things would get better...

6
1942: 1661
1941: 1300
1940: 1000
NUMBER OF SHIPS SUNK

They did not. But slowly radar and DEPTH CHARGES were improved. Special long-range aircraft were developed to hunt U-boats. The SECRET CODES of U-boats were worked out. By the end of 1943, more U-boats were sunk than Allied ships. From 1943, no Royal Navy battleships or aircraft carriers were sunk at all.

The importance of the Battle of the Atlantic

When we look back on the Battle of the Atlantic, we can see how important it was.

It was big. It dwarfs the Battle of Britain. It was fought over a vast area, for almost all of the war. It involved millions of people and thousands of ships. Conditions at sea were very bad. Losses were huge. Around 56,000 Allied MERCHANT SEAMEN had their ships sunk and around 25,000 of the sailors drowned. There were 39,000 Germans in U-boat crews and 28,000 of them died.

It was significant.

- As a result of winning the Battle of the Atlantic:
  - Allied ships blockaded Germany's ally, Italy. They cut off 64 per cent of its supplies.
  - From mid-1943, millions of troops and tons of equipment were transported across the Atlantic. These made it possible for the Allies to LIBERATE France from Nazi control on D-Day (see page 147).
- If Britain had lost, it would have run out of food and industrial and military resources. It would have been defeated.

4

The war will be decided in the Atlantic. If Germany cannot win there, he cannot win anywhere in the end.

The situation got worse in 1941. Britain's IMPORTS were at only 40 per cent of their normal peacetime levels. And war meant Britain needed more imports, not less! Churchill met with US President Roosevelt in May 1941. Roosevelt agreed that the Atlantic was vital.

7

Discussion

Look back at your answers to the Focus task on page 141. Would you give more space or less space in your exhibition to the Battle of the Atlantic than to Dunkirk or the Battle of Britain?

Focus task

Write short 'thought bubbles' for Churchill (of no more than 30 words) for at least three of the frames in the story strip. If you find it hard to choose, go for frames 4, 6 and 7. Before you start, think about:

- why the war at sea was so frightening to Churchill
- why he was so pleased at any successes
- why he was so worried by any setbacks.

7.4 Britain and the bomber war against Germany

Aim to remember:

- two ways in which bombing helped the Allies win the war
- two reasons why people have criticised the bombing.

Key words **controversial; firestorm; high explosive; incendiary; morally justified**

From 1942 onwards, British and American bomber planes flew over Germany. Night after night they bombed industrial and military targets. They also carried out terror raids against German towns and cities. In 1943 the centre of Hamburg was destroyed when RAF bombers dropped HIGH EXPLOSIVE and INCENDIARY bombs. The resulting FIRESTORM killed 40,000 people, made one million homeless and destroyed almost 75 per cent of the city.

SOURCE 1

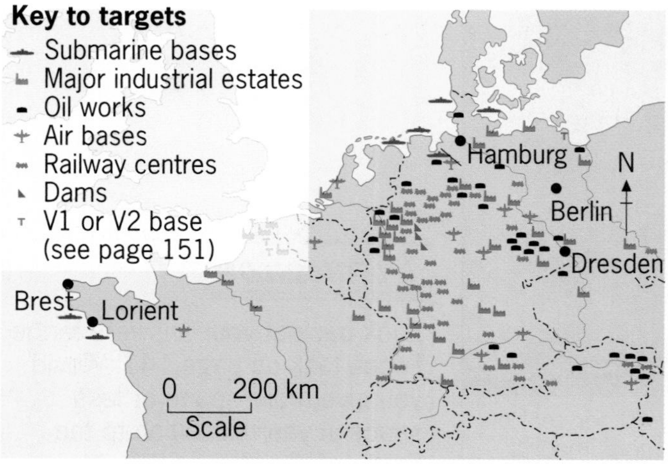
Key to targets
Submarine bases
Major industrial estates
Oil works
Air bases
Railway centres
Dams
V1 or V2 base
(see page 151)
Hamburg
Berlin
Dresden
N
Brest
Lorient
0
200 km
Scale

Targets of the Allied bombing campaign.

SOURCE 2

Oil works in Hamburg on fire after attacks by bombers in 1944.

SOURCE 3

Victims of an air raid on Berlin, December 1943, laid out in a sports hall.

The bombing – right or wrong?

The man behind Britain's bombing campaign was Arthur 'Bomber' Harris. He and Churchill believed that large-scale bombing of Germany was one of Britain's important contributions to the war. However, Harris is a CONTROVERSIAL figure. In the 1990s, when a statue of Arthur Harris was put up in London, it led to serious protests.

Why is bombing such a controversial subject? There are two big questions:

- Was it effective?
- Was it MORALLY JUSTIFIED?

Focus task

1 Work in pairs or small groups. The twelve statements below give you information about the bombing. Using your own copies of these statements, sort them into these categories:

Effective	**Justified**
Not effective	**Not justified**

2 Write two short paragraphs to explain your opinion on:

a) Was the bombing effective?
b) Was the bombing morally justified?

1 Bombers often failed to hit the right target. For example, in 1942 American and British bombers attacked the French ports of Brest and Lorient. They were being used by the Germans as submarine bases. The bombers flattened the towns and killed many French civilians. The submarine bases were almost untouched.

2 When most of the bombing took place in 1943–44, Germany's industrial production rose dramatically.

3 Few people argued **during the war** that bombing was morally wrong.

4 Germany and the Allies both bombed enemy towns and cities.

5 In January 1945, Germany's Armaments Minister, Albert Speer, reported that bombing severely held back his plans to increase production.

6 After the war, 91 per cent of Germans said the hardest aspect of life in the war was the bombing.

7 Many Allied military leaders believed that it would have been better to use the bombers on the battlefields rather than on Germany itself.

8 The bombing campaign tied up Germany's air power in defending the country. This was a big help to the USSR's forces in defeating Germany's armies on the ground.

9 Leading historian Professor Richard Overy said: 'Bombing denied German forces approximately half their battlefront weapons and equipment in 1944. It is difficult not to regard this margin as decisive.'

10 Many German workers stopped going to work because they were afraid of air attacks.

11 The main victims of bombing were innocent civilians.

12 Throughout 1943–44, the Allies lost ten to fifteen per cent of their planes and crews in the bombing raids. Losses were so high that the campaign was almost stopped in 1943.

7.5 The end of the war in Europe

As you work through these pages, try to remember:

- two ways in which Britain contributed to D-Day
- one example of the contributions of other countries.

Key words Commonwealth; Red Army; rout

The Second World War was huge. It was fought in dozens of countries. You have been focusing on Europe. While the Allies were bombing Germany:

- American, British and COMMONWEALTH troops drove the Germans out of North Africa in 1942
- the Allies invaded Italy and drove it out of the war by September 1943
- important events were taking place in the USSR on what is known as the Eastern Front.

The Eastern Front

On the Eastern Front, the USSR and Germany were locked in one of the most bloody battles ever known in human history. Both sides suffered badly but, in the words of Churchill, the Soviet Union eventually 'tore the heart out of the German army'. Most historians agree that this was the most important battleground of the Second World War.

SOURCE 1

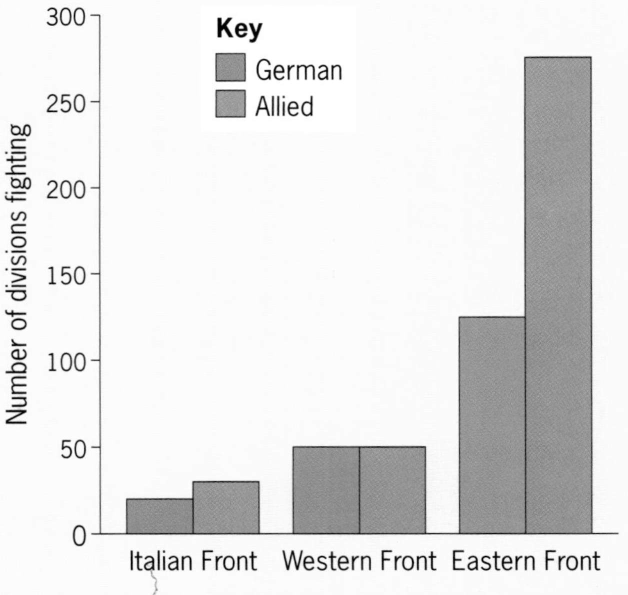

300
250
200
150
100
50
0
Number of divisions fighting
Key
German
Allied
Italian Front
Western Front
Eastern Front

The number of divisions fighting on different fronts in Europe in the Second World War.

This is how it happened

In 1941, Hitler invaded the Soviet Union. German forces were very successful – they destroyed almost all of the RED ARMY's tanks and planes. They killed two million Soviet soldiers. However, severe winter weather then slowed their progress.

Over the winter, the Red Army reorganised. It learned from its defeats. Soldiers were ordered not to give up even a tiny piece of Soviet soil. Any soldier who retreated at all was executed.

In one of the most extraordinary turn-arounds in the history of war, the Red Army stopped the German advance and then began to drive back the German army bit by bit.

From 1941 to 1944, 85 per cent of the German army was occupied on the Eastern Front. By 1945, the Germans were being ROUTED and Russian troops were advancing quickly into Germany.

The Western Front

Throughout the war, Stalin desperately wanted Britain and the USA to set up 'a second front' – to invade France and attack Germany from the west.

This was only possible once the Battle of the Atlantic was won. By the summer of 1944, the time had come for the Allies to try to liberate the countries of Western Europe from Nazi control.

D-Day

On 6 June 1944 the Allied commander, US General Dwight Eisenhower, ordered an attack on the beaches of Normandy. The Allies were up against strong German defences. Despite this, Operation Overlord (the attack) was a great success. By 11 June, the Allies had landed over 300,000 American, British and Commonwealth troops. They were supplied by sea and were protected by the navy and the Allies' much stronger air power.

VE Day

For the next eleven months, the Allies gradually pushed the Germans back (see Source 2). Hitler killed himself on 29 April. Germany finally surrendered on 8 May 1945. That day is known as VE (Victory in Europe) Day.

SOURCE 2

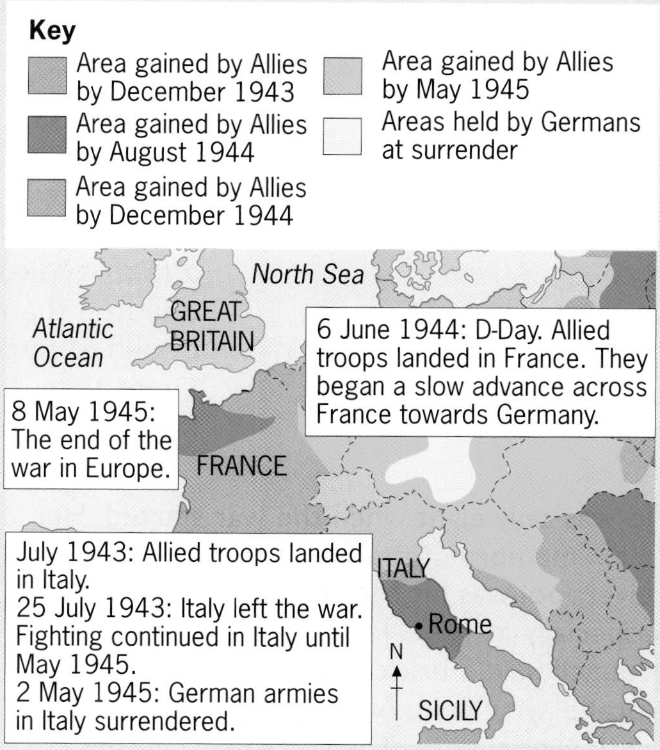
Key
Area gained by Allies by December 1943
Area gained by Allies by August 1944
Area gained by Allies by December 1944
Area gained by Allies by May 1945
Areas held by Germans at surrender
North Sea
Atlantic Ocean
GREAT BRITAIN
6 June 1944: D-Day. Allied troops landed in France. They began a slow advance across France towards Germany.
8 May 1945: The end of the war in Europe.
FRANCE
July 1943: Allied troops landed in Italy.
25 July 1943: Italy left the war.
Fighting continued in Italy until May 1945.
2 May 1945: German armies in Italy surrendered.
ITALY
Rome
N
SICILY

The war in Western Europe 1943–45.

Focus task

The Second World War in Europe

The museum you advised in the Focus task on page 141 has come to you for more help. Its exhibition is intended to show key aspects of the Second World War in Europe. You must advise the museum on how to use its space. It has one room 30 metres by 20 metres. Movable partitions can be used to create mini-galleries or rooms. It wants you to suggest:

- how many sections there should be in the exhibition
- what the theme of each section should be
- how big each section should be (they do not all have to be the same size)
- a title for each section (a question and a sentence summing up what is in the section)
- which sources and artefacts should be included in each section.

You could plan the layout of the exhibition using graph paper or drawing or design software. You could also use presentation software to draw up audio-visual displays.

Part B The Home Front 1939–45

7.6 The Edwards family in the Second World War

You need to be able to explain at least four examples of how the war changed people's lives.

Key words blackout; evacuee; reserved occupation

We have talked to one family about their life during the war. They are the Edwards family from Liverpool. Tom and Annie Edwards had seven daughters: Theresa, Pauline, Margie, Geraldine, Eileen, Josephine and Carmel. They were a fairly typical family of the time, although they had more children than most. Annie ran the house. Tom was a qualified nurse. He had served on the Western Front in the Great War. The person we talked to most was Josephine, the second youngest daughter. She was always called Jo.

Jo was only eight when the war started. Her main memory of the war is the air raids. Liverpool was hit hard by the Luftwaffe, especially in 1941. Jo remembers that the council built a brick air-raid shelter on the local playing field. Also it always seemed to be dark everywhere. The BLACKOUT curtains were shut tight. You could be fined if lights could be seen from your house.

Even today, Jo gets very upset when she remembers the air raids. During one raid, an incendiary (fire bomb) hit her house. It fell through the roof into her parents' bedroom. Tom and a neighbour managed to put out the fire, but the bed and bedding were ruined. An official came to look at the damage. Within a few days Annie received a slip of paper. She took it to the post office and got money to replace the damaged bed and bedding. Pretty good in the middle of a war, don't you think?

Jo was just a bit too old to be an EVACUEE, so she doesn't know much about that. However, she heard lots of tales from her friends and sister. Overall, she was glad she did not get evacuated. However, she was jealous of the evacuees in one way. They got beautiful new rucksacks in which to carry their belongings. Jo thought the bags were lovely. They were almost worth getting evacuated for!

Several of Jo's sisters worked during the war. Before the war, it was unusual for many women to work. But during the war, you got some pretty funny looks if you did not work.

- **Pauline** worked in the Ministry of Food in the centre of Liverpool.
- **Theresa** worked in a factory on the edge of the city. Conditions there were very bad. Quite a lot of the women caught tuberculosis.
- **Eileen** was one of the first women in Britain to work for the fire service. She was conscripted into the Auxiliary Fire Service in 1941.

Tom was not conscripted into the army. As a qualified nurse, he was in a RESERVED OCCUPATION. Like most people, he worked very long hours. He would often work a twelve-hour shift, then do his turn as fire warden on the roof of the hospital. This meant watching for incendiary bombs.

Focus task

How did the war change people's lives?

1 Read through the story of the Edwards family. Make some notes on the following aspects of life during the war:
- Conscription
- Air raids and air-raid precautions
- Food shortages and rationing
- War work
- Propaganda and censorship
- Evacuation.

You could work in pairs or small groups and divide this work between you.

2 With a partner, put the six aspects in order of importance from the Edwards' point of view. The first on your list will be the thing that affected the Edwards family the most. The last on your list will be what affected them the least.

If one fell, he had to put out the fire with sand.

Jo doesn't remember much about school. She says she remembers being hungry more! In the early years before the Americans arrived, there was little to eat – early 1941 was the worst period. Milk was often in short supply. You had to scrape by – one egg per person every two weeks, for example! The only thing that never seemed to run out was jam.

One of Jo's friends, Frank, remembers the bread and jam as well. Frank's mother had died before the war so he was looked after by his brothers and sister. They often ate bread and jam because their dad was a rotten cook! Frank and his dad had an allotment. They also used all of their garden to grow vegetables and keep chickens. They used to swap the vegetables they grew for things they needed from their neighbours. One man in the street kept pigs. The children collected scraps like potato peelings and gave them to him for the pigs.

We asked Jo about propaganda. At the time, most people seemed to think that the posters, newspapers and radio programmes were just giving information or helpful advice. Propaganda was the sort of thing the Nazis did! Frank remembers the censorship, in a way. His house was near to an anti-aircraft gun. He got a long lecture from his father and the ARP wardens (air-raid protection; see page 158) not to go blabbing about the gun. That was hard, as it was quite exciting having one next door!

Were the Edwards family typical?

Key words **Blitz; prefabricated**

On pages 148–49, you studied one family's experience of war. From pages 150–51 find:

- one way in which the Edwards were a typical war-time family
- one way in which their experience was different from the national picture.

Timeline: the Second World War on the Home Front

1938	
March	Military conscription introduced in Britain
1939	
June	Women's Land Army set up
August	Government passes laws giving itself emergency powers in case war starts
September	Blackout introduced; evacuation begins; petrol rationing introduced; all men aged 27–41 conscripted into the armed forces
October	The government launches the 'Dig for Victory' campaign
December	The government announces a 100 per cent increase in road deaths since September due to the blackout
1940	
January	The government introduces food rationing; people are encouraged to keep chickens and rabbits in their gardens for food
February	A 20m.p.h. speed limit is introduced in towns
April	Lord Woolton becomes Minister of Food
May	The Home Guard is formed; road signs are taken down so as to confuse the Germans if they invade
June	The government distributes leaflets telling people what to do if the Germans invade
July	The tea ration falls to two ounces per week; 50 per cent of men aged 20–25 are now in the armed forces
August	The government bans cakes with icing due to the sugar shortage; London is bombed
September	The London BLITZ begins
October	The government estimates that 25,000 Londoners are homeless as a result of bombing
November	Coventry is flattened in the Blitz
December	Manchester is bombed

1 Using the information in the timeline, see if you can guess when each of these posters might have been produced.

A

You never know
who's
listening!
CARELESS TALK
COSTS LIVES

1941	
January–March	The worst period of food shortages of the war
March	Labour Minister, Ernest Bevin, introduces the Essential Work Order – everyone must work
April	Plymouth is blitzed
May	The end of the London Blitz after the heaviest air raid of all
June	Clothing is rationed
July	The coal ration is reduced
November	The government introduces controls on milk
December	Conscription is introduced for men aged 18–26
1942	
January	Fuel shortages; the first US troops arrive
February	Soap is rationed
March	Petrol is rationed to essential users only; food imports are now half of peacetime levels; the government introduces a new wheatmeal loaf
July	Sweets are rationed
August	The government issues PREFABRICATED furniture
October	The sweet ration goes up; road signs are put back up
December	The housing shortage due to bombing means that about 2.5 million people are homeless
1943	
January	The government announces that over one million over-65s are in work
July	The battle against the U-boats turns in favour of the Allies (see pages 142–43)
1944	
January	More air raids on London; the government announces plans for a National Health Service
June	V1 flying bombs hit towns in England; over one million people are evacuated from south-east England; one-third of the working population are now in the armed forces
September	The first V2 rockets hit London; blackout restrictions are eased to 'dim out'
October–November	More V2 rockets hit London
1945	
January	Britain's armed forces reach 4.68 million, including 437,000 women
March	The last V2 rocket attack
April	Blackout ends
May	End of war in Europe

B

Beat
'FIREBOMB
FRITZ'
BRITAIN
SHALL NOT
BURN
BRITAIN'S FIRE GUARD IS BRITAIN'S DEFENCE

C

PART-TIME
WAR WORKER
JUST A GOOD AFTERNOON'S WORK

British war-time posters.

Activity

1 Look back at your notes on the Edwards family.
   a) List features on the timeline that were also mentioned in the story on pages 148–49.
   b) List features on the timeline that were not mentioned in the story.

2 Do you think the Edwards family can tell you all you need to know about life on the Home Front? Write two paragraphs to explain your answer.

7.7 How did government action affect people?

Try to remember:

- one way in which the government organised workers
- at least two ways in which the war affected women.

Key words assembly line; bulletin; prejudice

As you have seen in the timeline on pages 150–51, the government gave itself special powers in August 1939. It extended those powers during the war. Step by step, the government controlled people's lives as no government had ever done before.

Conscription

Men and women were conscripted for military service and for essential war work at home. Most men aged 18–41 went into the army. However, there were some reserved occupations. Skilled workers in essential industries and some medical workers were exempt. Workers with specialist skills – anything from electronics to demolition – might also be exempt.

The biggest impact of conscription was on women. By the summer of 1941, over half of the working population was employed by the government. It was still not enough, so women were conscripted. This meant that they had to register for war work at a labour exchange. Unless they were ill, or had small children, they were then sent to work in industry or the auxiliary forces.

There were 7.5 million women working in 1939 out of a total population of 40 million. Of these, 260,000 were working in the munitions industry in 1944. There were reports of some women who worked 80 to 90 hours per week on aeroplane ASSEMBLY LINES.

Millions of women became involved in the war effort in other ways, as air-raid wardens, fire officers, evacuation officers, and so on. Many looked after evacuees who were sent to live in their homes. The war also brought large numbers of women into the armed services, many of whom served overseas.

Even so, PREJUDICE remained. Women earned less than men. When the war ended, many women were forced out of skilled jobs back into the home or into lower grade work.

1 Why would electronics and demolition workers be useful on the Home Front?

Focus task

Did the government do enough?

Work in pairs or small groups.

Today we often hear radio or TV news BULLETINS that accuse the government of not doing enough about some important issue. Now imagine that a government minister during the war has been accused of not doing enough to make sure people are protected and that Britain wins the war. How do you think the minister would respond?

Over the next eight pages, you are going to prepare briefing notes for the minister to help him reassure the people of Britain that they are being protected.

Each note should be a series of bullet points on a card. Each card should be small enough to fit into the palm of your (or the minister's) hand. You can use the cards later for revision.

SOURCE 1

Women pilots moved aircraft from one location to another and were often first to fly aircraft. Few of these women worked in the air industry after the war.

SOURCE 2

British women officers often give orders to men. The men obey smartly and know it is no shame. For British women . . . proved themselves in this war. They have stuck to their posts near burning ammunition dumps, delivered messages on foot after their motorcycles have been blasted from under them. They have pulled aviators from burning planes . . . There isn't a single record of any British woman in uniformed service quitting her post, or failing in her duty under fire. When you see a girl in uniform with a bit of ribbon on her tunic, remember she didn't get it for knitting more socks than anyone else in Ipswich.

A War Department booklet for American soldiers coming to Britain in 1942.

2 Would you say that Sources 1–3 provide evidence that women overcame prejudice or that prejudice against women remained strong? Explain your answer.

SOURCE 3

Additional duties for female deputy managers

The Deputy Manager, being a woman, can assist the Manager, particularly if he is a male, by undertaking control of the female employees:

- *Reporting to the Manager as to whether or not our instructions regarding leaving the counter are being carried out.*
- *That the female staff cloakroom is kept in proper order.*
- *That hand-bags are kept in the Office, if there is no Office, in the place fixed by the Manager.*
- *Supervising the general appearance, tidiness, cleanliness, etc. of the female staff, with particular reference to the condition, repair and replacement of overalls, etc.*
- *Acting as liaison between the Manager and staff. (Managers must remember that in so many matters women will only talk properly to other women.)*

From a bulletin sent out by the Head Office of Sainsbury's to its branches in 1943. These bulletins were sent out regularly.

3 Write your first note about how you will keep industry running if so many men are going off to fight.

Industry

Activity

Look back at the story of the Edwards family (pages 148–49). Choose one paragraph from the story that would make a good source for this page. Write a suitable source caption to go with it.

Food, rationing and shortages

Key words **black market; coupons**

You need to be able to explain:

- two examples of food shortages
- one example to show that rationing was effective.

You have seen on pages 150–51 how Britain almost ran out of supplies. This was caused by German U-boat attacks on merchant ships. As a result, the government encouraged people to keep animals and grow food. Boy scouts and girl guides collected food scraps to feed pigs. Playing fields, railway embankments and the grounds of major public buildings were ploughed up. Private gardens were also turned over to vegetables – even window boxes were used to grow lettuces. Source 4 gives some idea of the success of these measures.

SOURCE 4

Date	Wheat (bushels)	Barley (bushels)	Oats (bushels)	Potatoes (tons)	Turnips and swedes (tons)	Mangolds (tons)	Sugar-beet (tons)
1935	33.5	34.7	44.9	6.3	12.2	18.8	9.1
1940	34.6	38.3	47.8	8.5	14.5	18.3	11.1
1945	60.3	59.2	63.7	16.2	26.4	36.5	18.6

War-time food production in the UK.

Even so, food soon ran short. Prices also rose steeply. Women could spend four times the usual amount of time shopping for food and still go home with nothing. Rationing was introduced early in the war. It was controlled by the Ministry of Food. Even the royal family had their own ration books. Rationing actually benefited many of the poorest in society. Because the government controlled prices, they could afford better food than they had in peacetime!

Rationing soon went beyond food. Almost every essential article could only be bought with COUPONS. This meant petrol, clothes, even sweets! Clothing coupons could only be used to buy government-approved clothes. These had a Utility Mark (see Source 5).

Rationing and shortages affected different people and different areas in different ways.

- Very large families with large numbers of ration books did not suffer from shortages in the same way as smaller families or families with no children.

- In rural areas, vegetables were usually quite easy to come by.
- In Northern Ireland, bacon and pork were not rationed.
- Some foods were in short supply, particularly sugar, tea and fruit from overseas.
- Fuel was always desperately short. Milkmen went back to using the horse and cart. Most people walked or cycled.
- The government did not like to admit it, but there was a strong BLACK MARKET. This became worse when US servicemen brought goods to Britain and sold them.

1 What would you have found hardest about rationing?

2 Write your second note about how the government used rationing to help the war effort.

Food

SOURCE 5

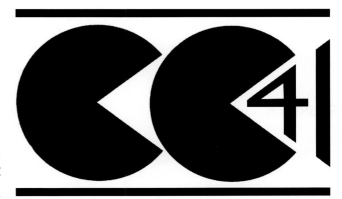

The Utility Mark was a guarantee that goods were made from recycled materials or had been made without wasting resources.

Activity

This picture shows the standard weekly ration for one adult in May 1941.

1 Compare this with your own diet today. Make a list of the differences between this diet and your own. Organise your list under the headings:
- Quantity
- Quality

2 Explain which diet you prefer, and why.

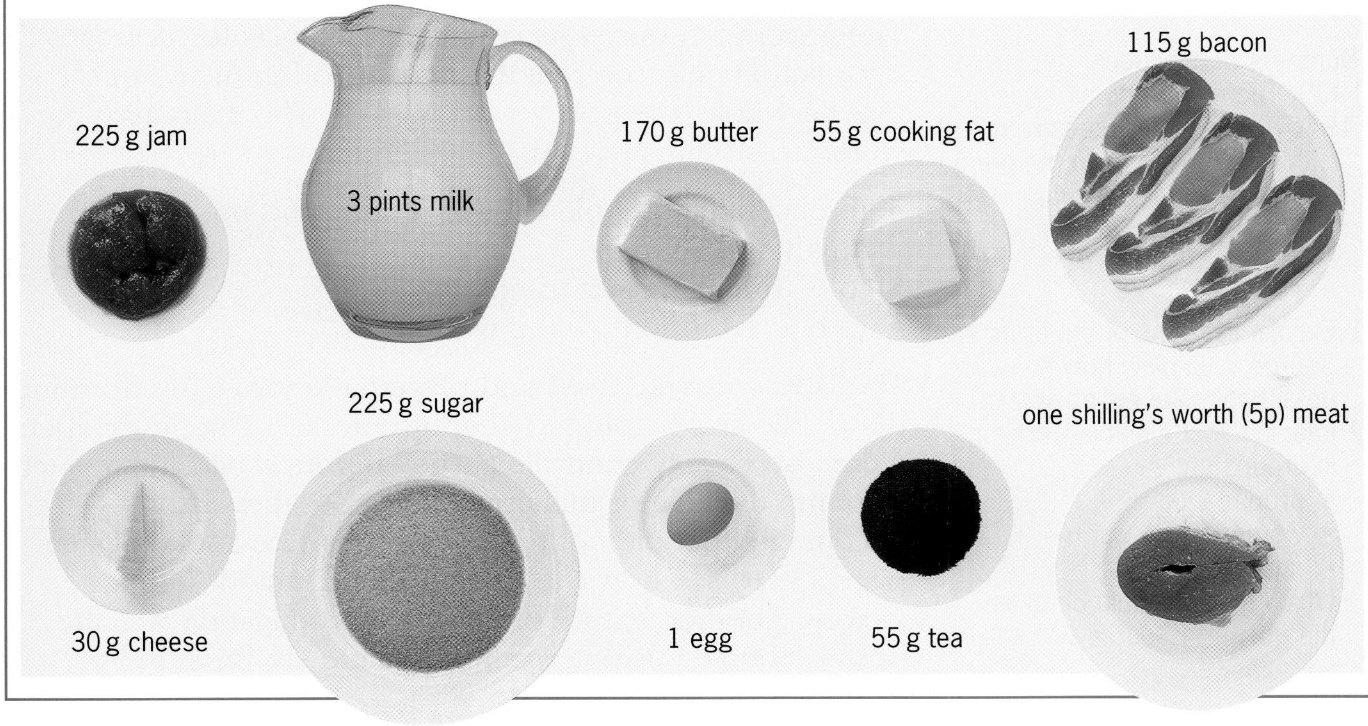
225 g jam
3 pints milk
170 g butter
55 g cooking fat
115 g bacon
225 g sugar
one shilling's worth (5p) meat
30 g cheese
1 egg
55 g tea

Try to remember:

- one effect of evacuation
- one reason to control information
- one example of propaganda.

Evacuation

In September 1939, around 1.5 million people, mainly school children, were moved from areas at high risk of bombing. These were the main cities, industrial areas, ports and air fields. Many returned home after the first evacuation, but there were two more periods of evacuation during the war. The main one was during the Blitz in 1940. The other came in 1944 when V1 flying bombs and V2 rockets were falling. Evacuation was distressing for families who were split up, but what were the other effects?

- Evacuation must have saved thousands of lives.
- Many women could work because they did not have to look after their children. This helped the war effort and gave women new opportunities.
- Different social groups were brought together. Youngsters from tough inner-city areas saw the countryside, often for the first time. Many comfortable people outside the cities learned how bad conditions in the cities were.

SOURCE 6

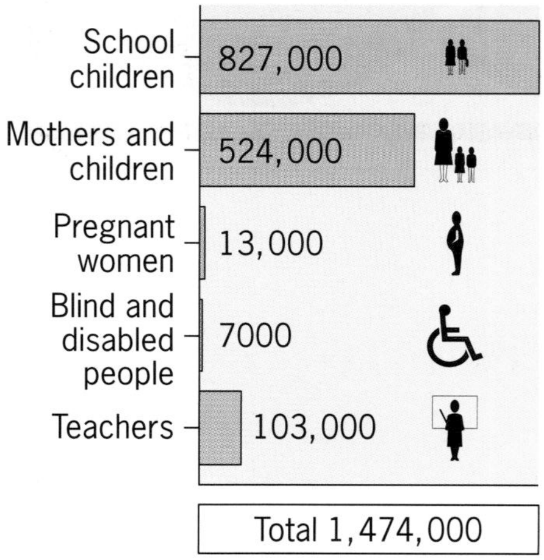
School children
827,000
Mothers and children
524,000
Pregnant women
13,000
Blind and disabled people
7000
Teachers
103,000
Total 1,474,000

Numbers of evacuees, September 1939. There were no air raids until 1940 so many evacuees returned home in the period September 1939–spring 1940.

1 Make your third note about what the government is doing to protect children.

Children

Propaganda and censorship

The government used its emergency powers to control information and to create the right mood in the country. On the whole, the policy worked well. The main aims were:

- to encourage people to save money and not to waste anything
- to warn people not to gossip
- to boost support for the war effort.

The BBC censored itself and played a key role in informing the public and helping to keep up morale. The newspapers were also closely controlled. They reported bad news, such as bomb damage or military defeats, but they also encouraged people not to be downhearted. Look back to page 138 to see how the press turned Dunkirk into a victory. Another feature of war-time propaganda was the poster. Source 7 is one example. There are three more examples on pages 150–51.

1 Explain the aims of the artist in Source 7. Explain how he uses details to make his points.
2 Imagine your class is working in groups on:
- propaganda
- women in the war
- evacuation.

Which group should be given the poster in Source 7? Explain your answer.

SOURCE 7

TAKE THEM BACK!
TAKE THEM BACK!
TAKE THEM BACK!..
DON'T do it, Mother—
LEAVE THE CHILDREN WHERE THEY ARE

A war-time poster about evacuation.

Activity

The propaganda guide

Look through pages 150–57 in this chapter and find at least five propaganda sources. Copy and complete this table to analyse them.

1 In columns 1 and 2, note and describe each source.

2 In column 3, put each source into one of the following categories:
a) preventing waste
b) being careful not to damage the war effort
c) keeping up morale.

3 In column 4, explain why you have put the source in that category.

Source (include page number)	Brief description	Category	Explanation

SOURCE 8

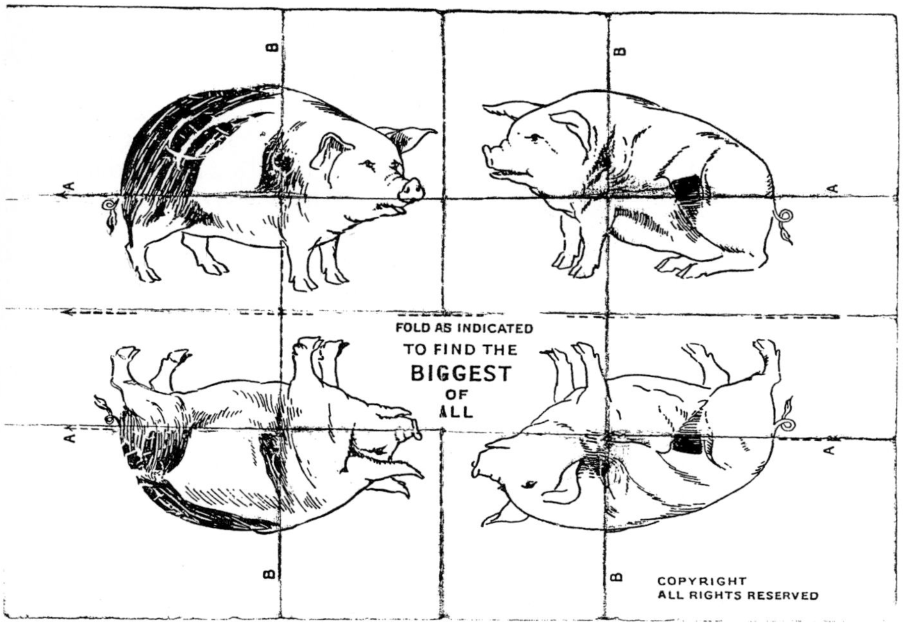
FOLD AS INDICATED TO FIND THE BIGGEST OF ALL
COPYRIGHT ALL RIGHTS RESERVED
A
B

A propaganda exercise aimed at children.

3 Write your fourth note about how the government has used propaganda to help the war effort.

Propaganda

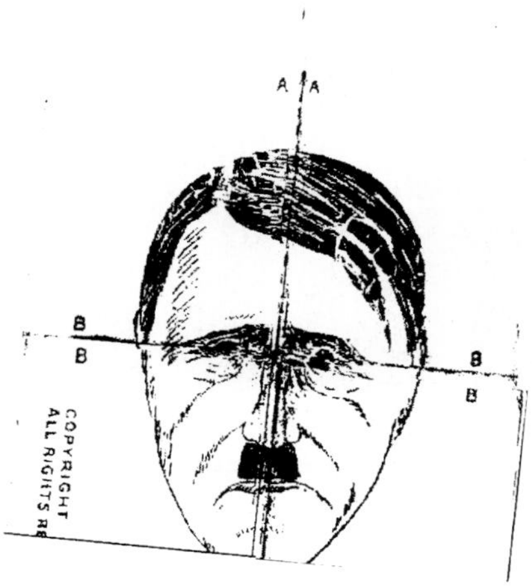
A
B
COPYRIGHT

You need to be able to:

- describe at least two actions the government took to prepare for air raids
- explain at least one way that protection was effective or ineffective.

Air-raid protection

Key words **Anderson shelter; gas mask; Morrison shelter**

Apart from invasion, the greatest threat to British people was the air raid. The government took swift action to protect the population from this deadly new form of war.

- Everyone was given a GAS MASK and shown how to wear it.
- A new force was created for air-raid protection (ARP). It was about 500,000 strong in 1939. These ARP wardens supervised the blackout. They also organised patrols during raids to check for incendiary bombs.
- The government provided two million ANDERSON SHELTERS (named after the minister in charge). They could be set up in back gardens.
- In 1941, the government provided 500,000 MORRISON SHELTERS. These could be set up indoors, usually under the stairs.

1 As a general rule, people in Britain resented ARP wardens, but they did not resent rationing. Why do you think this was?

Activity

Look at Source 9. Make your own list of features for a well protected house. Write the list in the style of a government information leaflet (but remember it will be a handy resource for revision!).

SOURCE 9

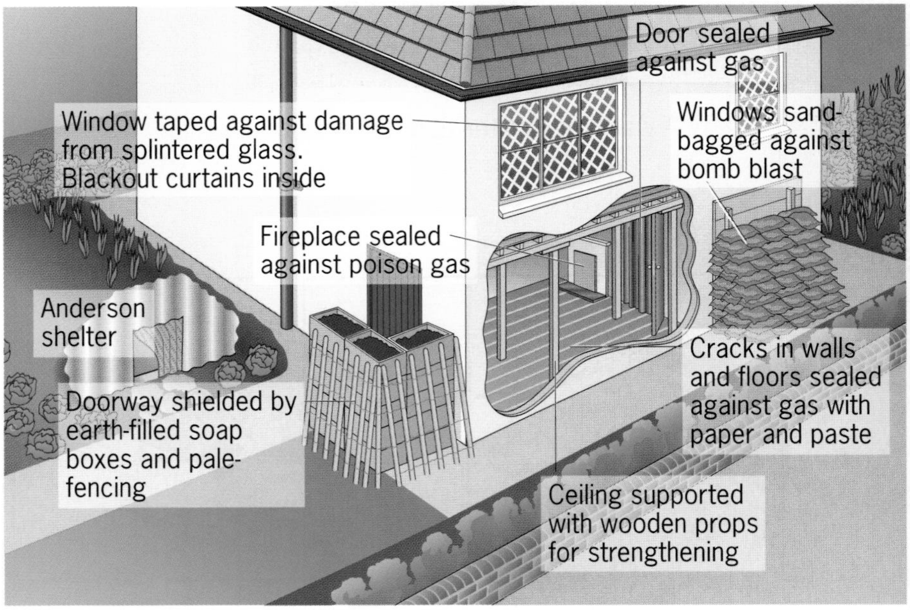
Door sealed against gas
Window taped against damage from splintered glass. Blackout curtains inside
Windows sand-bagged against bomb blast
Fireplace sealed against poison gas
Anderson shelter
Cracks in walls and floors sealed against gas with paper and paste
Doorway shielded by earth-filled soap boxes and pale-fencing
Ceiling supported with wooden props for strengthening

An artist's impression of a war-time house well prepared for air raids.

SOURCE 10

Painting kerbs for drivers and pedestrians to see in blackout conditions.

Blackout

Another air defence measure was the blackout. Homes had to black out, but so did shops, businesses and even trains and cars. ARP authorities could fine people up to half a week's wages for not obeying the blackout. The number of road accidents doubled in September 1939 due to the blackout but, in time, people got used to it.

SOURCE 11

Interviewer: Was the blackout very strict?

Oh, terrible. One night I went for a loaf of bread, and somebody had left a little cart out on the road, and I walked into it and fell over because I couldn't see.

Interviewer: Can you talk about ARP patrols?

Oh yes, one night we had a gentleman knocking on the door, and he said 'Will you please turn your light out or shut your curtains, you've a light showing' which we had, but I didn't know, we were getting ready for bed. It was only early evening, about 7.30 . . .

From an interview in 1995 with residents of Hebden Bridge, near Halifax.

SOURCE 12

A school playground in Catford, London, hit by a bomb.

Despite the precautions, the air raids took a terrible toll. When the Blitz began in 1940, London and other cities suffered terribly. This was the first war where Britain suffered more civilian than military casualties. There were not enough shelters, especially in the densely packed working-class areas of the cities. Anderson shelters protected people from flying glass, but not from falling houses. Source 13 shows how the Blitz affected Liverpool.

SOURCE 13

		Killed	Injured
1940	August	37	73
	September	221	357
	October	106	90
	November	305	192
	December	412	382
1941	January	43	23
	February	2	7
	March	101	99
	April	36	105
	May	1453	1065

Casualties in Liverpool 1940–41. The city's port, docks and warehouses made it a target for bombs.

2 Write your final note about how the government has tried to protect the population from bombing.

Bombing

Focus task

Do you agree with the Edwards family?

Look back at the Focus task on page 149. Here is what the Edwards family said was their order of importance for the six aspects of life:

1 Air raids and air-raid precautions
2 Food shortages and rationing
3 Evacuation
4 War work
5 Conscription
6 Propaganda and censorship.

Now you have studied the Home Front in detail, do you think most people in Britain would agree with the Edwards? Write a list for British people in general, explaining the order.

8 The coming of the Cold War 1945–49

8.1 Why did the USA and the USSR fall out after 1945?

These two pages will help you to:

- explain what the Cold War was in one sentence
- give one example of how Communist and capitalist beliefs are different.

Key words capitalism; standard of living; superpower

By the end of the Second World War, the USA and the USSR were the world's two SUPERPOWERS. This means they were stronger, better armed and more successful than all other countries. They were clearly in a different league from other powers, such as Britain and France.

Good news

The good news for world peace was that in 1945 these two superpowers were allies – working together in the battle against Hitler. In May 1945, they met each other in Berlin.

SOURCE 1

EAST
MEETS
WEST

American and Soviet soldiers shaking hands in Germany in 1945. The USA and the USSR fought together as allies against Germany during the Second World War.

Bad news

The bad news for world peace was that:

Within one year of the photograph in Source 1, the Soviet and American leaders were accusing each other of breaking the promises they had made during war-time.

Within two years, the American President was promising his help to anyone who would stand up to the USSR.

Within four years, it looked very likely that the two war-time allies would declare war **on each other**.

The conflict never came to war, but for almost 50 years it was a Cold War. The two sides never fought, but they spied on each other, criticised each other in the media and helped anyone who opposed the other side.

So why did these former friends fall out?

The big reason: different beliefs

In the past, the USA and the USSR had always been very suspicious of each other. They had totally different beliefs about how a country should be run (see Factfiles below). They were allies during the war only because they had the same enemy – Hitler's Germany.

SOURCE 2

THE COMMON DANGER
VICKY

A British cartoon from 1941.

Focus task

Use the information on this page to help you write a 25-word caption for Source 2.

Factfile

USA

USA CAPITALIST AND DEMOCRATIC
ELECTIONS
INDUSTRY
PRIVATE
INDIVIDUAL RIGHTS

★ American society was based on two key ideas: democracy and CAPITALISM.
★ Democracy meant that the American President and Congress were elected in free elections. They could be voted out if the American people were unhappy with them.
★ Capitalism meant that property and businesses were owned by private individuals and companies.
★ The USA was the world's richest country, **but** there were extremes of wealth and poverty.
★ For Americans, the rights and freedoms of individual Americans (for example, free speech, freedom to start a business) were more important than everyone being equal.
★ The majority of Americans believed passionately in the American way. They felt that Communism threatened their way of life.

Factfile

USSR

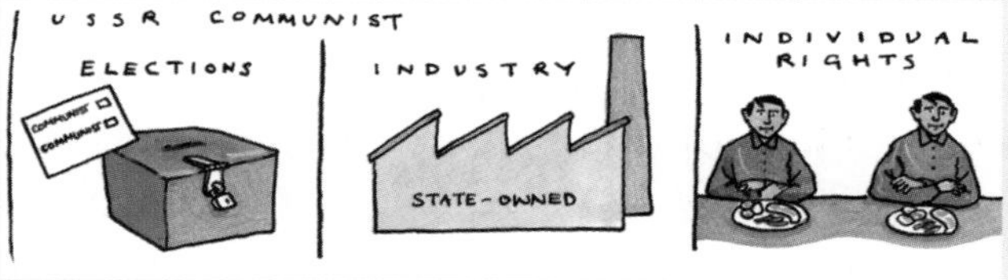
USSR COMMUNIST
ELECTIONS
INDUSTRY
STATE-OWNED
INDIVIDUAL RIGHTS

★ Soviet society was based on Communist ideas.
★ It was a one-party state. There were elections, but Soviet people could only elect Communists.
★ Industry was organised and run by the state.
★ Unemployment and extreme poverty were rare, but the general STANDARD OF LIVING of most Soviet citizens was much lower than for the average American.
★ Communists believed that the rights of individuals were less important than the good of society as a whole. As a result, there were many restrictions on the individual's freedom to travel, read certain books, start a business, etc.

Can you see the problem?

Both sides had reasonable, sensible, but **totally different** viewpoints.

With such different beliefs, you would expect them to disagree. However, different beliefs don't explain why they fell out **so badly** and **so quickly**. To understand that, read on …

The Allies fall out, 1945

From these two pages, aim to give two examples of Truman and Stalin disagreeing in 1945.

Key words **atomic bomb; personality clash; sphere of influence**

Agreements at Yalta

In February 1945, Stalin (USSR), Churchill (UK) and Roosevelt (USA) met at **Yalta**. At that time, the war was going well and it was clear that the Allies were going to win. The three leaders met to plan what to do about Germany and Europe once the war ended.

President Roosevelt got on reasonably well with Stalin. However, Churchill and Stalin got on badly. Churchill was suspicious of everything Stalin did. Stalin said that Churchill would pick your pocket for a kopek (a very low value Soviet coin). Despite these PERSONALITY CLASHES, they reached several important agreements. For example:

- they agreed that Eastern Europe would be regarded as a Soviet 'SPHERE OF INFLUENCE'

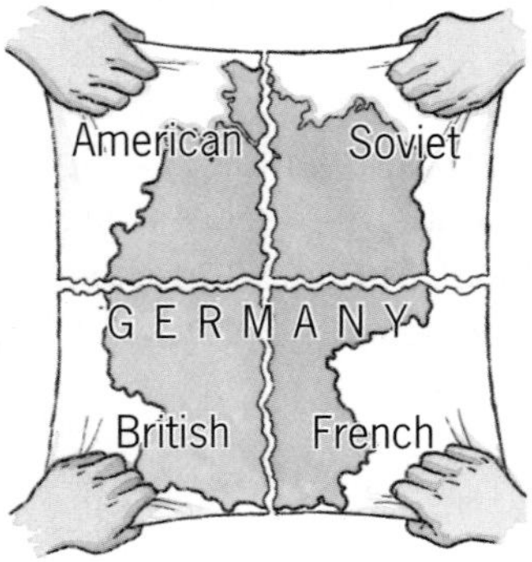
American
Soviet
GERMANY
British
French

- they agreed to divide Germany into four zones – British, French, American and Soviet

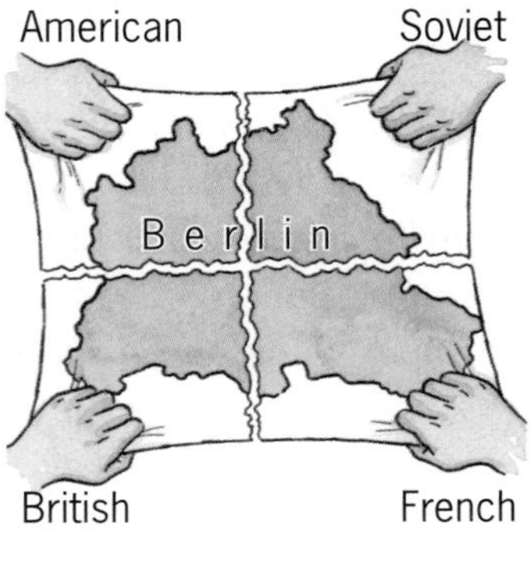
American
Soviet
Berlin
British
French

- they agreed to divide Berlin in the same way.

Disagreements at Potsdam

The Allied leaders met again at **Potsdam** in July–August 1945. This conference did not go nearly so well as Yalta, for the following reasons.

- The war in Europe was over – so the glue that held the alliance together was no longer there.

ALLIANCE

- The USA had a new leader – Roosevelt had died and Harry Truman had replaced him as President. Truman was much more anti-Communist than Roosevelt. Truman and Stalin found it very hard to understand each other.

- The Americans had developed an ATOMIC BOMB – this worried the Soviet Union.

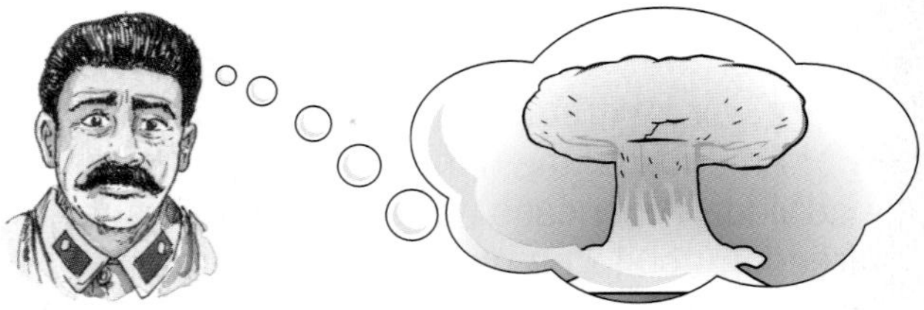

- Soviet troops were occupying most of Eastern Europe – this worried the USA.

The atom bomb

During the Potsdam conference, Truman told Stalin that the USA had successfully developed an atomic bomb. This new bomb was the most powerful weapon ever known. Source 3 shows how the two superpowers remembered this conversation very differently!

SOURCE 3A

This is the place I told Stalin about the Atom Bomb, which was tested on July 16, 1945 in New Mexico. He did not realise what I was talking about!

Notes written by Truman on the back of a photo of himself and Stalin at the Potsdam conference.

SOURCE 3B

Truman decided to surprise us at Potsdam . . . He took Stalin and me aside and informed us they had an extraordinary new weapon . . . It's difficult to say what he was thinking, but it seemed to me he wanted to alarm us. Stalin reacted quite calmly and Truman decided he hadn't understood. The words 'atom bomb' were not spoken, but we immediately guessed what he meant.

Soviet Foreign Minister Molotov's memories of the same event.

Churchill, Truman and Stalin at Potsdam.

Discussion

1 Look at Sources 3A and 3B, then decide which of the following statements you agree with.
- Truman was trying to scare Stalin.
- Stalin didn't understand about the bomb.
- Stalin knew about the bomb, but he was not going to let Truman see he was worried.
- Truman and Stalin clearly did not trust each other.

Use evidence from the sources to support your answer.

> **Can you see the problem . . . again?**
> Think about what was going on at Potsdam. It was not that one side was wrong and the other right. Both sides had reasonable, sensible, but **totally different** viewpoints. They saw their own actions as reasonable, but they saw the other side's actions as threatening.

Disagreement 1: what to do about Germany

This issue caused **big** tensions at Potsdam.

Stalin said he wanted to make Germany pay huge compensation ($10 billion) to the USSR. This was a new demand. He had not asked for this at Yalta. Stalin felt that this demand was perfectly justified. He did not care if compensation crippled Germany. The Soviets had lost 30 million people in the war. The Germans had flattened villages, towns and whole cities. Stalin would not admit it to Truman, but the war had left the USSR with almost no money or resources.

Truman opposed Stalin's demand for compensation. He did not understand that Stalin still felt threatened by Germany. Truman wanted Germany to recover and become a stable, democratic state. He did not want to repeat the mistakes made by the Treaty of Versailles when attempts to cripple Germany helped cause another war. Truman also felt that Germany would not be able to pay any compensation to the USSR if it was crippled. Stalin couldn't understand Truman's attitude. He wondered why the USA was so keen to rebuild Germany. Was it to threaten him?

Activity

How might each of the leaders have finished off these sentences?

We must not punish Germany harshly because . . .
We must not let Germany become strong because . . .

Make it your goal to explain why Truman and Stalin disagreed about Eastern Europe (one viewpoint each).

Disagreement 2: Eastern Europe

Key words Cominform

Stalin and Eastern Europe: justified or not?

The biggest political disputes between the USA and the USSR were about Eastern Europe.

In 1945 the Allies had agreed that Eastern Europe would be 'a Soviet sphere of influence'. To the Americans, this meant that Eastern European countries should be friendly towards the USSR. However, they should also be free to elect their own governments in democratic elections.

That was just not good enough for Stalin. He did not trust any government unless he was in charge of it. His Red Army troops helped Communists to take power in each of the Eastern European states. Then he set up an organisation called COMINFORM to control these new governments. He told them how to run their countries and how to deal with the Americans. The Americans protested against Soviet actions, but it did little good.

- To Stalin, control of Eastern Europe made sense. In the twentieth century, the USSR had twice been invaded through Eastern European countries. If he controlled the region, nobody would be able to invade through it.
- To Truman, Stalin's control of Eastern Europe was evidence that Stalin was building an empire. He clearly wanted to take over the rest of Europe as well.

1 Sources 4 and 5 look at the USSR's actions in Eastern Europe very differently. Explain the main differences between the two views.
2 What points and evidence could you use to support each view?
3 Is it possible to blame just one side for the clashes over Eastern Europe? Explain your answer.

SOURCE 4

Let us not forget that the Germans invaded the USSR through Finland, Poland, Romania, Bulgaria and Hungary. Why is it so surprising that the Soviet Union, anxious for its future safety, is trying to make sure that friendly, loyal governments are in these countries?

Stalin's view of his policy in Eastern Europe.

SOURCE 5

I am more than ever convinced that Communism is on the march on a worldwide scale, and only the USA can stop it.

A comment by US Senator Arthur Vandenberg in April 1946. Vandenberg was Chairman of the Senate Foreign Relations Committee. This meant that he had a big say in President Truman's policy.

Now try to explain why Stalin and Truman saw MARSHALL AID differently (one viewpoint each).

Key words civil war; containment; Iron Curtain; Marshall Aid; Truman Doctrine

The Truman Doctrine

In March 1947, Truman made a speech that became known as the TRUMAN DOCTRINE. He promised to help any country that was threatened by a Communist take-over. Truman's policy of stopping the spread of Communism became known as CONTAINMENT. He started straight away by sending money and equipment to help anti-Communist forces in a CIVIL WAR in Greece (see Source 7).

Marshall Aid

Truman also worried about Communism spreading to democratic countries in Europe. Bombing and fighting had destroyed roads, water supplies and other essential services. Truman feared that Communists would play on people's misery by making promises to improve their lives. This would gain them support. In 1947–48, it looked as if Communists might take power in Italy and France.

Truman decided to use the USA's mighty economic power. He ordered US general, George Marshall, to come up with an economic aid plan. It became known as Marshall Aid (or the Marshall Plan). The USA put $17 billion into helping Europe's shattered economies recover. Food, machinery, animals and countless other items were shipped to democratic countries in Europe (see Source 6). Truman wanted people to get back to work, make money and feel good about democracy.

SOURCE 6

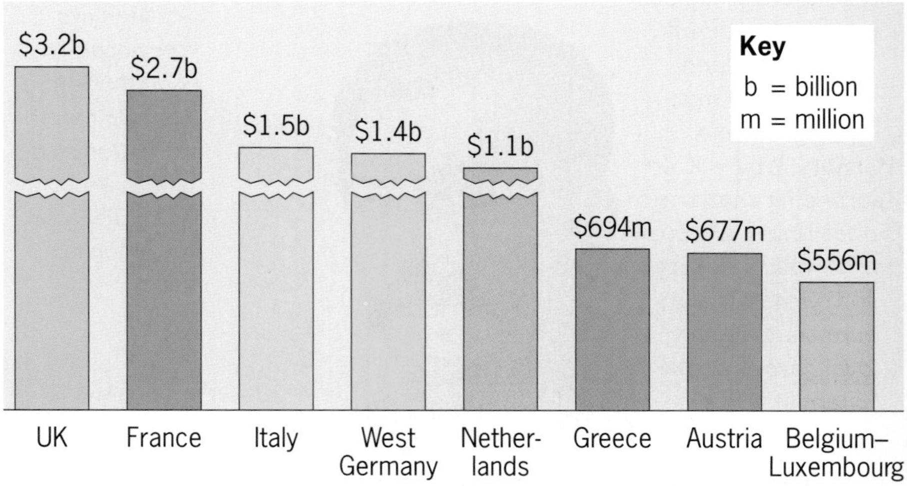
$3.2b
$2.7b
$1.5b
$1.4b
$1.1b
$694m
$677m
$556m
Key
b = billion
m = million
UK
France
Italy
West Germany
Nether- lands
Greece
Austria
Belgium–Luxembourg

Marshall Aid, April 1948 to June 1952 (Denmark, Norway, Turkey, Ireland, Sweden, Portugal and Iceland also received aid).

People reacted to Marshall Aid in different ways:

- Some saw it as a very generous gesture by the American people.
- Some saw it as a mixture of generosity and American self-interest. The USA wanted Europe to recover so that American industries could sell their goods there.
- Others saw it as a defence against the spread of Communism. For example, Italy did not receive any Marshall Aid until a non-Communist government took power in 1948.
- Stalin saw Marshall Aid as a threat. He believed that the USA was trying to dominate Europe by making it dependent on American handouts. He banned the Eastern European states from accepting Marshall Aid.

1 In what ways was Marshall Aid similar to and different from Stalin's actions in Eastern Europe? Explain your answer fully.

Can you see the problem . . . yet again?
It should be clear as daylight to you now – both sides had reasonable, sensible, but **totally different** viewpoints. The USSR and the USA both thought its own actions were perfectly reasonable. But they both saw the other's actions as threatening. This mistrust lies at the heart of the Cold War.

SOURCE 7

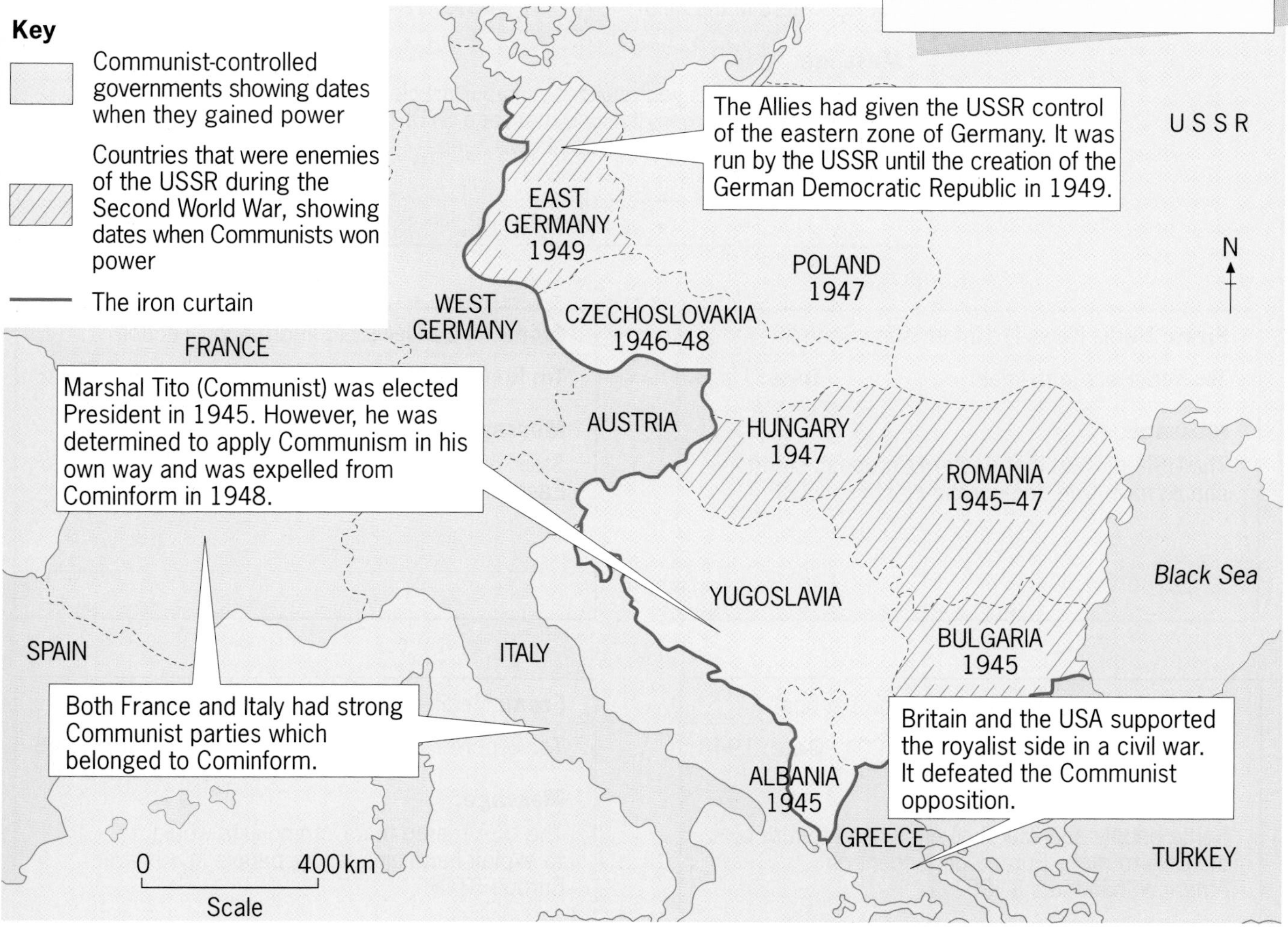

Key
Communist-controlled governments showing dates when they gained power
Countries that were enemies of the USSR during the Second World War, showing dates when Communists won power
The iron curtain
The Allies had given the USSR control of the eastern zone of Germany. It was run by the USSR until the creation of the German Democratic Republic in 1949.
USSR
EAST GERMANY 1949
POLAND 1947
N
WEST GERMANY
CZECHOSLOVAKIA 1946–48
FRANCE
Marshal Tito (Communist) was elected President in 1945. However, he was determined to apply Communism in his own way and was expelled from Cominform in 1948.
AUSTRIA
HUNGARY 1947
ROMANIA 1945–47
Black Sea
YUGOSLAVIA
SPAIN
ITALY
BULGARIA 1945
Both France and Italy had strong Communist parties which belonged to Cominform.
Britain and the USA supported the royalist side in a civil war. It defeated the Communist opposition.
ALBANIA 1945
GREECE
TURKEY
0
400 km
Scale

A map of Eastern Europe showing the IRON CURTAIN. Winston Churchill first used the term 'Iron Curtain' in a speech in the USA in March 1946. After this, it became the widely-used name for the border between Communist Eastern Europe and the West.

Focus task

The media played an important role in the development of the Cold War. Both sides wanted to convince their own people that they were in the right. Your task is to understand how they might have done this.

Write two separate newspaper reports of the events in Europe 1947–48:

1. An American view of the Soviet take-over of Eastern Europe
2. A Soviet view of the Truman Doctrine and Marshall Aid.

Remember that you are writing from only one point of view in each case.

For each report, describe five events, developments or views given by political leaders.

Each telegram on these pages has a point that you might be able to use. For each point, ask yourself:

- Am I clear about what happened?
- Can I use it in report 1?
- How can I use it to make the USA look reasonable and the USSR look unreasonable?
- Can I use it in report 2?
- How can I use it to make the USSR look reasonable and the USA look unreasonable?
- What events have I left out? Why have I left them out?

From: Media News Ltd Information Section
To: Reporters in the field | **Date:** 1948
Message:
You asked for points you could use in your article STOP We have too many for one message STOP Keep checking messages as points will keep coming STOP

From: Media News Ltd Information Section
To: Reporters in the field | **Date:** 1948
Message:
The USA insisted that Eastern European states should have free democratic elections STOP

From: Media News Ltd Information Section
To: Reporters in the field | **Date:** 1948
Message:
Stalin helped Communists take control of Eastern European states STOP

From: Media News Ltd Information Section
To: Reporters in the field | **Date:** 1948
Message:
Some people saw Marshall Aid as an attempt by the USA to make Europe dependent on American handouts STOP

From: Media News Ltd Information Section
To: Reporters in the field | **Date:** 1948
Message:
The USA feared that Communists would try to exploit hardships facing people in post-war Europe STOP

From: Media News Ltd Information Section	
To: Reporters in the field	**Date:** 1948
Message: The USSR was simply trying to make itself secure for the future STOP	

From: Media News Ltd Information Section	
To: Reporters in the field	**Date:** 1948
Message: Many American politicians believed that the USSR was trying to take over Europe STOP	

From: Media News Ltd Information Section	
To: Reporters in the field	**Date:** 1948
Message: The Truman Doctrine aimed to stop Communism spreading to any more countries STOP	

From: Media News Ltd Information Section	
To: Reporters in the field	**Date:** 1948
Message: The USSR had been invaded by German troops moving through Eastern European states STOP	

From: Media News Ltd Information Section	
To: Reporters in the field	**Date:** 1948
Message: The USA gave $17 billion to help rebuild Europe's economies STOP	

From: Media News Ltd Information Section	
To: Reporters in the field	**Date:** 1948
Message: The USSR suffered many more casualties than any other state in the war STOP	

From: Media News Ltd Information Section	
To: Reporters in the field	**Date:** 1948
Message: Truman sent money to support anti-Communist forces in Greece STOP	

From: Media News Ltd Information Section	
To: Reporters in the field	**Date:** 1948
Message: Some people saw Marshall Aid as a generous gesture STOP	

From: Media News Ltd Information Section	
To: Reporters in the field	**Date:** 1948
Message: Only non-Communist governments received Marshall Aid STOP	

From: Media News Ltd Information Section	
To: Reporters in the field	**Date:** 1948
Message: The USA agreed to Eastern Europe being a Soviet sphere of influence STOP	

8.2 Why did the superpowers clash over Berlin 1948–49?

From these pages, aim to explain:

- how the Western Allies started to rebuild Germany
- one reason why this alarmed Stalin
- two important consequences of the Berlin Blockade.

Key word currency

SOURCE 1

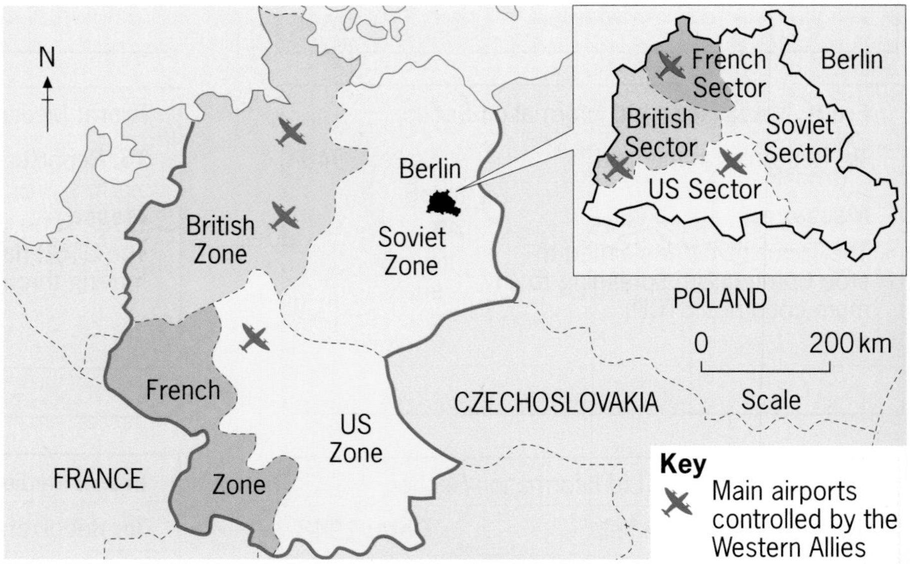
N
British Zone
Berlin
Soviet Zone
French Zone
US Zone
FRANCE
CZECHOSLOVAKIA
POLAND
0 200 km
Scale
French Sector
Berlin
British Sector
Soviet Sector
US Sector
Key
Main airports controlled by the Western Allies

A map of Berlin and West Germany in 1948.

Berlin after the war

After the war Germany was in ruins. By 1948 the American, French and British leaders decided it was time to start rebuilding Germany. American General Lucius Clay reorganised the CURRENCY and got German industries working again. Germans began going back to work and earning money.

The Berlin Blockade

To Stalin, it seemed that the Americans were rebuilding his old enemy. He could not stop the Allies, but he thought he could make a point by forcing them out of Berlin. In June 1948, he cut the rail and road links from the Allied zones to West Berlin. He also disrupted water and power supplies. It was a clever scheme. If the Allies stayed in Berlin, the people of Berlin would suffer. But the Allies responded with a brave and imaginative plan. For almost a year, they supplied Berlin by air with coal, food and medicine (see Source 4). The Western media praised the courage and endurance of the air crews. The Soviet media criticised the constant flights as unsafe. Stalin eventually gave up and lifted the blockade in May 1949.

SOURCE 2

The Western powers are transforming Germany into their strongpoint. They are making Germany part of a military and political block aimed at threatening the Soviet Union.

From a report sent to Soviet minister Molotov in March 1948.

SOURCE 3

If we mean that we are to hold Europe against Communism, we must not budge. I believe the future of democracy requires us to stay here in Berlin unless we are forced out.

US General Lucius Clay, June 1948.

SOURCE 4

An RAF transport plane being unloaded in Berlin, 1948.

The consequences of the Berlin Blockade

The Berlin Blockade was an important political dispute. It showed how stubborn each side could be. Stalin thought he was making a stand because the Americans were threatening him. The Americans suspected Stalin was getting ready to invade West Berlin.

1 Look at Source 4. What caption do you think might have appeared with this photograph in:
a) an American newspaper
b) a Soviet newspaper?

Focus task

You are going to prepare an ICT presentation about the causes of the Cold War.

Stage 1

Copy and complete a table like this – using your work on pages 160–71.

Factor	**Ways that the Soviets caused tension**	**Ways that the Americans caused tension**	**Which country was most to blame: S or A or B (B = both equally)**	**Explanation**
Different beliefs				
Personality clashes				
Disagreements over the future of Germany				
Disagreements over Eastern Europe				
Truman Doctrine and Marshall Plan				
The Berlin Blockade				

Stage 2

Now think about **which factors** were most to blame. All the factors in column 1 were important. But which do you think was **most** important? Put the factors into priority order. This will be easiest if you are working on a computer. If not, then cut up your chart and repaste it.

Write a paragraph or some bullet points to explain why you have put your top factor first.

Stage 3

Think about **which side** was most to blame **overall**. Look at your decisions in column 4. Choose the side you think was most to blame. Write a paragraph or some bullet points to explain your choice. If you think both sides were equally to blame, explain why.

Stage 4

Now use your notes to prepare a presentation. (Keep your notes. They will be useful for revision.)

9 Cold War – Hot War 1950–72

9.1 A touch of Cold War madness

These pages introduce you to the topic of the Cold War. Try to remember at least one of the examples in this section and **why** the Cold War affected this event.

Key words **CIA; KGB; paranoia; psychic; telepathic**

SOURCE 1

Look closely at Source 1. The atmosphere is tense. The hopes of a mighty superpower rest on the shoulders of each man. Each has been training his mind for years for this confrontation. Each is backed up by bodyguards and special advisers appointed by the government.

Both men also have electronic listening devices (bugs) sewn into their clothes, which are being taped by secret agents listening nearby. Among the minders are dark-suited agents from the CIA (American secret service) and the KGB (the Soviet Union's secret service). In the watching crowd, it is rumoured that there are PSYCHICS. They have been hired by the CIA and KGB to use their TELEPATHIC powers to confuse the man on the opposite side.

Who are these heroes? Great soldiers? Or great politicians trying to save the world? Actually, no! They are chess players! The year is 1972; the event is the Chess World Championships; the players are Bobby Fischer and Boris Spassky; the context is the Cold War; the atmosphere is one of PARANOIA.

You might find it hard to believe that all this effort went into a game of chess, but in the mad Cold War atmosphere the USA and the USSR went to great lengths to beat the other side at anything. Chess mattered because being the best at chess meant you were clever. But other things mattered, too. The Olympic Games mattered – you had to win the most medals. Science mattered – you had to make the best discoveries. The Moon mattered – you had to get there first. In fact, everything mattered.

If you were an American, you saw Communism or Soviet influence increasing wherever you looked. If you were a Soviet, you saw American or capitalist evil spreading everywhere. And if you didn't stop them, no one would.

1 There was a famous phrase for the Americans' habit of seeing Communist influence wherever they looked – 'Reds under the beds!' Can you think of a Soviet equivalent?

So . . .
If your enemy made a new weapon … you had to make a better one.
If your enemy helped one side in a far-away war … you had to help the other side.
If your enemy did something nice … you had to find a nasty side to it.
If your enemy did something nasty … you milked it for all it was worth.
If you lost an argument … you never admitted it. It was better simply to walk out.

SOURCE 2

SOURCE 3

UNION OF SOVIET
SOCIALIST REPUBLICS
U.S.S.R

Activity

1. Test your understanding of Cold War madness. Look at Sources 2 and 3. How can you explain what you see?
2. Do some extra research of your own and find five more pictures of Cold War madness. The internet is an excellent source. Try searching the websites of the Hulton Archive, the Public Record Office, and news organisations such as the BBC and ABC News.

Test your understanding by writing one sentence each to explain:

- MAD
- why people thought there might be a NUCLEAR WAR.

Activity

People sometimes say that truth is stranger than fiction. These two pages contain a number of facts and sources about the nuclear threat marked ✓ or ✗. There is one false item among them (either a wrong fact or a made-up piece of evidence).

1. Decide which is the false item.
2. Give some reasons why you think it is false.
3. Explain which sources or facts you are sure are right.
4. Explain why you are sure they are right.

✓ or ✗

MAD

Both the USA and the USSR supported a theory called MAD. This stood for Mutually Assured Destruction. Another name for it was the nuclear DETERRENT. The idea was that instead of getting rid of your nuclear weapons because they were dangerous, you built lots of them. This meant that neither side would dare launch a nuclear attack because the other side would RETALIATE and both sides would be destroyed.

Nuclear madness

Key words **civil defence; deterrent; hydrogen (H) bomb; missile; nuclear shelter; nuclear war; retaliate**

The previous two pages may have made the Cold War seem **ridiculous**. These two pages should remind you that it was also very **dangerous**. The USA and the USSR had hundreds of nuclear weapons pointing at each other. These MISSILES were unstoppable. They could be fired at enemy cities from the other side of the world, and could kill millions of people in a few minutes. Some people said that a nuclear war between the superpowers would destroy the human race completely.

SOURCE 4

✓ or ✗

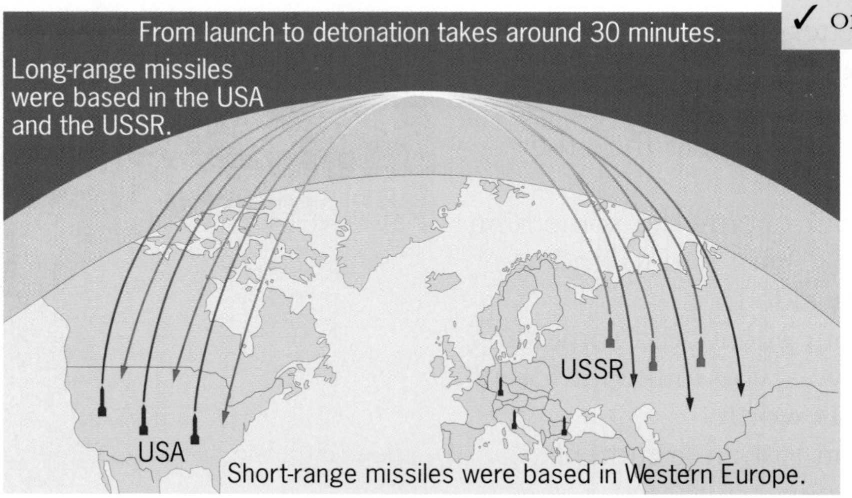
From launch to detonation takes around 30 minutes.
Long-range missiles were based in the USA and the USSR.
USSR
USA
Short-range missiles were based in Western Europe.

A map showing the location of American and Soviet missiles. Short-range missiles from Western Europe could hit the USSR in minutes.

✓ or ✗

SOURCE 5

An American B52 bomber. The USA had a nuclear branch of its air force called the Strategic Air Command (SAC). SAC kept twelve of these giant B52 bombers in the air, armed with nuclear weapons, 24 hours a day, 365 days a year – just in case.

✓ or ✗

Power crazy?
The head of SAC in the 1960s was General Thomas Power. Power once said, 'At the end of the war if there are two Americans and one Russian left alive, we win.' General Curtis Le May, the man who led SAC before Power, thought Power was mentally unstable. (Some people thought Le May was crazy!)

SOURCE 6

✓ or ✗

ATOMIC BOMB SHELTERS
financed BY the GOVERNMENT
STOP for DETAILS!

A billboard put up by a Californian swimming pool manufacturer in the early 1960s. He expanded his business by building NUCLEAR SHELTERS as well. His slogan was: 'Due to known conditions, ACT NOW!' Lots of celebrities had their own shelters built where they could survive for weeks following a nuclear attack.

✓ or ✗

SOURCE 7

When a nuclear war gets
underway
And the rockets come
falling down
All the bloody politicians
who started it will scuttle
off underground
And when they finally
re-emerge
With no life to be found
They can administrate the
rubble and they can
order each other around.

A song from the mid-1960s protesting about the nuclear arms race.

SOURCE 8

✓ or ✗

THE
Hydrogen Bomb
WHAT THE HYDROGEN BOMB DOES
What YOU could do
WHAT YOU CAN DO NOW Join the Civil Defence Corps or the Auxiliary Fire Service. They will teach you how to help yourself and others if war should come.
What CIVIL DEFENCE can do!
THE HEADQUARTERS SECTION
THE WARDEN SECTION
THE RESCUE SECTION
THE WELFARE SECTION
THE AMBULANCE & CASUALTY COLLECTING SECTION

A British CIVIL DEFENCE poster from 1965. The poster explains the effects of a HYDROGEN BOMB and provides advice on how to survive a nuclear blast.

✓ or ✗

H-bomb test
When the USSR tested its H-bomb in 1961, the Soviet leader swore all the scientists to secrecy, but then deliberately gave a full set of results to the USA. He wanted the Americans to fear the power of the Soviet bomb.

SOURCE 9

✓ or ✗

Evening Standard

Mr. K: If West show readiness to settle German treaty problem we won't insist on deadline

THE BIGGEST BOMB IN THE WORLD

50-million tons —Russia will explode it soon

'WE HAVE ONE TWICE AS BIG: WE WON'T LET IT OFF . . . IT MIGHT BREAK OUR OWN WINDOWS'

MOSCOW, Tuesday.—The biggest and most awesome blast ever to be set off by man is planned for the end of this month, Mr. Krushchev revealed today. Russia will explode a 50-megaton hydrogen bomb on October 30 or 31, he said.

Rocket-rattling 'sickening' says Philip

NUCLEAR SUBS

LORD BLANDFORD AND TINA PLAN A PARIS WEDDING

THE RUSSIANS DON'T HEAR THE NEWS

HENLYS SPECIAL LAND-ROVER SHOW

A newspaper account of the Soviet Union's test explosion of a hydrogen bomb (H-bomb) in October 1961. H-bombs were many times more powerful than atom bombs. This explosion was the largest man-made explosion in history.

You will look at three disputes in this chapter. Make sure you:

- know the basic outline of each dispute
- can explain one way in which the disputes were similar to each other
- can describe one way in which they were different from each other.

Containment case studies

You already know that disputes between the superpowers were inevitable because they had fiercely different beliefs. The USSR supported Communist movements all over the world. It wanted to spread Communism. The USA tried to contain Communism – to stop it spreading. It wanted to spread capitalism instead. It supported capitalist countries all over the world.

You are going to examine three case studies of the USA trying to contain Communism:

- the Korean War 1950–53
- the Cuban Missile Crisis 1962
- the Vietnam War 1964–72.

The Cuban Missile Crisis 1962
Outline:
Similarities with the other two case studies:
Differences from the other two case studies:
The Korean War 1950–53
Outline:
Similarities with the other two case studies:
Differences from the other two case studies:
The Vietnam War 1964–73
Outline:
Similarities with the other two case studies:
Differences from the other two case studies:

9.2 Containment case study 1: the Korean War 1950–53

Label the four stepping stones to American involvement in Korea without looking at this book.

Key words **Security Council; United Nations (UN)**

The Cold War was a war of threats and propaganda, but there was also quite a lot of hot war (real war) as well. The Americans and Soviets never fought each other face to face, but they fought each other indirectly. In 1950, Americans found themselves involved in a vicious and very real war against Communist forces in Korea. This is how it happened.

Step 1: China goes Communist
The Cold War was not just a conflict between the USA and the USSR – it was a conflict between capitalism and Communism.

In 1949, China went Communist. China was the most powerful country in the Far East and it had the largest population in the world. The USA now faced another huge Communist power.

1

Step 2: The USSR leaves the United Nations (UN)
Communist China was already a member of the UN, but its leader Mao Tse Tung wanted China to be on the UN Security Council, which was the part of the UN that made most of the decisions. The Security Council was dominated by capitalist countries. The USSR was the only Communist country on the council. Stalin wanted China to be on the Security Council, but he was outvoted. Stalin was furious, and he pulled out of the UN in protest.

2

Step 3: Communist North Korea invades South Korea
Meanwhile, Communism was gaining support in other parts of Asia. For example, Korea was divided into Communist North Korea and anti-Communist South Korea. In 1950 North Korea invaded the South. By September 1950, it was about to defeat the South.

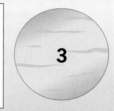

3

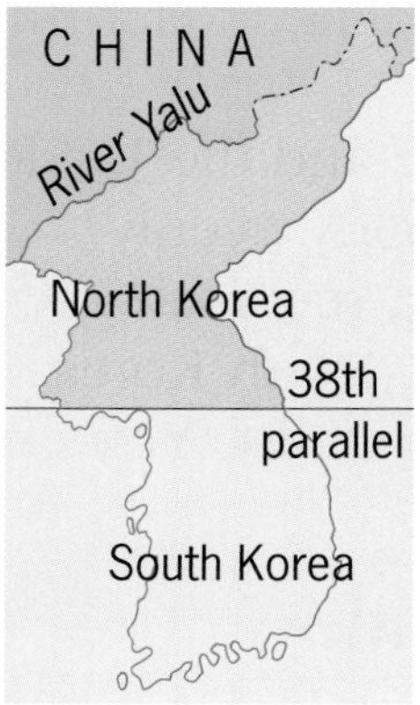
CHINA
River Yalu
North Korea
38th parallel
South Korea

Step 4: The UN takes the side of the USA
Do you remember President Truman's policy of containment? Truman felt that he could not allow Communism to take over South Korea. He managed to get the UN to condemn the North Korean invasion. He even managed to get it to send forces to help the South Koreans push the Communists out of their country. You probably wonder how he managed this. One of the main reasons was that the USSR was not there to object. It was still boycotting the UN over the issue of China's membership.

4

The Korean War

Make sure you can list at least two important effects of the Korean War.

The Korean War

SOURCE 1

IN MEMORY OF THE
LEAGUE of NATIONS
DIED OF
LACK OF EXERCISE
FACING WANTON AGGRESSION
United Nations

A cartoon by David Low, a famous British cartoonist. Low was well known for criticising appeasement in the 1930s. The figure on the right is President Truman.

1 What is the cartoon in Source 1 saying about the actions of the USA and the UN?

A UN force (mainly soldiers from the USA) joined the war alongside South Korea. The Americans pushed the North Koreans back. In fact, they went further than this. American Commander General MacArthur ordered his forces into North Korea. By late 1950, UN forces were approaching the border of China.

In January 1951, Chinese troops joined the war on the North Korean side. The USSR supplied them with weapons and equipment. They pushed the Americans back. At this point, General MacArthur called for Chinese cities to be bombed. He even said that the USA should use nuclear weapons if necessary. President Truman sacked MacArthur in April 1951.

With the Americans supporting one side and the USSR and China the other, the two sides were fairly evenly matched. By early 1953, the war reached a stalemate.

All sides signed a ceasefire in July 1953. North Korea stayed Communist. South Korea stayed capitalist. You could say the result was a draw!

Physical consequences of the Korean War

The war devastated many parts of Korea. The total casualties were about 1.4 million. About half a million of these were South Korean civilians. The UN lost 35,000 soldiers, 30,000 of whom were American.

Political consequences of the Korean War

In this chapter, we are most interested in the political consequences of the war – which means the way of thinking about the Cold War that followed from it.

The Korean War started as a local dispute, which then drew in the superpowers. The USA was directly involved (Americans made up most of the UN forces), and the USSR was indirectly involved (supplying weapons). It grew into a major war with the threat of nuclear warfare. How would this affect the superpowers' views on:

. . . China?
China had become an important new power. You'd expect the USA to be worried by this but it might surprise you that Communist USSR was also worried. The Soviets wanted to be the leading Communist state, and wanted China simply to support their policies. However, it was clear that the Chinese leaders had their own ideas.

. . . containment?
The Americans were divided over whether this first attempt to 'contain' Communism had been a success or a failure. Communism had been stopped but things had very nearly gone wrong and it had cost them massive amounts of money and high casualties. They would be more cautious about getting involved in local conflicts in the future.

. . . the UN?
The USA had taken over the UN. In fact, at one stage it seemed as if General MacArthur alone was acting as if he was the UN. The USSR would be very wary of the UN in future.

. . . nuclear weapons?
At one stage the US President had threatened to use nuclear weapons. The nuclear threat made the USSR more determined to develop powerful nuclear weapons of its own. Neutral countries became more worried, too.

. . . acting tough?
Korea convinced the American leaders that the only way to deal with the Communists was to be tough.

Focus task

What were the lessons of the Korean War?

The American President has called in one of his advisers: 'So tell me, Chuck, what lessons do you think I should learn from Korea?'

1. Decide which statements Chuck might have made. Note down any evidence from this case study that supports the statement.
2. Which statements do you think Chuck would not have made? Give reasons for your answer.

Watch out for China. It's big trouble.
These Communists are a push-over.
You've got to act tough.
Nuclear weapons are the future.
Don't get too involved in local disputes in future.
Leave important decisions to your army generals. They know best.

9.3 Containment case study 2: the Cuban Missile Crisis 1962

Aim to remember two pieces of evidence which show that people expected a nuclear war in 1962.

Why were people so worried in October 1962?

In October 1962, many people thought that the end of the world was near.

SOURCE 1

H
USA
H

A cartoon from the *Daily Mail*, 29 October 1962.

SOURCE 2

The first time I fell in love with poetry – Mr Valentine was reading Keats' 'La Belle Dame Sans Merci' out loud to us . . .

It was the time of the Cuba crisis and everybody was scared, even the grown-ups. No-one on the bus to school talked much, but those who did talked about nothing else and everyone's face was grim.

On a placard outside the newsagents, black block capitals spelled WAR INEVITABLE. Even the newsreaders on television looked scared when they talked about 'the grave international situation'.

As Mr Valentine read to us about . . . the lake where no birds sang . . . we really expected that death. And the bombs might come falling. The poem hurt us. Everyone in the class felt it, even the science boys and the maths geniuses who hated English, and the sporty class captain and Mr Valentine himself. You could feel it in the silence and the shared held breath when the voice stopped.

The memories of poet Liz Lochead, who was a Scottish school student in October 1962. The poem she talks about is a haunting and mysterious story.

SOURCE 3

It was a beautiful autumn evening, the height of the crisis, and I went up into the open air to smell it, because I thought it was the last Saturday I would ever see.

Robert McNamara talking about the evening of 27 October 1962. McNamara was one of US President Kennedy's closest advisers during the Cuban Crisis.

Activity A

Looking at one source closely

1 Look at Source 1 closely. You probably know what general point the cartoon is making, but think about **how** it makes that point. Explain the meaning of each of these details in the cartoon:
- what each man is sitting on
- the sweating forehead
- the arm wrestling
- the buttons on the table.

2 Now write a paragraph summing up the cartoon's message. Include specific examples from your answers to question 1.

SOURCE 4

THE YOUNG ONES IN REVOLT

– school strikes in protest at actions of superpowers

The two Ks – Kennedy and Khrushchev – will get a cable [telegram] from Britain's young ones in revolt today.

The sender: Robin Mariner, 18-year-old head boy at Midhurst, Sussex, grammar school, and leader of a strike by 40 of the school's sixth formers yesterday. The strikers told their headmaster, Mr Norman Lucas, after morning assembly that they would not attend classes for two days.

From an article in the *Manchester Guardian*, 25 October 1962.

Cuban Crisis timeline

14 October	The USA finds out that there are Soviet nuclear missiles in Cuba.
21 October	The USA announces that it will blockade Cuba to stop any more missiles arriving. The US army prepares to invade Cuba to get rid of the missiles that are there.
22 October	President Kennedy goes on national television to tell the American public what is happening. There is panic buying in American supermarkets.
	The Soviet leader, Khrushchev, tells his advisers to expect an American invasion of Cuba and to fight back if it happens.
25 October	American warships stop a Soviet ship. This is technically an act of war. The Soviet ship is only carrying oil so the Americans let it through.
26 October	Over 120,000 American troops assemble near the Florida coast.
27 October	Khrushchev offers to remove the Cuban missiles if the USA promises not to invade Cuba and if the USA removes its missiles from Turkey.
	Kennedy agrees.
28 October	Khrushchev announces that the USSR will remove its missiles from Cuba in order to protect world peace.

SOURCE 5

On October 27th I went and telephoned my wife and told her to drop everything and get out of Moscow. I thought then that the American bombers were on their way.

The memories of Fyodor Burlatsky. He was a Soviet journalist but he also carried secret messages for the Soviet government.

Activity B

Comparing sources

3 Does Source 1 sum up the same views as are in Sources 2–5? Write your answer by explaining:

a) what views are in each of Sources 2–5

b) whether Source 1 agrees or disagrees

c) how well you think Source 1 sums them up.

Activity C

Using the sources to support an argument

Read through these statements carefully:

A Nuclear war was very close in October 1962.

B The media thought nuclear war was very close in October 1962.

C Ordinary people thought that nuclear war was very close in October 1962.

D People 'in the know' thought nuclear war was very close in October 1962.

Each statement is making a slightly different point – they are similar, but not identical. For each statement explain:

- which sources support the statement
- why you feel the statement is supported by these sources.

Think carefully about each statement and be precise in your answers. You will find the timeline helpful.

Extension

Many people who were teenagers or older at the time of the Cuban Crisis remember it vividly. Write a short paragraph explaining why this might be.

From these pages, you should be able to explain:

- one reason why the USA disliked Castro's government
- one reason why Khrushchev put nuclear missiles in Cuba
- one reason why the USA objected.

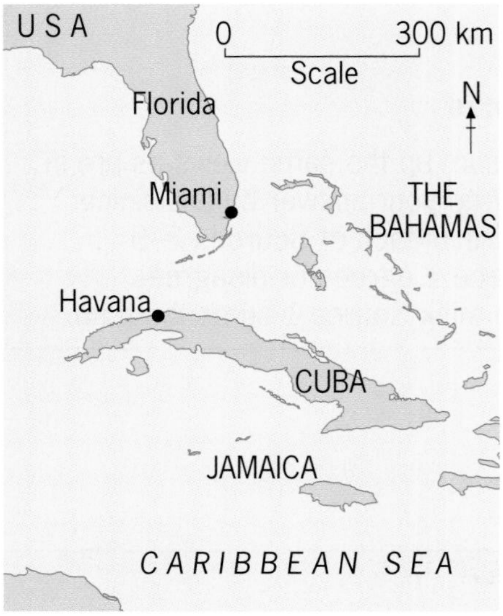
USA
0
300 km
Scale
N
Florida
Miami
THE BAHAMAS
Havana
CUBA
JAMAICA
CARIBBEAN SEA

A map of Cuba.

Why was Cuba so important?

Key words **'back yard'; launcher; spy plane**

Cuba is an island in the Caribbean Sea. In the 1950s, the USA regarded the Caribbean (and Central America) as its territory. Americans dominated Cuba. They went there for holidays. They owned big businesses. They had a large military base at Guantánamo Bay.

In 1959, it all went badly wrong for the USA. It had been supporting the man who ruled Cuba, Fulgencio Batista. He was corrupt and unpopular but he was not a Communist. The problem came when Fidel Castro, a Communist, led a successful revolution against Batista.

The USA was furious. It wanted to get rid of Castro quickly. American governments gave money and equipment to Cubans who opposed Castro. In April 1961, these Cubans landed in Cuba at the Bay of Pigs. They planned to overthrow Castro. However, the whole operation was a disaster. American President John F Kennedy was humiliated.

Soviet leader Nikita Khrushchev enjoyed the USA's embarrassment. He was pleased that there was a Communist state in the USA's 'BACK YARD' and he supplied Cuba with food, advisers and weapons. On the other hand, Khrushchev knew that if the USA decided to invade Cuba and remove Castro there was little he could do about it. So one reason he wanted nuclear missiles on Cuba was to scare off the USA from invading Cuba.

Khrushchev had another reason, too – Turkey. You might think this is getting too complicated, but actually this part is quite simple. The USA had missiles in Turkey. Turkey was close to the USSR. Cuba was close to the USA. This was typical Cold War logic – act tough, look strong. So, having missiles in Cuba was no different from the USA having missiles in Turkey.

SOURCE 6

The American missiles in Turkey are aimed at us and scare us. Why not throw a hedgehog in Uncle Sam's pants? Our missiles in Cuba will be aimed at the USA, even though we don't have as many of them. They will still be afraid.

Khrushchev speaking in private to other Soviet leaders, September 1962.

1 Read Source 6. Khrushchev called the missiles in Cuba 'a hedgehog in Uncle Sam's pants'. What do you think the Americans would have thought?

SOURCE 7

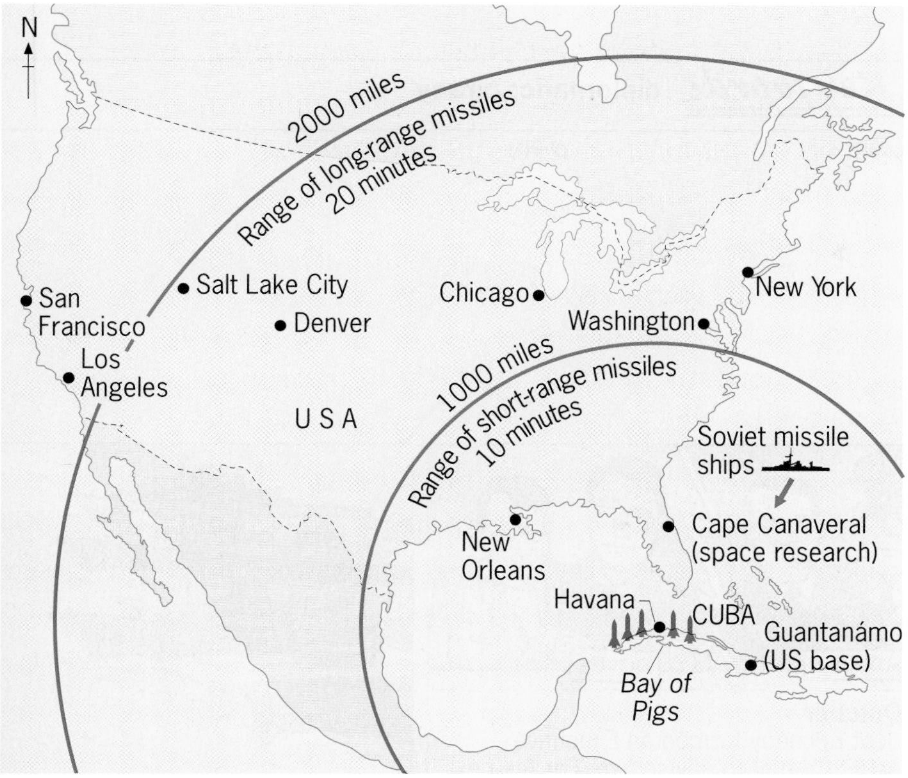
N
2000 miles
Range of long-range missiles
20 minutes
San Francisco
Salt Lake City
Denver
Chicago
New York
Washington
Los Angeles
USA
1000 miles
Range of short-range missiles
10 minutes
Soviet missile ships
Cape Canaveral (space research)
New Orleans
Havana
CUBA
Guantanámo (US base)
Bay of Pigs

A map showing the range of missiles based in Cuba. Cuba was as close to the USA as Turkey was to the USSR.

SOURCE 8

ЗАПРЕЩАЮ ДРУЖИТЬ
С СОВЕТСКИМ СОЮЗОМ!
USA

A cartoon from 1960. The notice held by the US Secretary of State says to Castro in Cuba: 'I forbid you to make friends with the Soviet Union.'

The Cuban Crisis

During September 1962, Soviet ships took 40 nuclear missiles to Cuba. Khrushchev also sent a huge amount of equipment to build missile LAUNCHERS, with experts to help the Cubans set them up. He even sent troops, tanks, jet fighters and anti-aircraft missiles to protect the nuclear missiles. About 5000 Soviets went to Cuba along with the missiles. It was pretty hard to hide all of this.

On 14 October, an American U2 SPY PLANE took a series of photographs of Cuba. It was the beginning of a two-week crisis that took the world to the brink of nuclear war. The story of the crisis is summarised on the next two pages.

2 Do you think Source 8 is pro-American or pro-Communist? Use the evidence in the cartoon to help you decide.

The story of the crisis

From these two pages, try to remember:

- two pieces of evidence that suggest the world was close to nuclear war
- one reason why Kennedy was happy with the outcome of the crisis
- one reason why Khrushchev was happy with the outcome of the crisis.

Key words diplomatic; piracy

14 October
A U2 spy plane took pictures of missile sites in Cuba.

HAWKS
DOVES

16–20 October
US President Kennedy formed an Executive Committee (ExComm) to advise him. For the next three days, ExComm argued about what to do. Some members of ExComm (the Hawks) wanted tough action such as:

- a 'surgical' (very precise) air attack to destroy the missile launch sites
- an invasion of Cuba.

Other ExComm members (the Doves) wanted less tough steps such as:

- DIPLOMATIC pressure
- secret contact with the USSR to see if the two could do a deal.

21 October
ExComm finally came up with a plan. The US navy was to blockade Cuba. This meant stopping all ships going to Cuba. No more military equipment would be allowed in. It was risky. Stopping a Soviet ship was technically an act of war. Kennedy admitted to his brother Robert that it was 'one hell of a gamble'.

DEFCON 2

24 October

- Secretary General of the UN, U Thant, called on both sides to compromise.
- Khrushchev ordered Soviet ships to stop heading for Cuba (but not to turn back).
- US armed forces went to level DEFCON 2. This was the only time in the entire Cold War they got so close to war.

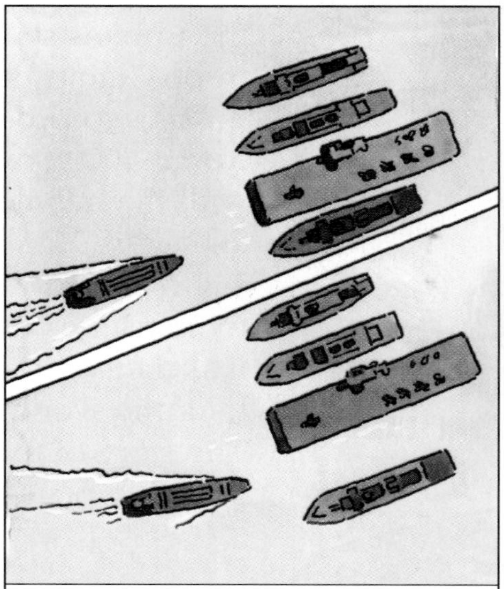

25 October
US warships stopped the first Soviet ship. It was only carrying oil so they let it through.

26 October

- Over 120,000 US troops assembled near the Florida coast. An American invasion of Cuba looked likely.
- Kennedy told ExComm that he wanted a deal to end the crisis. The Hawks still wanted an invasion.
- Kennedy got a letter from Khrushchev. The letter offered to remove the missiles if the USA promised not to invade Cuba. Most of ExComm wanted to accept the offer.

Discussion

1 You considered these four statements on page 181:

A Nuclear war was very close in October 1962.

B The media thought nuclear war was very close in October 1962.

C Ordinary people thought that nuclear war was very close in October 1962.

D People 'in the know' thought nuclear war was very close in October 1962.

Now that you know more about the crisis, which do you think is the most accurate statement?

2 Some people say that the Cuban Missile Crisis made the world a safer place. Do you agree? Explain your answer.

22 October
- US armed forces were put on alert to level DEFCON 3, short for Defence Condition 3. (DEFCON 1 meant all-out war with the USSR.)
- President Kennedy went on national television to tell the American public what was happening.
- In Moscow, Khrushchev was more and more sure that the USA would invade Cuba. He told his advisers, 'They can attack us and we shall respond. This may end in a big war.'

This blockade is PIRACY!

23 October
- Khrushchev condemned the US blockade. Secretly, he was glad that the USA had not invaded Cuba.
- Castro ordered Cuban forces to get ready for an American invasion.
- A fleet of Soviet ships approached Cuba carrying more missiles.
- There was a panic buying in US supermarkets as people prepared for war.

27 October
- Probably the most tense day of the crisis. Cuban forces shot down a US spy plane.
- Khrushchev sent another letter to Kennedy. It made the same offer but **also** insisted that the US missiles be removed from Turkey.
- Kennedy did not agree immediately. But he admitted that, 'Khrushchev has us in a pretty good spot here, because most people will regard this as a reasonable proposal.'
- Kennedy accepted Khrushchev's offer but insisted that the agreement to remove missiles from Turkey was to be kept secret.

For the sake of world peace . . .

27 October
Khrushchev announced that the USSR would remove its missiles from Cuba in order to protect world peace.

Who won?

The Cuban Crisis was desperately tense. In the end, however, both sides could claim a victory.

Victory according to Khrushchev

Khrushchev could claim that he had a promise from the USA to leave his ally Cuba alone. In addition, American nuclear missiles were quietly removed from Turkey in 1963.

Victory according to Kennedy

Kennedy could claim a success for the policy of containment. He had stood up to Khrushchev and his decisive action removed the threat of nuclear missiles based in Cuba.

Victory according to planet Earth

Perhaps the most important outcome of the crisis was that the USA and the USSR set up a 'hot line'. This was a direct phone link between the American President and the Soviet leader. Both realised that they had got very close to war.

In 1963, they agreed to a Nuclear Test Ban Treaty. It was a small but important step towards reducing the threat of nuclear destruction.

9.4 Containment case study 3: the Vietnam War 1964–72

From these pages, aim to recall:

- two reasons why Communists were trying to take over South Vietnam
- two reasons why the USA got involved in Vietnam.

Key words guerrilla; peasant; Viet Cong

Why did the USA get involved in Vietnam in the 1960s?

SOURCE 1

VIETNAM
LAOS
CAMBODIA
BURMA
THAILAND
INDIA

The domino theory in Asia. American governments were sure that China and the USSR were planning to spread Communism to countries in Asia. If one country fell to Communism, the others would fall like a row of dominoes.

SOURCE 2

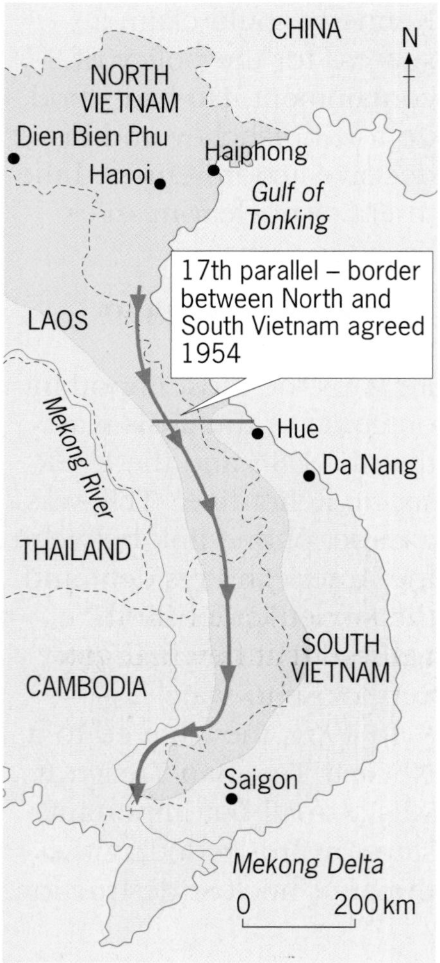
CHINA
N
NORTH VIETNAM
Dien Bien Phu
Haiphong
Hanoi
Gulf of Tonking
17th parallel – border between North and South Vietnam agreed 1954
LAOS
Hue
Da Nang
Mekong River
THAILAND
SOUTH VIETNAM
CAMBODIA
Saigon
Mekong Delta
0 200 km
Key
Communist-controlled areas in the mid-1960s
Ho Chi Minh Trail

Vietnam and surrounding countries.

Background: up to 1954

Here's a very quick summary of the background.

- Before the Second World War, the French ruled Vietnam. Then the Japanese took over. The Communist leader Ho Chi Minh fought the Japanese. Most of the Vietnamese peasants supported him.
- When the Japanese were defeated, the French tried to take back Vietnam. Ho Chi Minh fought them too. The Americans supported the French because they did not want Vietnam to become Communist under Ho Chi Minh (see Source 1).
- Even with American help, the French could not beat Ho Chi Minh. In 1954 they asked for peace talks.
- Vietnam was then divided into two new states. North Vietnam became Communist, under Ho Chi Minh; South Vietnam was led by Ngo Dinh Diem. He was anti-Communist, so the Americans supported him.

1954–64: The USA supports Diem

The USA supported Diem with money, equipment and military advisers who trained South Vietnamese troops. The advisers were soldiers, but they were not 'combat troops'.

Diem's regime was corrupt. It was unpopular with Vietnamese PEASANTS. As a result, Communists in South Vietnam (known as the VIET CONG) began to build up support. They got help from Ho Chi Minh in North Vietnam. In the early 1960s, they started attacking the South Vietnamese army. They also attacked government buildings and officials, including some Americans. They used hit-and-run GUERRILLA tactics, which were very effective. By 1962, they controlled much of the countryside. During 1963 and 1964, this guerrilla war continued and tension rose between North and South Vietnam.

1964 onwards: the USA sends combat troops

President Kennedy had been wary of getting more deeply involved in Vietnam. He was killed in 1963. The new President, Lyndon Johnson, decided that the USA had to get serious about Vietnam or get out. The decisive moment came in 1964 when North Vietnamese gunboats attacked American warships off the Vietnam coast.

In response, Johnson massively increased American involvement. From 1964, he sent hundreds of thousands of young American soldiers to fight in Vietnam (see Source 3). These figures do not include the warships, aircraft crews and other troops, or the secret operations run by the CIA or the South Vietnamese troops.

People thought, 'Surely the Viet Cong will never withstand such power?'

SOURCE 3

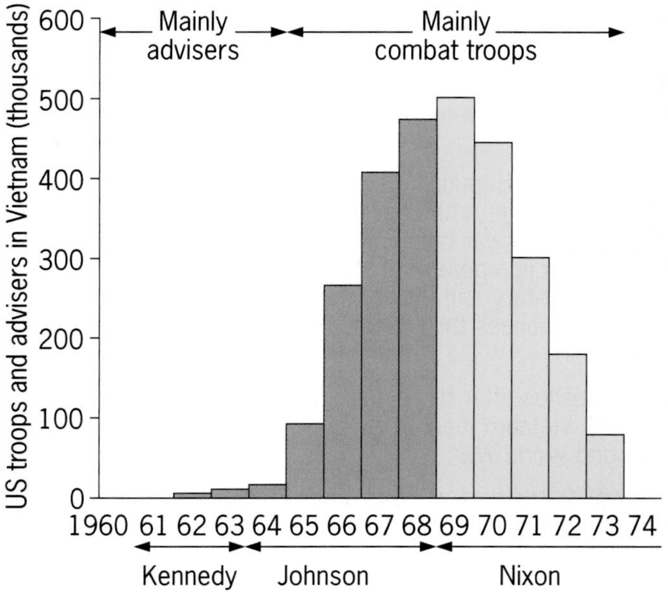
Mainly advisers
Mainly combat troops
US troops and advisers in Vietnam (thousands)
600
500
400
300
200
100
0
1960 61 62 63 64 65 66 67 68 69 70 71 72 73 74
Kennedy
Johnson
Nixon

US troops in Vietnam 1960–74.

Focus task

Why did the USA get involved in Vietnam?

You are a young news reporter. Your editor has asked you for a 100-word caption to go with this photo of American soldiers in Vietnam to explain why the USA is sending its young men to Vietnam. Your readers are very anti-Communist.

Make sure your caption includes these words:

- domino theory
- Ho Chi Minh
- Communism
- South Vietnam.

Find five reasons why the USA could not defeat the Viet Cong. Make sure you can recall:

- two or three strengths of the Viet Cong (with examples)
- two or three weaknesses of the USA (with examples).

Why couldn't the Americans defeat the Viet Cong 1965–69?

Key words **draft; embassy; search and destroy; supply route; Vietnamisation**

Timeline: American involvement in the Vietnam War

1954	Vietnam is divided into North and South Vietnam.
1959	The North Vietnam army creates the Ho Chi Minh Trail to carry supplies down to South Vietnam.
1960	North Vietnam creates the National Liberation Front of South Vietnam (usually called the Viet Cong).
1961	Around 16,000 American advisers help to organise the South Vietnam army.
1962–63	The Viet Cong use guerrilla tactics against South Vietnam's army and government. More American advisers and equipment arrive.
1964	North Vietnamese patrol boats fire on American warships in the Gulf of Tonkin. The American Congress gives President Johnson the authority to do whatever he thinks is necessary.
February 1965	Operation Rolling Thunder – a gigantic bombing campaign against North Vietnam. Factories and army bases are bombed, as well as the Ho Chi Minh Trail and the capital of North Vietnam, Hanoi.
March	The first American combat troops (3500 marines) come ashore at Da Nang.
June–September	A major Viet Cong offensive.
November	Battle in La Dreng Valley. The Communists suffer heavy losses.
1966	American forces build heavily armed camps. They control towns. The Viet Cong largely control the countryside.
1967	Continual running battles between American and Communist forces around the North–South Vietnam border. The Communists are unable to force out American troops.
January 1968	The Tet Offensive: a large-scale Communist attack on over 100 major towns and cities in South Vietnam. Even the American EMBASSY in Saigon is attacked. Some of the fiercest fighting of the war takes place. The city of Hue is nearly flattened by intense fighting. Tet is a defeat for the Communists but is also a major shock to the American military and public who thought the war was almost won. Intense fighting continues throughout 1968. Casualties on both sides mount.
October	Operation Rolling Thunder finishes after three and a half years. More bombs have been dropped on North Vietnam than all the bombs dropped on Germany and Japan during the Second World War.
1969	The USA begins its policy of 'VIETNAMISATION'. This means building up the South Vietnam army and withdrawing American combat troops. American air power continues to bomb North Vietnam.
	Intense fighting continues throughout the year. This includes the Battle for Hamburger Hill in May.
1970–71	The fighting spreads to Cambodia.
1972	Most American forces are now out of Vietnam. A major Communist offensive in March captures much ground. Most land is recaptured by the South Vietnam army by the end of the year.

Focus task

Good news. The air force has launched Operation Rolling Thunder. We are bombing Communist factories and fuel depots. We are bombing the Ho Chi Minh Trail. The Viet Cong will soon have no equipment and no reinforcements.
FEBRUARY 1965
Thanks Dan.
Good news. We beat the Viet Cong at La Dreng. They lost 2000 troops. We lost 300. They are no match for us in open combat.
NOVEMBER 1965
Thanks Dan.
Good news. We have total air superiority. Our aircraft are bombing all the Viet Cong strongholds.
JANUARY 1966
Thanks Dan.
Good news. We have over 400,000 young Americans fighting in Vietnam. And hundreds of thousands more can be DRAFTED when we need them.
MARCH 1966
Thanks Dan.
Good news. We've started 'SEARCH AND DESTROY' missions. Our teams fly into an area and search out and destroy the Viet Cong wherever they are.
MARCH 1967
Thanks Dan.
Good news. The Viet Cong's Tet Offensive has failed completely. They have suffered 100,000 casualties.
JANUARY 1968
Stop this Dan! We're spending loads of money on this war. So explain to me in words I can understand – why can't we beat them?

You are Lieutenant Dan. Everything you have told the Congressman in 1965–68 is correct. Now he's put you on the spot and you have to tell him why these measures have not worked as well as everyone had hoped.

On pages 190–91 is a collection of sources and comments to help you with your explanation.

Stage 1

Draw up a table like this one. Use the sources and the comments on the next two pages to complete it.

American tactic	Why it was not as effective as hoped	Evidence to support this conclusion
Bombing SUPPLY ROUTES		
Causing heavy casualties in open warfare		
Bombing Viet Cong bases		
Search and destroy		
Sending more troops		

Stage 2

Now it is time to get ready to meet the Congressman. Use your completed table to write three notes under each of these main headings:

1. Why air power does not have much effect on the Viet Cong
2. Why American troops are less effective than Viet Cong troops
3. Why the Viet Cong seem to have plenty of soldiers, weapons and supplies.

Use these sources to help you with the Focus task on page 189.

SOURCE 4

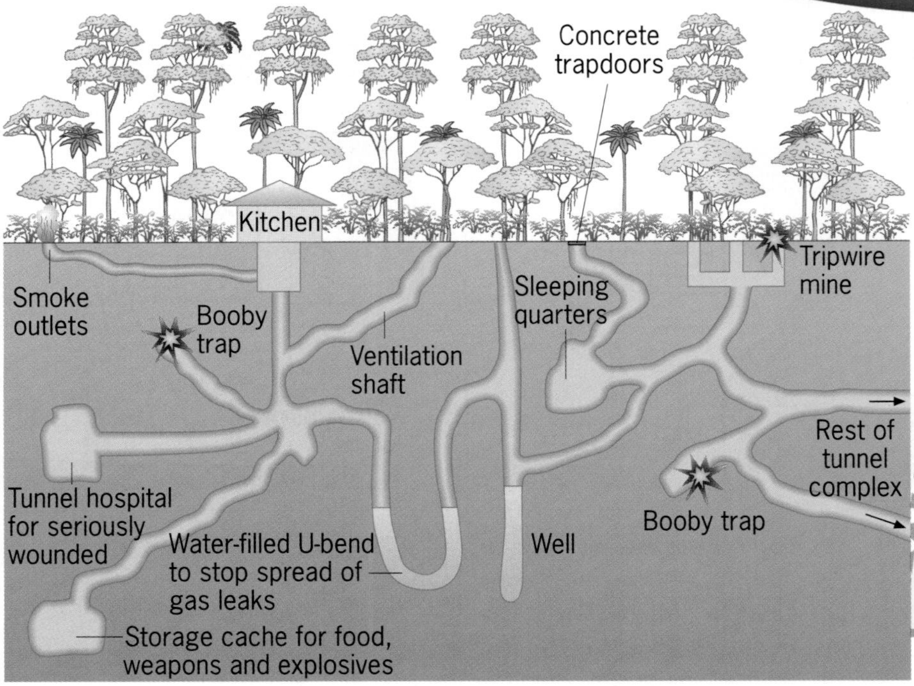
Concrete trapdoors
Kitchen
Tripwire mine
Smoke outlets
Booby trap
Sleeping quarters
Ventilation shaft
Rest of tunnel complex
Tunnel hospital for seriously wounded
Water-filled U-bend to stop spread of gas leaks
Well
Booby trap
Storage cache for food, weapons and explosives

A Viet Cong tunnel complex.

COMMENT

Bombing does not work very well against the Viet Cong. They hide themselves and their equipment in these tunnels. The tunnels are often mined or BOOBY TRAPPED in case enemy forces find them. The CIA estimate there are 240 kilometres of these tunnels.

COMMENT

The Viet Cong are fighting a guerrilla war. They avoid open combat. They attack American patrols then simply disappear into the villages or the jungle. Our soldiers cannot fight an enemy they cannot see.

Viet Cong fighters have control of the countryside. They execute peasants who co-operate with the South Vietnam government. They have killed an estimated 27,000 civilians. But they help any peasants who support them. They even help the peasants with their farming at harvest time.

SOURCE 5

A Viet Cong poster showing their hit-and-run tactics.

SOURCE 6

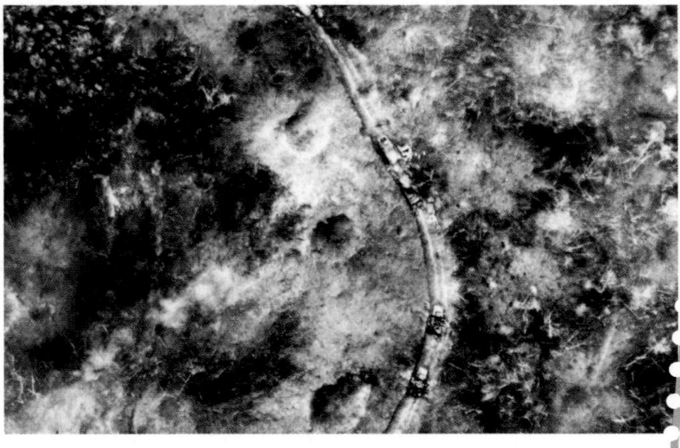

Viet Cong troops on the Ho Chi Minh Trail.

COMMENT

This is the main supply route for the Viet Cong fighters. Much of the equipment comes from China and the USSR. Our planes regularly attack the trail with bombs and CHEMICAL WEAPONS. However, as soon as the bombing stops, 40,000 Vietnamese people (mainly peasant women) work to repair the damage and keep supplies moving.

Key words booby trap; chemical weapons

COMMENT

Guerrilla and jungle warfare saps the morale of the American troops.

Forty per cent of American troops are drafted (conscripted). They only serve for one year so they are inexperienced. In contrast, Viet Cong fighters are usually experienced, they are on home ground and they are totally dedicated to their cause.

SOURCE 7

I remember sitting at this wretched little outpost one day with a couple of my sergeants. This one sergeant of mine said, 'You know Lieutenant, I don't see how we're ever going to win this.' And I said, 'Well, Sarge, I'm not supposed to say this to you as your officer – but I don't either.' So there was this sense that we just couldn't see what could be done to defeat these people.

Philip Caputo, a lieutenant in the Marine Corps in Vietnam in 1965–66.

SOURCE 8

A scene from the Tet Offensive, January 1968. The Viet Cong launch a huge attack on Saigon and many other major towns and cities in South Vietnam. They are beaten and suffer heavy losses.

COMMENT

We beat back the Tet Offensive easily, but it has shocked the American public. They thought the Viet Cong were almost beaten, then they launched this attack.

COMMENT

Viet Cong losses are much higher than American losses. However, the Viet Cong are prepared to accept heavy losses. The American public will not.

SOURCE 9

Vietnamese civilians massacred by American troops on a search and destroy mission at My Lai, March 1968. The search and destroy missions aim to find and kill Viet Cong fighters.

COMMENT

It is hard for the search and destroy missions to tell the difference between ordinary peasants and Viet Cong fighters. Civilians get killed by mistake. This massacre has shocked the American public and weakened support for the war.

Try to remember four key points from these two pages:

- two effects of the Vietnam War in Vietnam
- two main reasons why there was opposition to the war in the USA.

Why did the USA pull its soldiers out of Vietnam?

Key word veteran

By 1968, the war was a stalemate. The USA could not defeat the Viet Cong. The Viet Cong could not drive out the USA.

However, American public opinion could. As public support for the war drained away in the USA, the President began to scale down the American forces. By the end of 1973, they had left Vietnam completely. Why did the Americans pull out?

The media war

Newspaper and television journalists covered every aspect of the war in detail. The media brought the reality of war into people's living rooms.

- They reported the effects of American bombing on the Vietnamese people – they showed North Vietnamese civilians dead or homeless.
- They interviewed prisoners of war who had been tortured, and showed prisoners of war being executed.
- They filmed the effects of chemical weapons used by the USA.

SOURCE 10

The memorial to American Vietnam War VETERANS in Washington DC.

The media also showed the impact of the war on the USA itself:

- the body bags containing dead Americans. By the end of the war, the USA had suffered over 200,000 dead and wounded
- the cost of the war to the American economy – $20 billion a year.

The peace movement

It is no surprise that, with no end in sight, public opinion began to turn against the war. Students in American universities held demonstrations all over the country. They taunted President Lyndon Johnson with the chant:

'Hey, Hey, LBJ, how many kids did you kill today?'

We are not winning and can't win.

What we are doing to the Vietnamese people is immoral.

We don't want any more of our young people killed.

This war is tearing the USA apart and costing us dear.

Why are we trying to defeat Communism anyway? If they want to be Communist, let them.

Many of these students became 'draft dodgers' – they refused to serve in Vietnam. In November 1969, around 700,000 protesters marched on Washington DC. This was the largest single protest in American history. In March 1970, National Guard troopers shot dead four student protesters. This caused public uproar.

Not only students protested. In October 1969, about one million Americans joined a nationwide anti-war protest. Fifty members of the US Congress took part. Protest became more intense the following year. In April 1971, 2300 Vietnam War veterans held an anti-war protest in Washington.

The peace movement brought together all sorts of people who had different reasons for wanting the USA to get out of Vietnam, as you can see on the left.

Not all Americans supported the peace movement, of course. But it was obvious that the USA was not united in support of the Vietnam War.

SOURCE 11

END T
WA
IN VIET
SOCIAL

The Washington DC protest march, November 1969.

Activity

Many American school pupils got involved in the anti-war protests in the 1960s. You and your friends have got together to write a leaflet called 'Why the USA should leave Vietnam'. What will you say?

Try to remember two factors that helped the USA pull its forces out of Vietnam.

How did the USA get out of Vietnam?

Key words détente; honour; independence; orbit; summit

The USA was looking for a way to get out of Vietnam as early as 1968. This aim became stronger when Richard Nixon became President in 1969.

- From April 1969 to late 1971, he built up the South Vietnamese army. This policy was called 'Vietnamisation'. At the same time, Nixon steadily withdrew American troops (200,000 of them by 1972).
- Nixon's Secretary of State, Henry Kissinger, began talks with North Vietnam in 1969.
- Nixon pushed South Vietnam to compromise with the North. He also asked the USSR and China to get North Vietnam to compromise with the South.
- In March 1973, North and South Vietnam signed a peace agreement in Paris. The last American forces left Vietnam.

The fall of South Vietnam

Nixon was pleased with the deal. He talked about 'peace with HONOUR'. However, the peace did not last. North Vietnam invaded the South in December 1974. In April 1975, the South Vietnam capital, Saigon, fell to the Communists.

Détente after Vietnam

After the war, relationships between the superpowers improved. The USA was counting the cost of Vietnam. It was more cautious and was also trying to cut back on arms spending. China and the USSR fell out with each other and so both tried to get on better terms with the USA. Arms spending went down. Soviet and American leaders met at so-called 'SUMMIT' meetings. The Cold War seemed to be thawing. This period is known as DÉTENTE.

SOURCE 12

A cartoon from the *Daily Telegraph*, 30 January 1973.

SOURCE 13

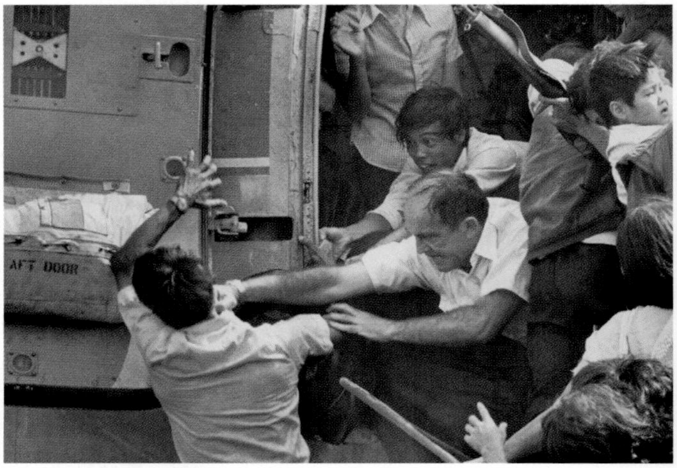

A scene at the American embassy in Saigon, April 1975. An embassy official is punching a man in the face to make him let go of the helicopter.

Activity

1. Sources 12 and 13 seem to contrast with President Nixon's claim that the USA achieved peace with honour. Explain fully how and why they do not support his claim.
2. Put yourself in Nixon's position and try to defend your claim. You could refer to:
   - why it was important to get out of Vietnam
   - what you think the main American achievements were in Vietnam.

Review task

Did containment work?

1 In Chapters 8 and 9, you have found out quite a lot about the American policy of containment. Now that you are an expert, read Sources 14–17 and fit the missing words into the correct source. Your teacher can tell you if you are right.

Missing words

lost another round
ORBIT
free peoples
INDEPENDENCE
us
our part of the world
defence
Chinese
symbol
other parts of the world
armed

SOURCE 14

It must be the policy of the United states to support [......] who are resisting take-over by [......] minorities inside their own countries or by outside pressures . . . The free peoples of the world look to [......] for support in protecting their freedom.

President Truman setting out the idea of containment in 1947.

SOURCE 16

Korea is a [......] to the watching world. If we allow Korea to fall within the Soviet [......], the world will feel we have [......] in our match with the Soviet Union.

The US State Department commenting on Korea in 1950.

SOURCE 17

If Khrushchev's going to get this mean on this one in [......], then we have no choice.

President Kennedy talking to his brother about Khrushchev's decision to put missiles in Cuba in October 1962.

SOURCE 15

First is the simple fact that South Vietnam, a member of the free world family, is striving to preserve its [......] from Communist attack. Second, South-East Asia has great significance in the forward [......] of the USA. For Hanoi, the immediate object is limited: conquest of the south and national unification. For Peking, however, Hanoi's victory would only be a first step towards [......] dominance of South-East Asia and towards exploitation of the new strategy in [......].

Robert McNamara, US Defence Secretary, speaking in 1964. Hanoi was the capital of North Vietnam; Peking was the capital of China.

2 Read through your completed Sources 14–17 carefully. Make a list of the concerns of American politicians between 1947 and the early 1960s.

3 Now look back over at least two of the three main Cold War confrontations you have studied in this chapter. For each one, fill out a table like this.

	Case study ...	Case study ...
Why was the USA concerned?		
What was American policy?		
What aspects of each event would the USA see as a success?		
What aspects would the USA see as a failure?		
Was this event a success or a failure for containment?		

4 Finally, decide whether you think the USA's policy of containment was an effective policy in 1947–75 and write two sentences to explain your view.

10 Eastern Europe 1953–89

10.1 How did Stalin and Khrushchev control Eastern Europe?

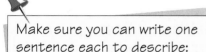

Make sure you can write one sentence each to describe:

- how Stalin ruled Eastern Europe
- one way in which Khrushchev appeared to be different to Stalin in 1955.

Key words **de-Stalinisation; loyal; luxury goods; NATO; peaceful coexistence; political prisoner; secret police; Warsaw Pact**

Key
Territory taken over by USSR at end of Second World War
Soviet-dominated Communist governments
Other Communist governments
USSR
Berlin
EAST GERMANY
Warsaw
POLAND
WEST GERMANY
Prague
CZECHOSLOVAKIA
FRANCE
SWITZERLAND
AUSTRIA
Budapest
HUNGARY
ROMANIA
Bucharest
Belgrade
YUGOSLAVIA
BULGARIA
Black Sea
ITALY
ALBANIA
GREECE
TURKEY
0 200 km
Scale

Stalin – tough guy?

Stalin ruled the USSR and Eastern Europe with an iron grip.

Each of the Eastern European states was supposed to be just a friendly ally of the USSR. Each state was supposed to be run by its own national Communist Party.

In fact, it was rather different. Stalin controlled the leaders, the economies, the SECRET POLICE and just about everything else in Eastern Europe. Only Yugoslavia was at all independent.

Activity

Which of the two leaders, Stalin or Khrushchev, do you think might have said the following?

> We must help the poor eat well, dress well and live well.

> Everyone imposes his own system (on a country) as far as his army has power to do so.

> You will do what I say, and you will appoint who I want.

> We must work together to protect each other from capitalist aggression.

> Peaceful coexistence between different systems of government is possible.

Support your choice with evidence from these two pages.

The Warsaw Pact

One topic appearing throughout this chapter is the WARSAW PACT – so let's be clear what this was. Just like Stalin, Khrushchev believed that the security of the USSR depended on keeping the countries of Eastern Europe strong and on the side of the USSR.

In 1949, anti-Communist countries had set up an alliance called the North Atlantic Treaty Organisation (NATO). In 1955, Khrushchev forced all of the Eastern European states to join a Communist alliance called the Warsaw Pact.
All members promised that if one state was threatened, they would help to defend it. The USSR was determined to keep all countries LOYAL to this pact. So to keep the alliance strong, Soviet troops were based in each country.

Khrushchev – nice guy?

Stalin died in 1953. In 1955, Nikita Khrushchev became leader of the USSR.

At first he seemed very different from Stalin:

- Khrushchev talked about 'PEACEFUL COEXISTENCE' – Communist countries living in peace with Western countries.
- He criticised Stalin for being a harsh dictator and released thousands of POLITICAL PRISONERS in the USSR.
- He brought in economic reforms to give people more food and LUXURY GOODS.

These policies were called 'DE-STALINISATION'. However, no one quite knew how far Khrushchev would go. Over the next 25 years, different Eastern European countries tested out the USSR to find out just how much freedom it would give them. On pages 198–211, you are going to find out how the Soviet Union dealt with protests in Hungary, Berlin, Czechoslovakia and Poland.

10.2 Why did Khrushchev send tanks into Hungary in 1956?

Check that you understand:

- two reasons why the Hungarians rebelled
- how Khrushchev reacted at first, then how he changed his mind.

Key words **collectivisation; freedom of speech**

Trouble in Hungary

In October 1956, anti-Soviet protests erupted in Hungary.

- Hungarians were fed up with their leader, Gerö, who had been chosen by the Soviet Union. They wanted to choose their own leader.
- There were thousands of Soviet troops in Hungary. The protesters wanted them out.
- Communist Party officials controlled everything from the police to factories to schools. The protesters wanted more say in how these were run.
- The AVO (the secret police) arrested anyone who criticised the government. The protesters wanted more FREEDOM OF SPEECH.
- Hungary's factories produced goods for the USSR instead of things Hungarians wanted to buy. The protesters demanded economic reforms to bring about a better standard of living.
- All farms were owned or controlled by the government and told what to grow. Their produce was also owned and distributed by the government. People wanted an end to this system called COLLECTIVISATION. Farmers wanted their land back.

Activity

Gerö,
get out!

1 The crowd in this picture has pulled down a statue of Stalin.
   a) Do you think this really happened? Was the crowd brave enough to do this or has the artist gone too far?
   b) How could you check if this is true?

2 Look at the list above of Hungarian complaints in 1956. Work with a partner to draw up some protest banners that might have appeared in the crowd. Remember, protest banners are usually two or three words long. For example, one banner might say 'Gerö, get out!'

Khrushchev's responses

25 October – crush it!

Gerö asked Khrushchev for the use of Soviet troops to crush the demonstrations. On 25 October, Khrushchev sent 30,000 troops to do just that. However, things did not go well. There was fierce fighting, and some of the troops seemed to sympathise with the protesters.

28 October – give in!

Khrushchev changed his approach. He sacked Gerö and appointed Imre Nagy as Hungary's new leader. Nagy was definitely the people's choice. He promised reforms in Hungary and this made the Hungarians happy. Nagy also promised to be a loyal ally to Moscow, which made Khrushchev happy. On 28 October, Khrushchev ordered Soviet troops to pull out of Hungary. However, he increased the number of Soviet troops on the Hungarian border.

Activity

Imagine Khrushchev is writing in his private diary. What might he have written about:

a) the day he got the request from Gerö (Was he in two minds over whether to help Gerö?)
b) the day he ordered in the troops (What did he expect to happen?)
c) the day he got the news of what had happened (Was he surprised, worried, angry? What might be in his mind to do next?)

1 Khrushchev often found himself in a no-win situation over Hungary. Look at his actions at the end of October 1956. How would his actions be seen by:

- the Hungarians
- a Soviet politician who believed in Stalin's way of doing things?

SOURCE 1

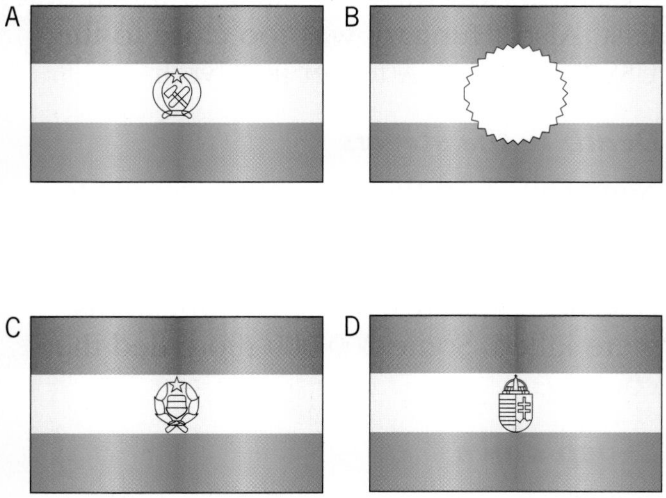
A
B
C
D

These four flags tell Hungary's story since the Second World War. Flag A is the Hungarian flag that the Communists introduced when they took power after the war. Flag B shows the changes the Hungarians made to the flag during the uprising in 1956. Flag C is the Hungarian flag after the Communists regained control, and Flag D is the flag after Communist rule ended in 1989.

SOURCE 2

Hungarians standing on a fallen statue in the centre of Budapest, 1956.

Test yourself to see if you can remember:

- two important changes brought in by Nagy
- two reasons why Khrushchev sent tanks into Hungary.

Key words clamp down; imperialist; rebellion

1 Make a list of all the actions taken by the Hungarians in October 1956.
2 Explain why it was amazing that Khrushchev accepted these actions.
3 Explain why some Soviet leaders were worried.
4 Do you think Khrushchev was a decisive or an indecisive leader?

Nagy's new Hungary

Nagy set about reforming Hungary. He introduced free elections so that non-Communists could try to get elected. He started giving land back to farmers and he got rid of the secret police.

Ordinary Hungarians began to set up their own local councils and took control of the police, factories and schools.

Khrushchev gives the go-ahead . . .

Amazingly, Khrushchev made an official statement on 30 October agreeing to what was happening.

. . . others are not so sure!

However, behind the scenes, many Soviet leaders were worried. They thought Nagy was being used by the Americans, or by opponents of Communism in Hungary, or by both!

Communist leaders of other countries in Eastern Europe were worried that the Hungarian protest would spread to their own countries if no action was taken.

SOURCE 3

The centre of Budapest, 1956.

What about the Warsaw Pact?

On 1 November, Imre Nagy declared Hungary to be a neutral country. He made it clear that Hungary was pulling out of the Warsaw Pact. This action made Khrushchev and others in the USSR sure that events in Hungary were part of an anti-Soviet plot. (In fact, there was no plot, but Khrushchev did not know what we know now.)

Will the USA help?

On 3 November, Soviet troops and tanks moved back into Hungary. Nagy called for help from the USA, but none came. The Western powers were already caught up in a dispute over the Suez canal in the Middle East. Also, Hungary was too close to the USSR for the USA to get involved.

Death in the streets

Nagy called on the Hungarian people to resist the Soviet forces. Hard fighting followed. There were over 2000 Soviet casualties and around 4000 Hungarians were killed. Some 200,000 more fled the country.

Clamp-down

A new Hungarian leader, Kádár, took control. He was backed by the USSR. In the months that followed, he CLAMPED DOWN on the REBELLION. Around 35,000 Hungarians were arrested and 300 were executed, including Imre Nagy.

Focus task

Why did Khrushchev send tanks into Hungary in 1956?

In December 1959, the Communist government in Hungary published a report on the events of 1956. Here is a summary of what it said.

Factor that caused the violence of 1956	Importance of the factor according to the Communists' report
Actions of the Hungarian governments before 1956	Essential factor
The actions of Imre Nagy	Very serious factor
Actions of opponents of Communism inside Hungary	The second most important factor
Actions of international IMPERALISTS, led by the USA, intended to stir up trouble	The biggest single factor

Look carefully at the conclusions of the report and the information on pages 198–200. Decide how far you agree with the report's findings. Draw up a table like this:

Factor	Evidence	Importance	Explanation

1 Look at each factor and note down any evidence from the last three pages that supports the view that it was a factor.
2 Decide whether you agree with the report's view on how important it was. Explain its importance in column 4.
3 Add new rows to your table listing any other factors that you think the report missed out – for example, the actions of the USSR or Khrushchev's de-Stalinisation policies.
4 Rearrange your new list of factors in order of importance. You could use a table like this:

Factors (in order of importance)	How/why this factor caused the violence of 1956	Evidence that supports the view that this was a cause of violence

Extension

5 Write your own report on why there was such violence in Hungary in 1956. Include all of the factors in your table. Remember to say how important you think each factor was.

Focus task

In the rest of this chapter, you are going to investigate three more case studies of Soviet control of Eastern Europe. Based on what you have read about Hungary, how do you think the Soviet Union will deal with each of the following situations?

Berlin 1961
In the heart of Communist East Germany is capitalist West Berlin. This city has always been a worry – now it is getting dangerous. It's full of American troops. The capitalist countries are pouring money into it to make it a boom town. The workers of East Germany look on jealously. Many of them want to leave East Germany to live in West Berlin where they can enjoy a much higher standard of living.

Czechoslovakia 1968
A new Prime Minister has been elected. He is a Communist and is loyal to the Soviet Union. But he has said that farmers, not Communist Party officials, should decide what crops to grow. He has allowed Czech journalists to interview political leaders on TV and radio and ask them awkward questions. What will the Soviet Union do?

Poland 1980
An illegal trade union has been set up, which has organised a wave of strikes all over Poland. The strike leaders are calling for more pay; a better standard of living; an end to censorship; workers to get the same welfare benefits as police and Communist Party workers; church services to be broadcast on radio and TV; workers to elect their own factory managers.

Write your ideas of how the Soviet Union will respond in columns 2 and 3 of a chart like this. Keep it and see if you were right. Then fill out column 4.

Situation	I think the Soviet Union will . . .	Explanation	What actually happened
Berlin			
Czechoslovakia			
Poland			

10.3 Why did Khrushchev build the Berlin Wall in 1961?

You need to be able to give:

- two reasons why Khrushchev built the Berlin Wall
- an explanation of each reason.

Key words **barricade; permit**

What was the Berlin Wall?

At the end of the Second World War, the Allies divided Berlin between them (see page 162). The USSR controlled East Berlin and the Americans, British and French controlled West Berlin. There was a border between the two sections of the city, but there was no wall. Berliners could travel back and forth between East and West. Many worked in the West and lived in the East; a few did the opposite. It was one of the few places in Europe where there was free access between the Communist world and the capitalist world.

Early in the morning of 13 August 1961, Soviet workmen arrived at the edge of the Soviet sector. They unloaded wood and barbed wire. Metre by metre, they built a wood and wire BARRICADE all along the border. By the end of the day, the city was split. Border guards had orders to shoot anyone who tried to cross without a PERMIT.

Within a week, buildings that lay on the Soviet side of the border had their windows bricked up. Within a month, the barbed wire fence was being replaced by a brick and concrete wall. In a very short time, the wall had high watch towers and machine-gun posts with armed guards, dogs and even minefields.

SOURCE 1A

The very early stages of the Berlin Wall, summer 1961.

SOURCE 1B

The Berlin Wall six to nine months after Source 1A.

How did people react to the wall?

Some people in East Berlin panicked. There was a scramble throughout the first day to get to the West. Within a week, there was a casualty. Rudolf Urban died trying to jump across the wall from an upstairs window. Many more deaths would follow.

West Berliners got pretty worried, too. It looked like the Soviet Union was squaring up for a fight. Khrushchev had already warned the Americans to get out of Berlin or face a war. This looked like one step towards it. West Berliners held a huge rally on 17 August calling on the American President, John F Kennedy, to keep troops in Berlin and not give in to Soviet bullying. Kennedy reassured them. In fact, he sent 1500 extra troops to the city.

Tension mounted; people waited; the world watched. On the tensest day – 27 October – Soviet and US tanks drew up on either side of the wall. They were only 100 metres away from turning a Cold War into a Hot War. But nothing happened. No shots were fired and the tanks backed off. The Americans did not try to reopen the border.

A tense stalemate followed. Kennedy said: 'It's not a very nice solution, but a wall is a hell of a lot better than a war.' And 28 years later, the wall was still there.

SOURCE 2

The tension rose rapidly because this was Americans confronting Russians. It wasn't East Germans. There was live ammunition in the tanks on both sides. It was an unexpected, sudden confrontation that in my opinion was the closest the Russians and the Americans came to going to war in the entire Cold War period.

The views of Colonel Jim Attwood of the US army based in Berlin. Attwood was describing the events of 27 October 1961 when Soviet and American tanks faced each other.

SOURCE 3

Bernauer Straße

East Berlin and French West Berlin police confront each other over a gap blown in the Berlin Wall by explosive laid on the East Berlin side, May 1962.

Why did Khrushchev build the wall?

The wall caused enormous and lasting tension between the USA and the USSR. Some people at the time thought that it might even spark off a full-scale nuclear war. So why did Khrushchev take such a huge risk? Here are two possible explanations:

- to keep the East Germans in
- to warn the West Germans and Americans to stay out.

1 This will stop East Germans leaving East Germany.
2 This will stop the capitalists trying to interfere in the affairs of East Germany. You have to act tough.

Focus task

Why did Khrushchev build the Berlin Wall?

You have two possible explanations why Khrushchev built the Berlin Wall. There is evidence to support them both. Unfortunately, it is all scraps, but sometimes that's all historians have to work with!

1 Look at the scraps of evidence and decide which explanation each scrap supports. A sorting grid will help you.

Explanation 1		Explanation 2	
Points for	**Points against**	**Points for**	**Points against**

Between 1948 and 1961, one sixth of the population of East Germany (2.8 million people) left Communist East Germany and fled to West Germany via Berlin.

In 1955, West Germany joined NATO and began to rearm.

In 1961, West German leader Konrad Adenauer called for East and West Germany to be united again.

At a meeting in Vienna in June 1961, Khrushchev told President Kennedy to pull American troops out of Berlin altogether or risk war.

Khrushchev wanted to strengthen his hold on East Germany. American forces based in West Berlin threatened that control.

Most historians think that Khrushchev was bluffing at the Vienna meeting! It was the first time he had met Kennedy, who had been President for only four months. Khrushchev wanted to test him.

Living and working conditions in West Germany were far better for most people than they were in East Germany.

Most people fleeing Communist East Germany were young, skilled workers or educated professionals, such as teachers, lawyers and doctors. East Germany needed these people to make its own economy successful.

10.4 Czechoslovakia 1968: a repeat of 1956?

From this section and pages 198–201, you need to be able to explain:

- two ways in which 1956 and 1968 were similar
- two ways in which they were different.

Key words Brezhnev Doctrine; planner

The Brezhnev Doctrine

Leonid Brezhnev replaced Khrushchev as leader of the Soviet Union in 1964. Brezhnev was not a reformer like Khrushchev. He believed that:

- the USSR should keep tight control of Eastern Europe
- Communist countries should be one-party states
- nothing should interfere with Communist Party control of people's lives
- Communist countries should be loyal to the Warsaw Pact.

His views later became known as the BREZHNEV DOCTRINE. These views faced their first test when Alexander Dubček became leader of Czechoslovakia in 1968.

Dubček

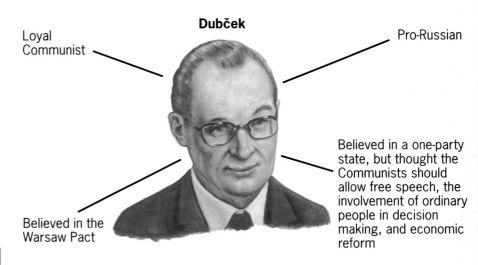

Loyal Communist
Pro-Russian
Believed in a one-party state, but thought the Communists should allow free speech, the involvement of ordinary people in decision making, and economic reform
Believed in the Warsaw Pact

Activity

Imagine you could read Brezhnev's personal diary. What might he have written in his diary on these dates?

Here are some suggested starters:

January 1968: New leader in Czechoslovakia called Dubček. I think . . .
February 1968: Dubček just made a speech to Czech farmers. I . . .
April 1968: This Dubček character is . . .

Dubček's reforms

Dubček was soon putting his beliefs into action.

- In his first speech (February 1968), he told farmers that **they** should decide what crops to grow – not Communist Party economic PLANNERS.
- In April 1968, he published the Action Programme. This gave more power to ordinary workers and managers in factories.
- He allowed Czech journalists to interview political leaders on TV and radio. The journalists asked very awkward questions about whether the USSR's influence was good for Czechoslovakia.

These events are known as 'the Prague Spring'.

Communist reactions

You might think that Dubček's views were quite reasonable. However, at the time, this kind of thing was unheard of in Eastern Europe.

Communist leaders in other Eastern European countries urged Brezhnev to stop Dubček. If Czechoslovakia had these freedoms, then people in Poland, Hungary and East Germany would want them as well.

Soviet politicians were also alarmed. Could they trust Dubček when he said he supported the Warsaw Pact? Could they control Dubček if he got rid of the secret police? Were the Americans supporting Dubček?

Brezhnev held a crisis meeting with Dubček between 29 July and 1 August. He demanded that Dubček clamp down on the media. Dubček agreed some restrictions. Then on 9–11 August, Dubček welcomed Yugoslavia's Marshal Tito to Czechoslovakia on a visit. This was not very clever. Tito was a Communist leader, but he refused to follow the orders of the USSR. The visit made Brezhnev wonder whether Dubček was going to behave like Tito.

The tanks roll in . . . again

On 21 August 1968, Brezhnev decided that enough was enough. He sent tanks and paratroopers into Prague. Half a million troops (including forces from East Germany and Hungary) soon followed. Moscow radio claimed that the Czech government had invited the Soviet troops. The Soviet troops thought they were helping Czechoslovakia to defeat American and anti-Communist forces, which were threatening the country.

Dubček called for calm. There was some resistance to the Soviet forces, but not as much as in Hungary in 1956. Estimates put the deaths at between 80 and 200.

SOURCE 1

Czechs arguing with Soviet tank commanders in Prague, August 1968.

The aftermath

Dubček and all his ministers were arrested and taken to Moscow. Dubček was replaced by Gustáv Husák whom Brezhnev trusted to follow the Soviet line. Dubček was given a new job in Turkey but, two years later, he was thrown out of the party and carefully removed from Communist history (see Source 2).

Husák restored strict party control over all aspects of Czech life. Soviet troops were placed in the country. The Czech people did not resist, or at least not openly. But in January 1969, the whole country ground to a halt, to show how people felt. The Czech ice hockey team beat the USSR. It was a small victory, but the massive celebrations showed the bitterness Czechs felt towards Brezhnev and the USSR.

SOURCE 2

This photograph was changed by Communist censors after Dubček was thrown out of the Communist Party. Dubček is marked with an arrow in the first picture.

Focus task

How similar were events in Hungary in 1956 and Czechoslovakia in 1968?

1 Look back over your work on Hungary (pages 198–201) and Czechoslovakia (pages 206–8). Complete a table like this to compare the two rebellions.

Feature of the rebellion	Hungary 1956	Czechoslovakia 1968
Aims of rebels		
Attitude of rebels to Soviet control		
Attitude of rebels to Warsaw Pact		
Attitude of Soviet leader towards the rebels		
Attitude of other Warsaw Pact countries		
Action taken by USSR		
Resistance to Soviet action		
Treatment of rebels		
Clamp-down		

2 Underline or highlight the similarities between Hungary and Czechoslovakia in one colour. Mark the differences between them in another colour.

10.5 How important was Solidarity in Poland?

Key words **incompetence; privilege**

From this section, aim to explain:

- two reasons why Solidarity became important
- one reason why it fell
- two reasons why you think it was an important organisation.

The rise of Solidarity

In the 1970s, Poland was heavily in debt. Poland's Communist leader, Gierek, tried to solve the problem by raising food prices and holding down wages. He hoped that this would bring the government extra income so that it could pay off its debts.

This may look like a sensible solution to the crisis, but workers in Poland did not see it that way. They felt that:

- government INCOMPETENCE caused the crisis in the first place
- most government leaders and police officials had luxury flats, private health care and other PRIVILEGES
- if workers had to pay for the country's problems, they should have a true say in how it was run.

The workers' unhappiness showed in the shipyards in the city of Gdansk in 1980. Heavy industries such as coal, steel and shipbuilding were very important in Poland, and they employed thousands of workers. The Gdansk shipyards became the centre of protest for all these workers. They set up a committee to demand a say in how the economy was run. Then in September, it joined with similar groups from across Poland to form a trade union called Solidarity. The union was controlled by the workers, not by the Communist Party.

Solidarity's demands

Solidarity soon became massively popular. It had a well-liked leader, Lech Walesa, and the full support of the Catholic Church, which was the most powerful organisation in Poland apart from the Communist Party. By January 1981, Solidarity had 9.4 million members. It looked as though Solidarity had real power – it was almost an alternative government. For example, Solidarity demanded that Gierek resign, and he did! He was followed by Kania. Solidarity demanded to be recognised as a legal organisation, and Kania did so.

In September 1981, a Solidarity CONGRESS was held. This was pretty amazing – a non-Communist organisation holding a huge congress in the middle of a Communist country! Speakers at the congress called on workers in other countries to set up their own unions.

CHURCH SERVICES TO BE BROADCAST ON RADIO AND TV
SOLIDARNOŚĆ
WORKERS, NOT COMMUNIST PARTY, TO ELECT FACTORY MANAGERS
WORKERS TO GET SAME WELFARE BENEFITS AS POLICE AND PARTY WORKERS
BETTER PAY
NO CENSORSHIP

SOURCE 1

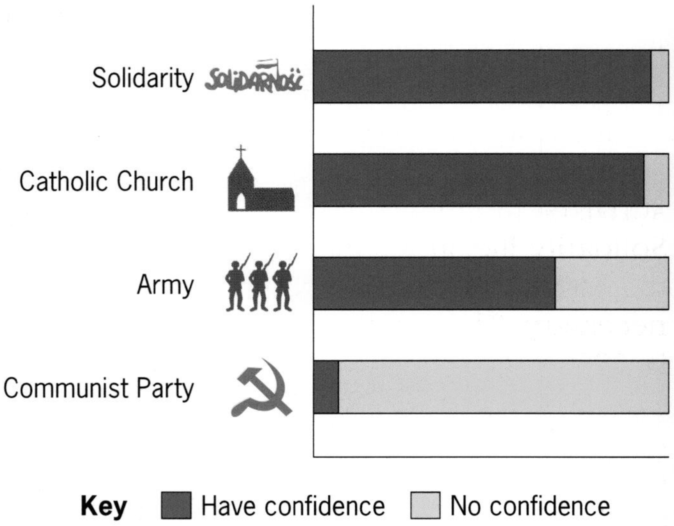
Solidarity
Catholic Church
Army
Communist Party
Key
Have confidence
No confidence

The results of an opinion poll in Poland, November 1981. People were asked whether they had confidence in key organisations in Poland. It is known that 11 per cent of those polled were Communist Party members.

Anti-Communist countries loved Solidarity. They enjoyed any development that challenged the Communists. There were millions of Americans who had Polish ancestors and they strongly supported Solidarity. Money flooded in. The Solidarity logo became a popular car sticker all over Western Europe! Walesa was interviewed on international news programmes as if he was a major political figure.

Activity

Why did Solidarity become an important force in Poland?

This table shows some reasons why Solidarity became a major force.

1 Complete your own copy of the table.
2 Choose one factor that you think is most important and explain your choice.

Factor	How this contributed to the rise of Solidarity
Government policies	
Privileges of government officials	
Religion	
Support from Western states	

Key words **activist; congress; martial law**

The fall of Solidarity

Unfortunately for Solidarity, it was not as strong as it thought. In October 1981, Poland got another new leader, General Jaruzelski, head of the army. Brezhnev told him that he would send Soviet troops into Poland if he did not clamp down on Solidarity.

Jaruzelski declared MARTIAL LAW in December 1981. He arrested Lech Walesa and around 10,000 other Solidarity ACTIVISTS. In January 1982, Poland's Parliament declared Solidarity illegal. Its members did not resist. They knew that the Soviet army would come in and help the Polish army if necessary. There was no violence as there was in Hungary in 1956 or Czechoslovakia in 1968.

As an organisation, Solidarity simply disappeared, although its former members continued to oppose the Communist regime in different ways – for example, they ran an illegal radio station.

However, the rise and fall of Solidarity carried two simple messages for all Communist governments in Eastern Europe.

- Many ordinary working people were fed up with living under Communist rule.
- Communist rule depended on Soviet military power. If the USSR stopped backing the Communist governments in Eastern Europe, they would crumble.

Focus task

How important was Solidarity?

1 You are planning a one-hour documentary about Soviet control of Eastern Europe 1948–81. Your programme should cover:
- Hungary 1956
- Berlin 1961
- Czechoslovakia 1968
- Poland 1980–81.

Work in a group to decide how much time you will give to each topic.

2 Write one paragraph to explain your decision.

Extension

3 Bad news! Your programme has to be cut to 30 minutes. You must either cut all topics by half or cut two topics altogether. Which option will you choose? If you cut two topics, which will you cut? To help you think this through, draw up a chart like this for each topic.

Reasons X is important	Reasons X is not important

4 Write another paragraph to explain your decision.

10.6 Why did Communism collapse in 1989?

From this section, you need to be able to explain:

- why some people think 'PEOPLE POWER' brought about the collapse of Communism
- two pieces of evidence that support this view.

Key words free travel; people power

You now know a lot about the Cold War.

- You have seen how it started (Chapter 8).
- You have seen how the Americans tried to contain the spread of Communism (Chapter 9).
- You have seen how the Soviet Union tried to contain the spread of capitalism and democracy in Eastern Europe (Chapter 10).

You now come to a story that ties it all together and finishes it off as well – the collapse of the Communist regimes of Eastern Europe.

Factor 1: people power

SOURCE 1

BERLIN WALL
Tom Johnston

"Ten years we've been tunnelling and finally we're FREE!"

A cartoon from the *News of The World*, 12 November 1989.

SOURCE 3

151
8

East Germans escaping to the West by train from Czechoslovakia.

SOURCE 2

A scene in Berlin, November 1989. East German border guards watch as East Germans smash huge chunks out of the wall with sledgehammers.

SOURCE 4

May
Hungary opens its borders with non-Communist Austria. Hungarians already have the right to FREE TRAVEL. However, many East Germans on holiday in Hungary start using this route to get to West Germany.

June–August
Protests against Communist rule in Poland continue throughout the summer. In August, Communist party leaders agree to truly free elections. Solidarity wins 99 out of 100 seats in Poland's Senate. Lech Walesa becomes Eastern Europe's first non-Communist leader since the Second World War.

September
Thousands more East Germans flee to West Germany through Hungary and Czechoslovakia. East German leader Erich Honecker asks Hungary and Czechoslovakia to close their borders. They refuse.

October
Soviet leader Mikhail Gorbachev visits East Germany and makes a key speech. He urges all Eastern European leaders to reform their countries. He makes it clear that the USSR will not use troops to keep them in power.

Hungary declares itself to be a democratic republic rather than a Communist republic.

November
Thousands of East Germans march on the Berlin Wall. Honecker orders troops to shoot at the demonstrators, but they refuse. Border guards join the crowds.

Giant demonstrations (over 350,000 people) in Czechoslovakia force the Communist leaders to resign.

Czechoslovakia opens its borders with the West. It also holds free elections.

December
Massive demonstrations lead to the downfall of the Communist regimes in Bulgaria and Romania.

NORWAY
FINLAND
N
SWEDEN
ESTONIA
RUSSIA
LATVIA
LITHUANIA
BELORUSSIA
Berlin
EAST GERMANY
Warsaw
POLAND
Prague
UKRAINE
WEST GERMANY
CZECHOSLOVAKIA
AUSTRIA
Budapest
HUNGARY
ROMANIA
Bucharest
Black Sea
Belgrade
YUGOSLAVIA
BULGARIA
ITALY
ALBANIA
TURKEY
0 200 km
Scale
Key
Territory taken over by USSR at end of Second World War
Soviet-dominated Communist governments
Other Communist governments

The collapse of Communism in Eastern Europe, 1989.

1. Source 1 is a joke, but it is based on real events. Which parts are true and which parts are over the top?
2. Choose five words that you think describe the mood in Source 2.
3. What does Source 2 tell you about how people felt about the wall? Explain your answer.
4. Source 3 shows people wanting to escape from East Germany. What does this say about people's attitude to their own country and its leaders?

Focus task

Why did Communism collapse?

When Communist regimes collapsed in 1989, people tried to think why. Many newspapers, journals and TV programmes came up with the same conclusion – people power.

1. Look carefully at Sources 1–4. List any evidence that supports the idea that people power brought about the collapse of Communism.
2. Make a separate list of any other factors that seem to be important.

In this section, try to pinpoint two problems in the USSR which led to the USSR changing its mind about Eastern Europe.

1 Put yourself in the position of someone like Lech Walesa in the mid-1980s (see page 211). If you had known about the USSR's problems, would the knowledge have made you:
- worried
- hopeful
- both?

Explain your answer fully.

Factor 2: problems in the USSR

During the 1980s, big changes were taking place in the USSR.

- **Economic disaster:** its economy was in a mess. The USSR could not afford to keep huge numbers of troops in Eastern Europe.
- **Social problems:** its people faced huge problems, especially in housing and health. The USSR needed to spend money on these problems rather than on controlling Eastern Europe.
- **Political problems:** its leaders were mostly old men who were ill. The USSR needed new leaders and new ideas.

The USSR no longer wanted to hold on to Eastern Europe.

Factor 3: Mikhail Gorbachev

Mikhail Gorbachev became Soviet leader in 1985. He was totally different from previous Soviet leaders. He set out two main ideas:

Perestroika *(restructuring or reorganising the USSR)*
- He brought reforms to the Soviet economy.
- He increased spending on health and housing programmes.
- He made huge cuts in the USSR's military spending.

Glasnost *(freedom or openness)*
- He did not try to hide his country's problems.
- He made it clear to the USA that the USSR would no longer compete with the USA. He now felt that the USSR's security depended on good relations with the USA.
- He encouraged people in the USSR to speak out and to suggest new ways of running the economy and the country.

What did Gorbachev's reforms mean?

The USSR had always controlled Eastern Europe to provide a security zone. Gorbachev turned this idea on its head.

- He said that the USSR could not afford to have millions of troops in Eastern Europe to keep it Communist.
- He believed that Communist leaders in Eastern Europe should bring in reforms similar to those he had introduced in the USSR.
- He made it clear in 1989 that Soviet troops would not put down demonstrations in Eastern European countries.

Today, Gorbachev is still regarded as a hero in the USA, Western Europe and Eastern Europe. However, he is less well regarded in Russia. Many Russians see Gorbachev as the man who lost their empire. It is easy to see why. Gorbachev started a process of change that could not be stopped. In October 1990, East and West Germany became one country again. Within months, other parts of the USSR declared themselves to be independent countries. It started with the Baltic states, but the process soon spread to the Ukraine and the Muslim republics in the south of the USSR. On 25 December 1991, Gorbachev announced the break-up of the USSR and he stepped down from being leader.

2 Look back at Source 4 on page 213. Make a list of the events in Eastern Europe that seem to be affected by what Gorbachev did.

Activity

Look closely at Source 5. Write a paragraph explaining why Gorbachev should be 'Man of the Decade'.

SOURCE 5

JANUARY 1, 1990
$2.50
MAN OF THE DECADE
TIME
Mikhail
Gorbachev

The cover of *Time*, a US magazine, January 1990, naming Mikhail Gorbachev as Man of the 1980s.

SOURCE 6

If interviews with 'the man in the street' can be believed, the former Soviet peoples consider him a failure. History will be kinder. The Nobel Prize he received for ending the Cold War was well deserved. Every man, woman and child in this country should be eternally grateful. His statue should stand in the centre of every East European capital; for it was Gorbachev who allowed them their independence.

From a report on Gorbachev's speech of 25 December 1991, which appeared in the US newspaper, the *Boston Globe*.

Make it your goal to explain one way in which Ronald Reagan helped Gorbachev to change the Soviet Union.

Factor 4: President Ronald Reagan and other Western leaders

Ronald Reagan became US President in January 1981. He was President until 1988. He had only one policy about the USSR – get tough. He criticised its control over Eastern Europe. He also increased the USA's military spending by $32 billion. He then challenged the USSR to keep up with American arms spending.

Reagan was generally very popular with the American people. He also had the support of other Western leaders such as Britain's Prime Minister, Margaret Thatcher, and France's President Mitterand. Reagan was extremely anti-Communist.

Reagan's tough tactics increased the USSR's problems. But, in a way, Reagan helped Gorbachev.

- It was clear by the late 1980s that the USSR could not compete with American military spending. This helped Gorbachev to push through his military spending cuts.
- Reagan got on quite well with Gorbachev himself. They met at summit conferences and discussed many issues. As superpower relations improved, the USSR felt less threatened by the USA. This meant there was less need for the USSR to control Eastern Europe.

SOURCE 7

President Reagan and Mikhail Gorbachev at their first summit meeting in Geneva, November 1985. They met again in 1986, 1987 and 1988.

SOURCE 8

'YOU PUT YOUR RIGHT HAND IN...
...YOU PUT YOUR RIGHT HAND OUT...
...YOU PUT YOUR RIGHT HAND IN...
...AND YOU SHAKE IT ALL ABOUT!'
SUMMIT HOKEY COKEY

A cartoon called 'Summit Hokey Cokey', first published in the *Daily Telegraph*, 9 November 1985.

Focus task

Why did Communism collapse?

Work in small groups to prepare a 'cheat sheet' on this question. Imagine you are going to cheat in an essay test. You cannot take a textbook or pile of notes into the test so you will have to get everything you need to jog your memory on to one side of A4 paper or less.

1 Your cheat sheet should be organised in paragraphs or sections.

Divide your group so that you are all studying at least two factors from this list:

- people power
- problems in the USSR
- Mikhail Gorbachev
- Reagan and other Western leaders.

2 Now research your factors. Come back with notes and ideas on how important your factors were.

3 As a group, plan what you will put in each essay paragraph on each factor. Here is a suggested format:

Ask . . .	**What we will say**
What is the theme of this paragraph? For example, people power	One important reason why the Berlin Wall came down in 1989 was people power.
How is it helping to answer the question?	People power helped to bring down the wall in several ways . . .
How can we show we are not just making it up?	There are several examples that support our view. They include . . .

Repeat this process for each paragraph. There is no need to write out in full what you plan to say in the essay. If you use a word-processor for this exercise, you can revise your plan and print out spare copies!

4 Now here is an extra challenge! Some of these factors are connected.

Factor	**People power**	**Problems in the USSR**	**Gorbachev**	**Reagan and other Western leaders**
People power				
Problems in the USSR				
Mikhail Gorbachev				
Reagan and other Western leaders				

Use a format like this to:

- note down any connections you can see
- choose two connections you will write about in an extra paragraph on connections (use the same format for this new paragraph as you used in stage 3).

5 Now plan an introductory paragraph. Use the same format for this plan as you used in stage 3.

Obviously you can't use your cheat sheet in a real exam, but it will help you revise!

Glossary

ABDICATE to give up a throne for example German Kaiser Wilhelm gave up his throne in 1918

ACTIVIST person heavily involved in a movement, for example a member of the Nazi party would be a Nazi activist

AGENT person who works for another person or organisation, for example an intelligence agent works for a government

AGGRESSIVE using force or threats, for example when Italy attacked Greece in 1923

AIRSHIP large balloon filled with gas which was lighter than air so it flew. The best known example was the zeppelin

ALLIANCE deal between two countries to help each other

ALLIES countries which are in an alliance

ALLOTMENT a small patch of garden

ALLY country which is friendly towards another country

AMMUNITION bullets or shells

ANDERSON SHELTER shelter made from thin iron and covered in earth – used during the Second World War

ANSCHLUSS joining Austria and Germany together into one country

APPEASEMENT giving way to another person or country, for example Britain and France letting Hitler take over territories in the 1930s

ARMAMENT building up a stock of weapons

ARMISTICE short-term end to fighting before a final treaty is signed

ARMOURED CAR military vehicle which was protected by metal plates but was lighter and faster than a tank

ARMS RACE competition between two or more countries to build more weapons than their rivals

ARTILLERY heavy guns

ARYAN type of human which the Nazis believed to be the master race

ASOCIAL person who did not fit the Nazis' view of normal society (for example homosexuals)

ASSEMBLY LINE method of producing goods in a factory where each worker does only one task over and over

ATOMIC BOMB powerful bomb first used in 1945 by the USA against Japan

ATTRITION wearing down, for example tactics of killing large numbers of enemy soldiers in the First World War was known as attrition

'BACK YARD' area of influence of a country, for example Cuba was seen as being in America's back yard

BAIL OUT abandon a plane or ship

BARBED WIRE barricade used in the First World War to stop trenches being attacked by enemy soldiers

BARRACKS place where soldiers are based, and usually live and train

BARRAGE large number of shells fired by heavy guns

BARRICADE obstacle designed to stop people getting through

BATTALION an army unit made up of several regiments

BAYONET sharp knife attached to end of rifles

BENEFIT help, or good effect

BLACK MARKET buying and selling goods illegally during war-time

BLACKOUT shutting down all lights so that enemy aeroplanes could not see where they were or what they were attacking

BLAST effects of bombs or shells or other explosions

BLITZ name given to German air attacks on British cities in 1940–41

BLITZKREIG German tactics used in the Second World War involving fast-moving troops and vehicles

BLOCKADE stopping supplies getting through, for example the Royal Navy blockaded Germany in the First World War and stopped food and equipment getting to German ports

BOER WAR war between British government and farmers called Boers who lived in South Africa. Lasted from 1899–1902

BOLSHEVISM beliefs of the Bolsheviks or Communists in Russia in the period 1900–24

BOMBARDMENT attack by large numbers of heavy guns

BOOBY TRAP trip wire or similar device attached to explosive or blade designed to injure attackers, for example Viet Cong tunnels in the Vietnam War were booby trapped

BOOM good times for business and the economy

BORDER POST place between two countries where guards check passports, etc.

BOUNDARY line between two states or areas within states

BOYCOTT refusing to trade or have other kind of contact with a country

BREAKTHROUGH event which brings about important change

BREZHNEV DOCTRINE views of USSR leader Brezhnev in the 1960s which stated that Communist control in Eastern Europe could not be challenged

BULLETIN short programme which brings news

CAMOUFLAGE using paint or cloth or both to disguise men or equipment

CAMPAIGNER someone who tries to get something changed, for example Suffragettes campaigned for women to get the vote

CAPITALISM economic system in which companies and individuals trade freely and in which some do well and others do badly

CAVALRY soldiers on horseback

CEASEFIRE end to fighting

CENSOR government official who reads letters, newspapers, etc. and decides whether they are giving away valuable information

CENSORSHIP controlling information published in newspapers, films, etc.

CHANCELLOR important government minister. In Germany the Chancellor was the head of the government. In Britain the chancellor controlled finance.

CHEMICAL WEAPONS weapons like poison gas in the First World War or substances which killed leaves on trees in the Vietnam War

CIA Central Intelligence Agency – the organisation which ran the USA's spies

CIVIL DEFENCE looking after civilians and their homes and protecting them from dangers like air raids or nuclear war

CIVIL SERVICE organisation which takes measures passed by governments and actually puts them into operation

CIVIL WAR war between people who live in the same country

CLAMP DOWN action (usually by governments) to stop a group causing trouble, for example Provisional Government tried to clamp down on Bolsheviks in Russia in 1917

COALITION group of people or countries working together

COLLECTIVE SECURITY policy of the League of Nations in 1920s. The idea was that all nations looked after each other's security so that any country which attacked another one would face the opposition of the rest

COLLECTIVISATION policy of Soviet leader Stalin in 1930s to bring small farms together into larger farms

COLONY territory ruled by another country, for example India was a British colony until 1947

COMINFORM organisation set up by Soviet leader Stalin to link the Communist parties in all countries under his control

COMMANDER leader, person in charge

COMMONWEALTH countries which used to be part of the British Empire and were still closely linked to Britain

COMMUNICATIONS methods of getting messages and goods from one place to another – can refer to radio, road, rail, sea, air, etc.

COMMUNIST belief of Communist Party members. Basic idea of Communism is that the whole community is more important than the individual and all members of the community should work for the good of the community

COMPENSATION giving money or goods to a person or country which had been harmed

COMPROMISE reaching an agreement where each side gives up something it wanted

COMRADESHIP feeling of being together – often seen among soldiers who fought together in the First World War

CONCENTRATION CAMP special centres set up by the Nazis to get rid of their opponents

CONFERENCE meeting where important issues were discussed

CONFORMING fitting in with what government or society expected

CONGRESS meeting of people, usually to discuss a big issue like how a country is run

CONQUER take over, for example Germany conquered much of western Europe in 1939–40

CONSCIENTIOUS OBJECTOR person who refused to fight in wars because they believed war was morally wrong

CONSCRIPTION making people go into the army by law

CONSTITUTION the rules used to run a country, for example whether it was a democracy, how long between elections, etc.

CONTAINMENT policy of the USA from 1947 onwards to stop Communists taking control of countries

CONTROVERSIAL causing arguments

CO-OPERATE work together

CORRUPT not honest, for example government officials taking bribes

COUNCIL group of people who run an organisation, for example the League of Nations Council contained the most important countries in the League

COUPONS tickets that allowed people to buy certain goods in war-time, for example coupons for meat – without these you could not buy meat no matter how much money you had

COURT-MARTIAL court of law run by the army

COVENANT agreement

CRISIS (pl. crises) serious event which caused tension or even war, for example Cuban Missile Crisis of 1962

CULTURE language, music, art, literature, etc. of a people which makes them unique

CURRENCY money

DECISIVE being able to make difficult choices

DEFENCE lawyer who presents the case in favour of a person accused of a crime

DEMOCRATIC (democracy) system of government in which people elect their governments and can get rid of them at the next elections

DEMONSTRATION way of showing protest about an issue

DEPRESSION bad times in the economy, causing businesses to fail and leading to unemployment

DEPTH CHARGES special bombs fired by ships to destroy submarines

DE-STALINISATION policy of Soviet leader Khrushchev in the 1950s moving away from the way Stalin had ruled and criticising Stalin's actions

DESTINY what fate said a person or nation was meant to achieve

DÉTENTE good relations

DETERRENT putting someone off – the main example of this was nuclear weapons. The USA and USSR both had nuclear weapons. This deterred (put off) the other side from using them

DICTATOR single ruler with complete power

DIPLOMATIC talking between countries by their representatives (diplomats)

DISARMAMENT *see* armament getting rid of weapons – this was supposed to happen at the end of the Second World War but did not

DIVISION separating, for example Germany was separated or divided into East and West Germany at the end of the Second World War
DOMESTIC SERVICE working as a cook, cleaner or similar job in a wealthy person's home
DRAFT similar to conscription – calling up men to serve in the army
DUCK BOARDS pieces of wood used in trenches in the First World War to try to keep feet out of the mud
DUGOUT underground area of a trench

ECONOMIC relating to business or money
ECONOMY the work and earnings of a country
EINSATZ special units used by the Nazis to kill Jews and Communists during the Second World War
ELECTION (general/local) event where people choose local or national leaders
ELITE top people in society, for example army generals, wealthy landowners, owners of big industries
EMBASSY building where countries have their representatives in another country
EMERGENCY POWERS ability to ignore normal political rules, for example President Hindenburg in late 1920s Germany used Emergency Powers to pass laws without consulting the Reichstag (the German Parliament)
EMPIRE land ruled over by another country, for example British Empire meant that Britain ruled large parts of Africa and India
ETHNIC race, for example particular races were said to have a particular ethnic identity
EUTHANASIA putting very sick people to death
EVACUATION taking people away from an area, for example British children in the Second World War were evacuated away from cities to rural areas
EVACUEE person who was evacuated
EVIDENCE information which supports a point of view
EXECUTED killed, usually for committing a crime
EXEMPT not affected by
EXPEDITIONARY setting off to foreign country, for example the British Expeditionary Force went to France in the First and Second World Wars
EXTREMIST person who holds very radical views on an issue

FACILITIES essential services
FASCIST party run by Italian dictator Benito Mussolini. A person belonging to that party. This term was also used to describe the Nazis
FATHERLAND Germany
FINAL SOLUTION Nazi plan to murder all the Jews and certain other racial groups in Europe. It began in 1942
FIRESTORM huge, intensive fire caused by bombing. Firestorms in Hamburg and Dresden killed tens of thousands of people
FOREIGN AFFAIRS relations between one country and other countries
FREE TRAVEL the right of a person to go anywhere without being checked on
FREEDOM OF SPEECH the right of a person to say his/her view without being attacked
FREIKORPS group of ex-soldiers who were powerful in Germany in the early 1920s
FRONT (Western Front/Eastern Front) where fighting took place
FÜHRER leader – name that Adolf Hitler liked to use when he was in power in Germany

GAS CHAMBER rooms used to murder Jews and other racial groups with poison gas in death camps in the period 1942–45
GAS MASK special equipment which allowed people to breathe during a gas attack
GENERAL senior commander in the army
GESTAPO secret police force in Nazi Germany

GHETTO area where Jews were forced to live in Poland in the Second World War
GLORIFY to celebrate something and make it seem exciting or glorious
GRANT to give something, usually land or loans of money
GUARANTEED promised
GUERRILLA fighter using hit and run tactics rather than fighting in large battles

HARD LABOUR punishment which usually involved prison and physical work like breaking rocks
HIGH EXPLOSIVE powerful type of shell or bomb
HINDENBURG LINE line of trenches and barricades built by German forces in the First World War
HINDSIGHT looking back from the present at the past
HONOUR a kind of reward, for example a medal
HONOURS SYSTEM range of rewards used in Britain to reward people who had made an important contribution to areas like politics, health, business, etc.
HOUSEHOLDER someone who owned or paid the rent for a whole house (as opposed to a room in the house)
HOUSEKEEPING feeding and clothing a family, paying the rent, etc.
HUMILIATED made to feel stupid
HUNDRED DAYS final stages of the First World War in which British forces won a series of victories against German forces
HYDROGEN (H) BOMB very powerful type of bomb, many times more powerful than an atom bomb
HYPERINFLATION prices increasing very fast

IDEAL strongly held view or belief
IMPERIALIST connected with empires – an imperialist was usually someone who was trying to get or keep an empire
IMPORTS goods coming into a country
INCENDIARY bomb which starts fires
INCOMPETENCE being unable to do something properly
INDEPENDENCE freedom to rule yourself, for example when a colony became independent from the country which used to rule it
INDUSTRIALIST owner of a big factory or industry
INFANTRY soldiers who fought on foot
INFERENCE working out what a piece of text or an image says
INFORM ON give away information about another person or movement
INHERITED passing from parents to children after the parent dies
INSTALMENT stage, for example a bill might be paid in instalments
INSURANCE protection against something happening
INTACT not damaged
INTERCEPT to cut in on, for example German radio signals to U-boats in the Second World War were intercepted by the British
INTERNATIONAL relating to more than one country
INTERPRET work out the meaning, for example historians looking at a range of sources and reaching a judgement based on those sources
IRON CURTAIN barrier between the communist Eastern European countries and the democratic western European countries which emerged at the end of the Second World War
ISOLATIONISM attitude in the USA at the end of the First World War in which the USA did not want to get involved in the concerns of other countries

JUDICIARY judges and other top officials in the law
JUSTICE fair treatment which allows a fair trial for someone who is accused of a crime

KAISER ruler of Germany in the early 20th century, up to 1918
KGB secret police service of the USSR

LABOUR one of Britain's main political parties – Labour represented ordinary working people

LABOUR EXCHANGE office where unemployed workers could find out about job opportunities

LAND MINE small bomb placed underground which blew up when people stepped on it

LANDMARK an important event

LAUNCHER machine for firing rockets – caused great concern to USA in 1962 when launchers were spotted in Cuba

LAWYER person who works with the law and tries to win cases

LEAGUE OF NATIONS organisation set up by President Wilson in 1919 to try and keep the peace in the world

LEBENSRAUM *living space* – Nazis claimed that Germans in the 1930s needed more living space and used this to justify their wars and invasions

LIBERAL one of the main political parties in Britain in the early 1900s

LIBERATE to set free

LIFELINE a chance of survival or of a better life, for example old age pensions in 1908 gave many old people a lifeline

LOAN money given to a person or country which had to be repaid, for example US loans to Germany in the 1920s

LONG TERM lasting a long time

LOOT to steal goods or money

LOYAL giving complete support

LUXURY GOODS items which are not necessary to stay alive, for example jewellery, fancy food, wine

MACHINE GUN specialist gun which fired hundreds of bullets a minute – first became important in the First World War

MALNUTRITION lack of food or very bad food leading eventually to death

MANUFACTURED GOODS goods made in factories, for example clothing, machinery

MARK German money

MARSHALL AID (Marshall Plan) package of money and equipment given to western European countries by the USA at the end of the Second World War to help their economies recover from the war

MARTIAL LAW rule by the army

MASTER RACE Nazi belief that some humans were inferior to others

MERCHANT SEAMEN sailors who worked on ships carrying goods (not warships)

MILITANT radical or extreme

MINE place where minerals like coal or iron were dug up

MINERAL RESOURCES coal, iron, copper, etc.

MINISTER senior politician in a government

MISSILE rocket-powered bomb which could hit targets many miles away

MODERATE reasonable, prepared to discuss an issue

MORAL CONDEMNATION criticism of a country which attacked another country

MORALE spirit of a country or people, mostly important in war-time

MORALLY JUSTIFIED action which can be said to be acceptable because it is right

MORRISON SHELTER indoor air-raid shelter produced by the government in the Second World War

MUNITIONETTES women who worked in munitions factories in the First World War

MUNITIONS bullets and shells

MUTINY disobeying authority, usually in the army or navy

NAÏVE easily misled or fooled

NATIONAL COMMUNITY Nazi aim for Germany in the 1930s – people would become members of the National Community totally loyal to Hitler

NATIONALISATION putting industries under control of the government

NATO North Atlantic Treaty Organisation – set up in 1949 as alliance of North American and Western European countries against the USSR
NAZI short for National Socialist, party of Adolf Hitler in the 1920s–40s in Germany
NEGOTIATE to talk and try to reach a solution to a problem
NEUTRAL not linked to any side in an argument or war
NO MAN'S LAND area between German and British/French trenches in the First World War
NUCLEAR SHELTER underground building built to withstand a nuclear bomb attack
NUCLEAR WAR war using nuclear weapons – bombs and missiles
NUREMBERG LAWS laws passed in Germany in 1935 which banned Germans from marrying or having relationships with Jews

OBJECTIVE aim
OFFENSIVE attacking
ORBIT in the Cold War the USSR was said to have many countries in its orbit (control)
OUTFLANK to get round the side – in 1914 the German and British/French forces tried to get around the side of each other's armies but failed
'OVER THE TOP' getting out of a trench in the First World War to attack an enemy trench

PACT agreement or deal
PARACHUTE silk sheet used to protect someone who jumped from an aeroplane – mainly used by pilots whose planes were hit or by paratroopers (soldiers who jumped from aeroplanes)
PARANOIA suspicion or fear
PARAPET top of a First World War trench which protected troops from blast or snipers
PASSIVE RESISTANCE not co-operating, but not actually fighting, for example going on strike
PATRIOTIC supporting your country
PEACEFUL COEXISTENCE living together without fighting
PEASANT farmer with small plot
PENSION payment to people who were too old to work
PEOPLE POWER impact of large numbers of ordinary people in terms of causing important changes
PERMIT a document that allows people to travel from one place to another, for example people needed a permit to cross the Berlin Wall
PERSECUTE to arrest or generally make life difficult for people, usually because of their beliefs
PERSONALITY CLASH argument caused by the fact that people dislike each other rather than political ideas
PHONEY fake
PIRACY illegal action
PLANNER government official who works out what action might be taken in particular circumstances
PLEBISCITE vote in which people decide on an issue
POISON GAS weapons first used in 1915 – common versions were chlorine and mustard gas
POLISH CORRIDOR area of land given to Poland after the First World War but which contained mainly German people – given to Poland so that Poland had access to a sea port
POLITICAL PRISONER someone put in prison for political views rather than committing a crime
POVERTY LINE way of measuring how well off people were – first used by social reformer Seebohm Rowntree in the late 19th century
PREFABRICATED already made – usually refers to buildings, for example roofs which were already built and then simply put together on site

PREJUDICE strong dislike, usually based on racial, religious or political views
PRESIDENT head of the government in many countries, especially the USA
PRIVILEGE wealth and luxury
PROPAGANDA information containing a particular message – governments used propaganda, especially in wars, to get people behind them
PROPORTIONAL REPRESENTATION system of voting where the number of seats for a party in the assembly is based on the number of votes they received in election – one example is Weimar Germany, where if a party like the Socialists got 30% of the vote, they got 30% of the seats in the Reichstag
PROSECUTION lawyer who accuses someone of a crime and tries to get them found guilty
PROTECTIVE CUSTODY putting someone in prison for their own good
PSYCHIC person with mental powers
PSYCHOLOGICAL relating to the mind
PUBLIC OPINION views of the general public – in the 20th century governments became more and more concerned with public opinion
PUTSCH revolt

RACIAL PURITY term used by the Nazis – racially pure people had only Aryan families and had never had relatives who were Jews or certain other races
RACIST someone who discriminates against others because of their race, for example being Jewish, or black
RADAR system used in Britain to detect aircraft approaching the country long before they reached it
RALLY gathering of people, usually to show support for a political party or to protest about something
RATIONING controlling the amount of particular foods and other goods which people could buy
RATIONS amount of food, clothing, etc. which people were allowed to buy in war-time
RAW MATERIALS goods like timber, rubber, etc. which were then used to make manufactured goods like cars
REARMAMENT *see* armament building up weapons, for example Hitler built up Germany's supplies of weapons in the 1930s
REBELLION refusing to obey the government
RECRUITMENT getting people into an organisation, for example trying to get people into the army in Britain in 1914
RED ARMY the army of the USSR from the 1920s onwards
RE-EDUCATION the Nazis' name for putting people with different political or religious ideas, or way of life, into concentration camps
REFORM changing something to improve it
REFUGEES COMMISSION organisation which was part of the League of Nations – its job was to help refugees to get home
REGIME type of government
REICH Germany
REICHSTAG German parliament
RELIABLE something which can be trusted
REPARATIONS payment to make up for damage or injury caused, for example Germany had to pay reparations to France and Belgium after the First World War
REPRESENTATION how people's views are given to the government, for example the Representation of the People Act in Britain allowed women to vote, so they were then represented in Parliament
REPUBLIC system of government which does not have a monarchy
RESERVED OCCUPATION job which was so important that men in the job were not allowed to join the army, for example coal miners at certain times in the First World War
RESISTANCE movements which fought against German occupation in the Second World War

RESOURCES materials that are useful to a country, for example in the Second World War Germany needed resources like oil, rubber and timber
RETALIATE to hit back
REVOLT to try to overthrow a government
REVOLUTION successful overthrow of a government, for example Russian Revolution of 1917
ROUT total defeat

SA Nazi storm troopers who attacked Nazis' political rivals in the 1920s
SANCTIONS measures to cut off one country from trading with other countries
SCARCE in short supply
SEARCH AND DESTROY type of mission used by US forces in Vietnam in 1960s – they searched for and tried to destroy enemy forces
SECRET CODE way of sending messages so that anyone listening in could not understand unless they knew the code
SECRET POLICE police force used against political opponents of the government
SECURITY safety
SECURITY COUNCIL organisation within the United Nations which contained the most powerful members of the United Nations
SELF-DETERMINATION ability of small countries to rule themselves
SEWAGE human waste
SHELLFIRE term for any kind of shooting by large or small artillery guns
SHELL SHOCK mental illness caused by blast from artillery shells
SHILLINGS money used in Britain up to 1971 – there were 20 shillings in a pound
SHORT TERM lasting a short time
SHRAPNEL type of shell which burst into metal fragments, designed to kill soldiers
SLAV eastern European peoples
SLAVE LABOUR workers used by the Nazis in the Second World War – they could be prisoners of war or racial groups like Jews or Gypsies
SNIPER soldier with accurate rifle who picked off enemy soldiers
SOCIALIST Socialists held political ideas which were similar to Communism but not as extreme – they believed in greater government involvement in everyday life, for example laws to protect workers from harsh employers
SOURCE any document, picture, song, film, etc. that historians can use to learn about the past
SPHERE OF INFLUENCE area where one country had a strong say in what happened, for example USSR controlled Eastern Europe after the Second World War because that was the Soviet sphere of influence
SPY PLANE aeroplanes used to take photographs of enemy countries – the best known was the U2 spy plane
SS organisation in Nazi Germany which ran concentration camps and many other aspects of security – headed by Heinrich Himmler
STABILITY situation which is calm and peaceful (stable)
STAGING POST step towards a particular aim to be achieved
STALEMATE situation where two sides are equally matched
STANDARD OF LIVING general conditions for people, usually shown by their ability to afford food, a place to live and a few luxuries
STERILISED stopped from having children
STORM TROOPERS Nazi organisation which attacked opponents of Nazis; also type of soldier in the First World War specially equipped for attacking trenches
STRATEGIC overall thinking, for example a strategic plan is a plan to win a war, but a tactical plan is a plan to win a battle
SUBMARINE ship which can sail below the surface, usually to attack enemy ships
SUFFRAGE the vote
SUFFRAGETTES radical women's group which campaigned to get women the vote

SUFFRAGISTS moderate women's group which campaigned to get women the vote
SUMMIT important meeting
SUPERPOWER the USA and USSR after 1945
SUPPLY ROUTE way of getting food, medicine, weapons, etc. to an army

TACTICS way of fighting a battle
TANK large armoured vehicle, first used in the First World War in 1917
TARIFF tax on goods coming into a country to make the goods more expensive
TELEPATHIC communicating from mind to mind without talking
TENSION bad feeling, for example in the years up to 1914 there was a lot of tension between Britain and Germany
TERRITORY land
TERROR fear
TORTURE hurting people to frighten them or to get information from them
TRADE UNION organisation which represented workers
TRADES UNION CONGRESS meeting of all of the trade unions in Britain
TRADITIONAL VALUES ideas about how homes should be run and families should live – traditional values usually meant the man working and the woman staying at home looking after children
TRAFFICKING transporting goods, usually referring to illegal transporting, for example trafficking drugs
TRAITOR person who works against his/her own country
TRANSMITTER equipment for sending radio signals
TRANSPORTED taken from one place to another
TREATY agreement between countries, often at the end of a war
TRENCHES deep ditches dug and repaired by soldiers to shelter from gunfire and shellfire – generally associated with the First World War
TRIAL when someone is accused of a crime and the evidence for and against them is investigated
TRIGGER event which causes other events to happen
TRUMAN DOCTRINE speech by US President Truman in 1947, in which he promised to help any country which wanted to oppose Communism
TUBERCULOSIS chest disease caused by damp conditions

U-BOAT German submarines from the First World War and the Second World War
UNEMPLOYMENT no work
UNION *see* trade union
UNITED NATIONS (UN) organisation set up after the Second World War to try to keep international peace

VETERAN person who has experience of something, for example war veteran
VIET CONG Communist group which fought to make South Vietnam a Communist country in the 1950s and 1960s
VIETNAMISATION policy of US President Nixon in late 1960s and early 1970s to build up South Vietnam forces and withdraw US forces from Vietnam
VOLUNTEERS people who offer to do something or join an organisation, for example men who agreed to go to war in 1914

WARDEN official who looked after a particular area, for example air-raid warden
WAR FOOTING getting ready for war
WAR-MONGERING threatening war or making it more likely
WARSAW PACT organisation of USSR and Eastern European countries set up in 1955 to oppose the USA and NATO
WELFARE looking after people
WORKHOUSE place for poor people who had no money and no place to live

Index

U

V

W

Y

Acknowledgements

The author would like to express his thanks to Phil Smith and his students at Coney Green High School, Radcliffe, Manchester, for their help in developing many of the materials in this book. The author would also like to thank his own GCSE students at Stafford College who helped to decide what worked for them!

Photo credits

Front cover *Main picture* Imperial War Museum, London, *tl* Imperial War Museum, London, *bl* and *br* Popperfoto; **p.v** *t* Illustrated London News Picture Library, *c* Mary Evans Picture Library, *b* News International Syndication; **p.vi** *t* Centre for the Study of Cartoons and Caricature, University of Kent/ Atlantic Syndication, *c* Topham Picturepoint, *b* The Art Archive/Imperial War Museum; **p.1** Popperfoto/Reuters; **p.2** AKG London/Erich Lessing; **p.16** *t* and *b* Illustrated London News Picture Library; **p.21** sketches by Private Jim Maultsaid of 35th Ulster Division published in *The Road to the Somme* by Philip Orr, Blackstaff Press page 193; **p.25** *t* Corbis UK Ltd, *b* The Liddell Collection, University of Leeds Library; **p.33** © National Library of Wales, unidentified photographer (PZ4257 Llyfr Ffoto LLGC: NLW Photograph Album 254 p.7); **p.35** Hulton Getty; **p.37** *t* Mary Evans Picture Library, *b* Punch Cartoon Library; **p.38** and **p.39** Mary Evans Picture Library; **p.40** British Newspaper Library; **p.41, p.42** and **p.43** Mary Evans Picture Library; **p.45** Mary Evans/ Fawcett Library; **p.47** Mary Evans Picture Library; **p.49** Topham Picturepoint; **p.50, p.51** *t* and *bl* Imperial War Museum, London, *br* Public Record Office; **p.52** Imperial War Museum, London; **p.53** Mary Evans/Fawcett Library; **p.54** Imperial War Museum; **p.55** Mary Evans Picture Library; **p.57** Tony Hall/ *The Liverpool Daily Post and Echo*; **p.65** Mary Evans Picture Library; **p.69** *t* Punch Cartoon Library, *b* News International Syndication; **p.71** *all* United Nations © DACS 2001; **p.82** *bl* Bildarchiv Preussischer Kulturbesitz, *br* Hulton Getty; **p.84** Ullstein; **p.85** Hulton Getty; **p.89** Centre for the Study of Cartoons and Caricature, University of Kent/Atlantic Syndication; **p.92** AKG London; **p.96** *t* Peter Newark's Military Pictures, *b* AKG London; **p.97** Süddeutscher Verlag Bilderdienst; **p.100** Randall Bytwerk's German Propaganda Archive, http://www.calvin.edu/academic/cas/gpa/; **p.101** London Evening Standard/ Atlantic Syndication; **p.106** Kobal Collection; **p.108** AKG London; **p.109** Archiv Gerstenberg; **p.111** Süddeutscher Verlag Bilderdienst; **p.112** Bildarchiv Preussischer Kulturbesitz; **p.113** AKG London Ltd; **p.114** *tl* Popperfoto, *bl* AKG London Ltd, *r* Bildarchiv Preussischer Kulturbesitz; **p.115** Staatarchiv, Bremen; **p.116** Press Association; **p.117** © Yad Vashem Photo Archive; **p.118** and **p.119** Randall Bytwerk's German Propaganda Archive, http://www.calvin.edu/academic/cas/gpa/; **p.130** *Evening Standard*/Atlantic Syndication; **p.132** Punch Cartoon Library; **p.133** Topham Picturepoint; **p.139** *l* The Art Archive/Imperial War Museum, *r* Hugo Jaeger/TimePix/Rex Features; **p.144** *r* Hulton Getty, *b* Imperial War Museum; **p.149** Ben Walsh; **p.150** Mary Evans Picture Library; **p.151** *both* Peter Newark's Military Pictures; **p.153** Imperial War Museum, London; **p.155** *t* Hulton Getty, *b* John Townson/Creation; **p.157** *t* Imperial War Museum, *bl* and *br* Tyne & Wear Archives Service; **p.158** Hulton Getty; **p.159** Popperfoto; **p.160** Associated Press/Topham; **p.161** Atlantic Syndication; **p.163** Hulton Getty; **p.171** Peter Newark's Military Pictures; **p.172** Associated Press; **p.173** *t* Corbis UK Ltd, *b* Corbis/Bettman/UPI; **p.174** Popperfoto; **p.175** *t* Popperfoto, *c* Public Record Office, *b* John Frost Newspaper Archive; **p.178** *Evening Standard*/Atlantic Syndication; **p.183** Pravda 1960; **p.187** Larry Burrows/TimePix/Rex Features; **p.190** Corbis UK Ltd; **p.191** *t* Corbis UK Ltd, *b* Associated Press/Topham;

p.192 and **p.193** Corbis UK Ltd; **p.194** *t* © *Daily Telegraph*/Centre for the Study of Cartoons and Caricature, University of Kent, *b* Corbis UK Ltd; **p.196** The Art Archive; **p.197** AKG London; **p.199** Hulton Getty; **p.200** Hulton Getty; **p.203** *l* Topham Picturepoint, *r* Popperfoto; **p.204** Popperfoto; **p.207** Czech News Agency; **p.208** *both* The Open University; **p.212** *tl News of the World*/John Frost Newspaper Newspapers, *bl* Piel/Gamma/Frank Spooner Pictures, *r* Popperfoto/Reuters; **p.215** TimePix/Rex Features; **p.216** *l* Topham Picturepoint, *r* © *Daily Telegraph*/Centre for the Study of Cartoons and Caricatures, University of Kent.

(*t* = top, *b* = bottom, *l* = left, *r* = right, *c* = centre)

While every effort has been made to contact copyright holders, the publishers apologise for any omissions, which they will be pleased to rectify at the earliest opportunity.